NEW VIEWS OF
BORDERLANDS HISTORY

NEW VIEWS OF
BORDERLANDS HISTORY

Edited by
ROBERT H. JACKSON

University of New Mexico Press
Albuquerque

Library of Congress
Cataloging-in-Publication Data

New views of borderlands history / edited by Robert H. Jackson.
p.   cm.
Contents: Colonial Chihuahua : people and frontiers in flux / Susan M. Deeds —
Demographic, social, and economic change in New Mexico / Ross Frank — Northwestern
New Spain : the Pimeria Alta and the Californias / Robert H. Jackson — Spanish colonial
Texas / Jesús F. de la Teja — The formation of frontier and indigenous communities :
missions in Califiornia and Texas / Robert H. Jackson — Marginals and acculturation in
frontier society / Peter Stern — The Spanish colonial Floridas / Patricia R. Wickman —
Some common threads on the northern frontier of Mexico / Robert H. Jackson.
Includes bibliographical references and index.
ISBN 0-8263-1937-8 (cloth). — ISBN 0-8263-1938-6 (pbk.)
1. Mexican-American Border Region—History.
2. Southwest, New—History.
3. Florida—History—Spanish colony, 1565–1763.
4. Frontier and pioneer life—Mexican-American Border Region.
5. Frontier and pioneer life—Southwest, New.
6. Frontier and pioneer life—Florida.
I. Jackson, Robert H. (Robert Howard)
F786.N49   1998
972'.1—dc21   98-24572
                                                                              CIP

CONTENTS

ILLUSTRATIONS

TABLES

Tables appear at the end of chapters on page numbers indicated

INTRODUCTION

ROBERT H. JACKSON

Spanish exploration and colonization of the region known today as the Borderlands began soon after discovery of the New World. Columbus organized the
first colony on Hispaniola in 1493 and 1494, and within twenty years Spanish
ships coasted the region later named La Florida in search of slaves and gold.
Within fifteen years of the conquest of Mexico (1519–1521), Spaniards explored
parts of what today is northern Mexico and the southwestern United States.
Hernán Cortés, the conqueror of the Mexica-Aztec tribute state in central
Mexico, organized expeditions to Baja California in the mid-1530s. Vessels
built at Cortés's Pacific Coast shipyard explored the California coastline in
1542–43 under the command of Juan Rodríguez Cabrillo. In 1540 Francisco de
Coronado lead a large army to discover what the adventurers hoped would be a
new and greater Mexico with fabled wealth, inspired by the legend of the Seven
Cities of Cibola, the reports of Alvar Núñez Cabeza de Vaca (a survivor of the
failed Narváez expedition to Florida who trekked from Texas to northwestern
Mexico after being shipwrecked on the Texas coast), and the exaggerations of
Fray Marcos de Niza sent to confirm Cabeza de Vaca's reports (see the chronol-
ogy at the end of this Introduction for a partial list of important expeditions to
Borderlands regions). During the sixteenth century most exploration and colo-
nization expeditions were organized as private ventures for profit.

The early expeditions to Florida and the Borderlands frontier region generally did not find what they had hoped to encounter: sedentary and hierarchical
native societies with great wealth in the form of gold, silver, and precious
stones. Instead, the Spaniards came across native societies that were either

I

hunter-gatherers or sedentary or semisedentary agriculturists. Politically, the different indigenous groups were organized into chieftainships, or as smaller bands. The sedentary indigenous societies supported elites and specialists, but did not have large stores of accumulated gold, silver, and precious stones that offered the conquistadors quick profits when taken as booty.

The narratives of the early explorations contain elements of high adventure, violence, suspense, and mystery that rival the best Hollywood action movies. However, after the first generation of conquistadors, the history of the Borderlands frontier was characterized by the creation of colonial societies composed of both Spanish settlers and local indigenous populations. The societies that evolved in Florida and northern Mexico mirrored the societies of heavily populated central Mexico, and what can be called the Spanish Caribbean colonial complex. Although similar institutions developed in Florida and the northern Mexican frontier, Florida was still distinct.

In some instances, institutions first evolved in Spain and then developed in new ways in Spanish America. The Spanish first introduced the *encomienda*—a grant of jurisdiction over a specific indigenous population that generally entitled the *encomendero* to tribute and labor—from southern Spain into the early Caribbean settlements. In other parts of Spanish America the conquistadors distributed the indigenous populations in encomienda grants shortly after conquest. The crown attempted to forestall the emergence of a New World feudal nobility. It issued the New Laws in 1542 to phase out the encomienda and eliminate the worst abuses associated with the institution, such as excessive labor and tribute demands. On the northern frontier of Mexico, the encomienda only existed in New Mexico prior to the 1680 Pueblo revolt.[1] By the early seventeenth century, privately funded and organized exploration and colonization largely ended, and in northern Mexico the colonial government assumed more responsibility for settling the frontier.

In other instances the Spanish modified existing indigenous institutions. They took advantage of the fact that native peoples already had a tradition of paying tribute and providing labor services to a hierarchical government. This certainly was the case in central Mexico. There, the Spanish grafted their own social concepts onto the existing Nahuatl tradition of tribute payments and labor services to the ruling lineages in each *altepetl* ("city state"). Following the conquest of the Mexica-Aztec tribute state, the Spanish organized a system of indirect rule that allowed each altepetl or individual corporate indigenous community with a ruling *tlatoani* lineage a degree of autonomy as long as the indigenous rulers complied with tribute and labor obligations.[2] The central Mexican system that evolved during the course of the sixteenth century served as the model or blueprint for the colonial system and society that evolved on the northern frontier of Mexico.

Initially, the Spanish envisioned the development of a corporate-type society with two distinct castes, each with unique rights and obligations. Spanish settlers constituted the *república de españoles,* while the indigenous peoples were the *república de indios.* The two castes had separate laws and courts, and the Spanish government legally defined the native peoples as minors (*niños con barbas*—"children with beards") under the special protection and jurisdiction of the crown. The indigenous population alone paid tribute and worked in *repartimiento* and other labor drafts, and were subject to legal discrimination and sumptuary laws. For example, natives were not to carry firearms or ride horses, and guild law closed certain professions to natives. On the other hand, indigenous community leaders very effectively used Spanish colonial law to benefit the communities, and individuals could escape stiff penalties for criminal offenses by pandering to the Spanish stereotypes of indigenous behavior.

The origins of Spanish Florida were very different. Several major expeditions explored Florida in the first decades of the sixteenth century, but permanent settlement only took place in 1565. In 1564, the French established Fort Caroline in northern Florida, near modern Jacksonville. The French outpost posed a threat to trade between Spain and the Caribbean carried in *flotas* (flotillas of merchant vessels escorted by warships) that skirted the Florida coast. Fort Caroline could have potentially served as a base for the interception of the flota. A privately organized expedition founded San Agustín (Saint Augustine) in 1565, and in the same year wiped out the French outpost. For the next two hundred years, San Agustín developed as a military outpost that served as the northern anchor of a Caribbean defense strategy built around large stone forts. Jesuit and later Franciscan missionaries established missions in northern Florida and the coastal regions of Georgia (Guale). After 1660, however, the English began to colonize the Carolinas, and for the next century Florida would become part of a contested region. English colonial forces destroyed most of the missions, and carried away hundreds of Indians as slaves. The destruction of the missions in the first decade of the eighteenth century reduced the Spanish presence to San Agustín and Pensacola. Unlike the settlements in northern Mexico, Spanish civil and religious officials in Florida answered to Havana, and not Mexico City.

As regards the indigenous populations of northern Mexico and Florida, Spanish policy was to transform the social organization, culture, religion and worldview, and political organization of the native societies. The Spanish government developed the mission as an institution to achieve the goal of transforming indigenous societies, in a cost-effective fashion, into a community populated by sedentary peasants paying tribute to the colonial government and providing labor through drafts such as repartimiento. Through a series of papal concessions known as the *real patronato*, the crown received virtually complete control over the Catholic Church in the New World. This enabled the government to use the members of certain missionary orders such as the Franciscans and Jesuits as representatives of both church and state, placed in charge of the acculturation programs in mission communities. The missionaries created new communities through *congregación*, the resettlement of native peoples in nucleated villages.[3] Although staffed by members of the Catholic Church, the mission was fundamentally a government institution funded by the Crown. The government had to authorize the establishment of each new mission.

Several factors motivated Spanish colonization of Florida and the northern frontier of Mexico, and the immediate cause for colonization profoundly influenced patterns of development. The discovery of gold and silver mines stimulated colonization in regions such as Nueva Vizcaya and Sonora, and led to disputes between missionaries and settlers, both of whom wanted to control the indigenous populations. The missionaries generally wanted to isolate and protect the Indians from what they saw as the corruption of Spanish society, whereas the settlers wanted access to a ready source of labor. The existence of mining camps, rural estates, and other settlements also offered natives an avenue for escaping from the paternalistic control of the missionaries. In other areas such as Florida, Texas, and California, colonization resulted from real or potential threats from colonial rivals. The apparent lack of wealth in the form of mines and weak or nonexistent links to regional markets limited settlement in these strategic borderlands. This forced the government to place greater emphasis on the missions to establish territorial rights by occupation. The Borderlands also witnessed different schemes to promote nonindigenous settlement, and with these came the more difficult task of balancing the competing demands and interests of the settlers and missionaries.

The mission was one of several frontier institutions that contributed to forging new colonial societies. The Spanish envisioned that the society of the frontier regions would include both assimilated Indians and Spanish settlers. The colonial government established *presidios* (military garrisons) to protect the missions and other settlements from hostile indigenous groups and potential colonial rivals such as the French and English. The presidios also became centers of nonmilitary settlement. The government attempted to promote communities near the presidios, and settlers also gravitated to these seeking protection from raids by hostile natives.[4] The government also promoted the peopling of the frontier through authorizing planned settlements, subsidizing settlers sent to the frontier, and awarding land grants. Sanctioning of the creation of formal local municipal government was also an important aspect of frontier policy designed to create more stable communities.[5]

The present volume examines colonial societies on the northern frontier of Mexico, which evolved from institutions in central Mexico, and contrasts that experience with what occurred in Florida, which was the northern extension of the Spanish Caribbean colonial complex and quite different from colonial Mexico. The book consists of two sets of essays. The first are detailed regional studies written by specialists in the history of each area. These address common themes: the structure of frontier society, demographic and settlement patterns, and economic development. The regional studies also contain the stories of common people who typified frontier experiences. The regional chapters offer a synthesis of the current state of historical knowledge for each region. But because the historical literature for each region is different, the discussion of these themes reflect the availability of materials historians have generally addressed, stressing issues unique to the history of each region. For example, sacramental registers for the California missions are very complete when compared to the same set of records for missions in Texas, New Mexico, or Sonora and southern Arizona. Sacramental registers simply have not survived for Florida missions. I believe an edited volume on the Borderlands has a number of benefits over the writing of a general synthetic history by a single historian.[6] A single author may be familiar with the major studies published for a specific region, but may not have the same familiarity with sources as does the specialist in each region. It is also easy to miss the nuances of debates and interpretations, particularly when the literature crosses disciplinary lines. Finally, the generalists may dwell on topics that are not currently emphasized in the specialized literature.

There are five regional studies in this volume, organized in the two sections of this book. The first section examines the northern frontier of Mexico. It opens with colonial Chihuahua, which was an important frontier region not acquired by the United States. Chihuahua is an example of a mining frontier on the far northern Mexican frontier, first settled in the second half of the sixteenth century. It is followed by chapters that document frontier regions later incorporated into the United States, presented in chronological sequence of settlement: New Mexico, Sonora and the Californias, and Texas. The first section of the book also contains two thematic monographic chapters that present recent advances in research. The first is a study of missions in California and Texas presented in a comparative context, built around the theme of the missions representing the process of the creation of indigenous communities formed along the line of central Mexico communities. The second is a study of social marginals and acculturation in frontier society, including the phenomenon of "white Indians" or Europeans who become members of indigenous society. It attempts to recreate for the reader the "lived experience" of Borderlands settlers.

The second section of the book consists of one essay on Spanish Florida, with a short introduction that fleshes out some of the similarities and differences with the northern Mexican frontier. It presents Florida as a different type of borderland that developed out of the Caribbean colonial complex, oriented more toward the defense of the Caribbean against Spain's European rivals.

The essays in this volume represent the most recent advances in Borderlands scholarship. The contributors combine extensive archival research with a synthesis of the secondary literature. This collection of essays supplements previous synthetic studies of the Borderlands, including David Weber's recent book, *The Spanish Frontier in North America*. With these final comments, I invite the reader to begin the journey of exploring the development of colonial societies on the fringes of the Spanish empire in America.

Chronology: Exploration and Colonization Expeditions to the Borderlands

NORTHERN MEXICO

NEW MEXICO
Fray Marcos de Niza, 1539
Francisco de Coronado, 1540–1542
Agustín Rodríguez-Francisco Chamuscado, 1581
Antonio de Espejo, 1583
Gaspar Castano de Sosa, 1590
Juan de Oñate, 1598, 1601, 1604–1605
Diego de Vargas, 1696
Pedro de Villasur,: 1720
Francisco Domínguez-Silvestre de Escalante, 1776

TEXAS
Juan Barroto-Antonio Romero, 1686
Alonso de León, 1686, 1687, 1688, 1690
Domingo Ramón, 1716

Martín de Alarcón, 1718
Marques de Aguayo, 1721–1722

ARIZONA
Francisco de Coronado, 1540
Eusebio Francisco Kino, 1681–1711

CALIFORNIA
Juan Rodríguez Cabrillo, 1542–1543
Sebastián Rodriguez Cermenho, 1595
Sebastián Vizcaino, 1602–1603
Gaspar de Portola-Junipero Serra, 1769
Juan Pérez, 1774
Juan Bautista de Anza, 1774, 1775–1776
de Garces, 1775–1776
Juan Francisco de la Bodega y Quadra, 1775
Gabriel Moraga, 1806, 1808, 1810, 1812–1814

LA FLORIDA

Juan Ponce de León, 1513
Alonso Alvarez de Pineda,: 1519
Pedro de Quejo, 1525
Panfilo de Narváez, 1528
Alvar Núñez Cabeza de Vaca, 1528–1536 (including Texas, New Mexico,
Arizona, and northwestern Mexico)
Hernando de Soto, 1539–1543
Tristán de Luna, 1560
Pedro Menéndez de Aviles, 1565
Juan Pardo, 1566–1568

NOTES

1. For an overview of the development of Spanish colonial institutions on the northern frontier of Mexico and in Florida, see Robert H. Jackson, "Relations With the Parent Country: Spanish," in *Encyclopedia of North American Colonies*, 3 vols. (New York, 1993), 1:317–26.

2. See Charles Gibson, The Aztecs under Spanish Rule: A History of the Indians of the Valley of Mexico, 1519–1810 (Stanford, 1964); James Lockhart, The Nahuas after the Con-

quest: A Social and Cultural History of the Indians of Central Mexico, Sixteenth through Eighteenth Century (Stanford, 1992). Examples of studies of Mexican regions other than the core of the Mexica-Aztec state include Robert Haskett, Indigenous Rulers: An Ethnohistory of Town Government in Colonial Cuernavaca (Albuquerque, 1991); Ronald Spores, The Mixtecs in Ancient and Colonial Times (Norman, 1984); John Chance, Conquest of the Sierra: Spaniards and Indians in Colonial Oaxaca (Norman, 1989).

3. For a more detailed discussion of the evolution of frontier mission programs, see Robert H. Jackson, *Indian Population Decline: The Missions of Northwestern New Spain, 1687–1840* (Albuquerque, 1994); Robert H. Jackson and Edward Castillo, *Indians, Franciscans, and Spanish Colonization: The Impact of the Mission System on California Indians* (Albuquerque, 1995). For studies of missions in other parts of Spanish America, see, for example, David Block, *Mission Culture on the Upper Amazon* (Lincoln, 1994); and the essays in Erick Langer and Robert H. Jackson, eds., *The New Latin American Mission History* (Lincoln, 1995).

4. Max Moorhead, The Presidio: Bastion of the Spanish Borderlands (Norman, 1975).

5. Jesús F. de la Teja, *San Antonio de Bexar: A Community on New Spain's Northern Frontier* (Albuquerque, 1995), is perhaps the best study of a frontier community in northern Mexico.

6. The best-known single author-synthetic histories of the Borderlands, including Florida, are the older study by John Francis Bannon, S.J., *The Spanish Borderlands Frontier, 1513–1821* (New York, 1970); and more recently, David Weber, *The Spanish Frontier in North America* (New Haven, 1992).

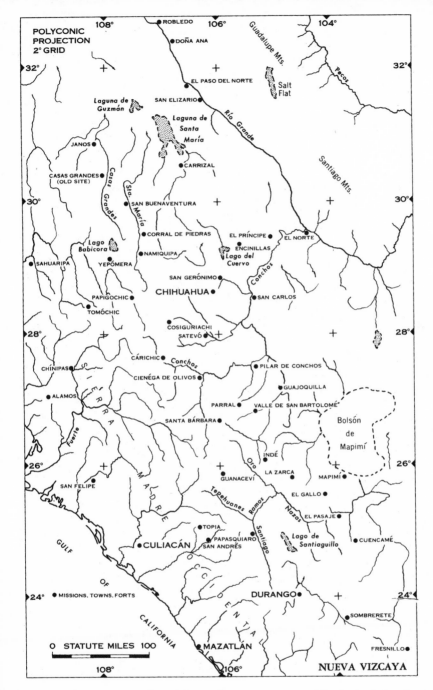

Map 1. Nueva Vizcaya. Adapted from John Francis Bannon, The Spanish Borderlands Frontier, 1513–1821. *Albuquerque: University of New Mexico Press, 1974, 78.*

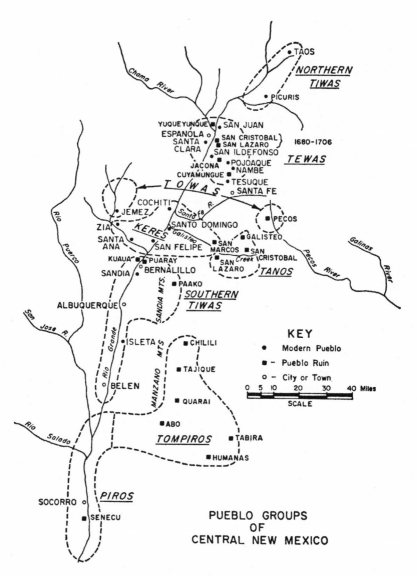

Map 2. Pueblo Groups at Contact, ca. 1540–1598. From Thomas D. Hall, Social Change in the Soutwest, 1350–1880, *Lawrence: Kansas University Press, 1989, Map V2, 79. Reprinted in Weber,* New Spain's Far Northern Frontier, *242.*

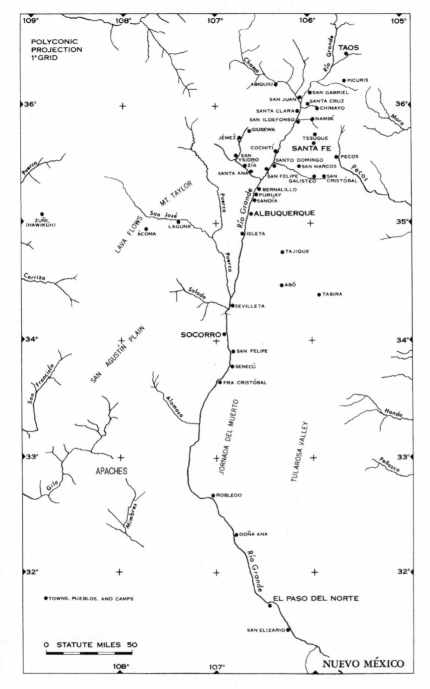

Map 3. Nuevo México. Adapted from John Francis Bannon, The Spanish Borderlands Frontier, 1513–1821. Albuquerque: University of New Mexico Press, 1974, 11.

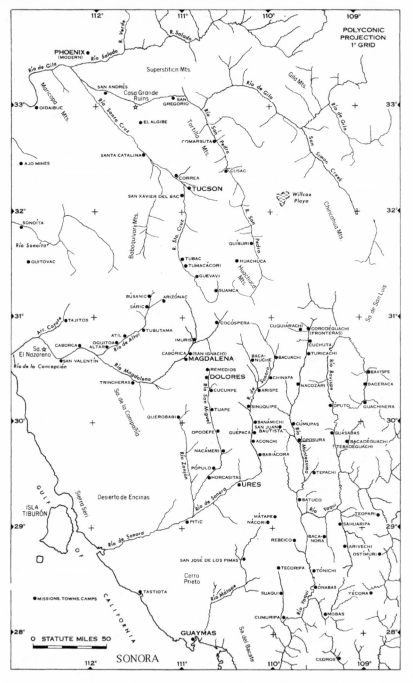

Map 4. Sonora. Adapted from John Francis Bannon, The Spanish Borderlands Frontier, 1513–1821. *Albuquerque: University of New Mexico Press, 1974, Primería Alta, 66.*

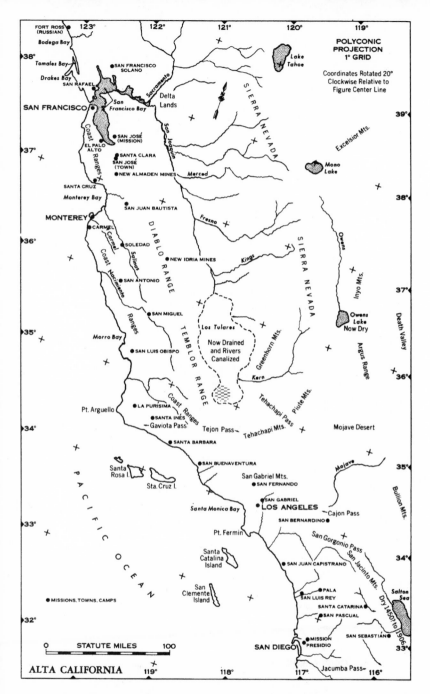

Map 5. Alta California. Adapted from John Francis Bannon, The Spanish Borderlands Frontier, 1513–1821. *Albuquerque: University of New Mexico Press, 1974,* 165.

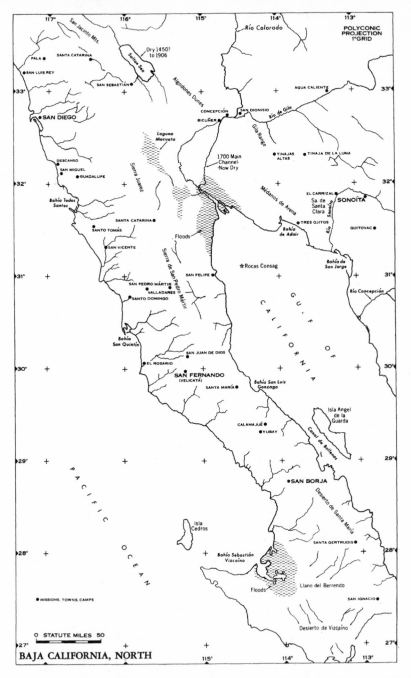

Maps 6a and 6b. Baja California. Adapted from John Francis Bannon, The Spanish Borderlands Frontier, 1513–1821. *Albuquerque: University of New Mexico Press, 1974, Baja California South, Baja California North, 144, 145.*

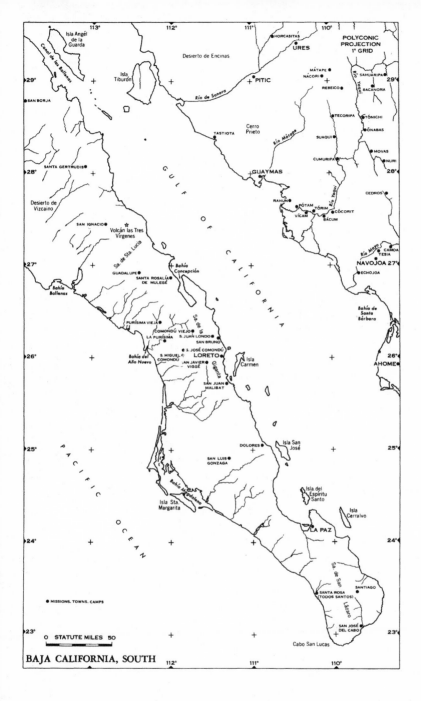

BAJA CALIFORNIA, SOUTH

15

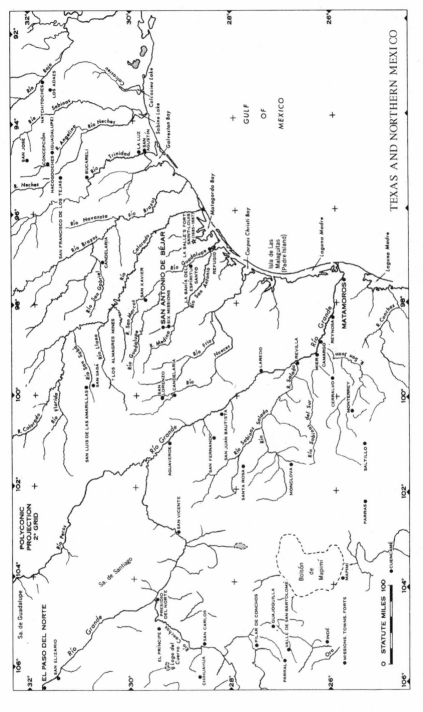

Map 7. *Texas and Northern Mexico. Adapted from John Francis Bannon, The Spanish Borderlands Frontier, 1513–1821. Albuquerque: University of New Mexico Press, 1974, Coahuila, Nuevo Léon, Nuevo Santander, and Texas, 113.*

TEXAS AND NORTHERN MEXICO

Map 8. *Principal Native Tribes of Lower La Florida at European Contact. Arrows indicate extended power spheres. Light lines indicate modern states. Illustration by Lynn Rogers.*

PART I
THE FRONTIER OF
NORTHERN MEXICO

CHAPTER ONE

COLONIAL CHIHUAHUA
Peoples and Frontiers in Flux

SUSAN M. DEEDS

In the middle of the eighteenth century, Juan Rodríguez de Albuerne, Marqués de Altamira and adviser to the Mexican viceroy on military issues, wrote a series of reports highly critical of Spanish frontier policy. He linked instability and the lack of sufficient economic productivity on the northern Mexican silver-mining frontier to Spain's failure to promulgate colonization by Spaniards or other *gente de razón* (non-Indians, literally people with reason). He lamented the low return on the high royal costs of subsidizing presidios and missions as the cornerstones of Spain's strategy for occupying the northern reaches of its colonial empire. With even a quarter of the funds spent on presidios guarding the royal road from Chihuahua to Mexico City (eight million pesos in the previous eighty years), he believed that the crown could have occupied the area with Spanish settlements and enterprises that would have been much more effective in persuading indigenous peoples to become efficient laborers and taxpayers. For peoples "who only comprehend what enters through the eyes," the habits of Spaniards were necessary to entice them from their "natural poverty" and "indolence."[1]

Altamira's opinions, while anticipating the so-called rational reforms aimed at increasing productivity and returns to the Spanish Bourbon kings of the late eighteenth century, were also firmly anchored in medieval Spanish notions of a civilized state, which contrasted the backwardness of the countryside with the ideal of urban sophistication. His judgments had racial connotations as well. Not even 150 years of missionary guidance had been sufficient to educate Indians who lacked reason. The guidance by Spanish example that he advocated could not overcome this "natural" state of affairs, but at least it could induce proper obedience.

The relative sizes of various ethnic groups figured prominently in late colonial official assessments of the north. The key to Spanish control was to tip the balance of power away from the native population through the proper demographic mix; increased Spanish presence in the midst of Indian groups would inevitably demonstrate the superiority of Spanish ways and produce a stable society.[2] If the argument appears simplistic to us today, it also misrepresents the complex evolution of the human landscape after initial contact between Indians and Europeans. Demographic factors did provide an important means for assessing the development of the northern frontier, although not in the ways officials would have recognized at the time. As we shall see, the flux in population movements in colonial Chihuahua has a corollary in the contentiousness of its social evolution.

The patterns of indigenous settlement observed as Spaniards began to arrive in the sixteenth century had already been evolving for centuries in reaction to cultural, ecological, and demographic factors. These patterns continued to change after contact in response to similar factors, although the invasion of Spanish microbes, soldiers, and ambitions added peculiar twists. It is possible to chronicle these shifts, at least from the early seventeenth century, when more detailed accounts began to be written by Spanish explorers, clergy, and officials.

The native population of Chihuahua at the time of Spanish arrival in Mexico in the early sixteenth century can only be roughly estimated, perhaps constituting between 200,000 and 300,000.[3] A century later that number had declined by as much as 50 percent to about 150,000. The Sierra Madre Occidental of western Chihuahua was home to various indigenous peoples; the most populous mountain-dwelling groups were Tarahumaras (Rarámuris) and Tepehuanes, whose settlements also extended into the valleys and plains east of the sierra. After contact, the sierra groups were described as semisedentary, changing *ranchería*[4] locations cyclically in accordance with cycles of agriculture and hunting and gathering. In the eastern semiarid plateau, more mobile Sumas-Jumanos and Conchos also cultivated some corn. The easternmost desert of the Bolsón de Mapimí harbored band groups such as Tobosos, Salineros, and Chisos, who, like the Apaches who moved into Chihuahua later, became even more nomadic with the introduction of Spanish livestock.[5]

Hunter-gatherers and farmers evolved patterns of mutual dependence long before Spanish arrival, interacting either through trade or intertribal warfare. Those relations were gradually disrupted as Spaniards penetrated the area, to be replaced by warfare between Europeans and Indian groups as well as new patterns of indigenous raiding on Spanish livestock, Spanish slave-raiding expeditions, and trade in European and Indian captives.[6]

Social organization varied somewhat between ranchería and band groups. Ranchería Indians used digging sticks to cultivate maize, beans, and squash along waterways. Although they hunted and collected wild plants, they did not depend as exclusively on these activities as did the band groups. Yet for all groups political organization was decentralized,[7] without formal links across bands or rancherías. Individual bands were guided by a headman/war chief, while ranchería affairs were directed by elders (*principales*) using moral persuasion except in times of conflict, when chief warriors may have exercised more political authority. War leaders earned their positions through demonstrations of bravery. Ritual specialists employed magical powers to cure and predict; ritual practices were aimed at assuring material survival through agriculture and warfare. Dreams were a source of knowledge and power, as were certain sacred spaces of the natural world. Where agriculture was practiced, households had individual use rights on communal croplands, but extended families cooperated in economic activities. Both men and women performed agricultural and gathering tasks; only men hunted with bow and arrow. Women prepared food, cared for children, and made textiles, pots, and baskets. Gender roles were complementary in economic activities, but with the exception of some female shamans, women occupied subordinate political roles. There was little class differentiation in ranchería and band societies, although some elders may have accumulated surplus goods and wives in the former.[8] These socioeconomic patterns changed after contact, depending upon the extent to which groups were incorporated into Spanish networks and institutions and the ways in which they were affected by the introduction of diseases brought by Europeans. Ranchería groups like the Tepehuanes, Tarahumaras, and some Conchos became more sedentary, practicing more intensive agriculture including stock-raising. Members of bands that escaped forced labor came to depend increasingly on raiding Spanish ranches. All groups were reduced by epidemic diseases, and some like the Conchos and Tobosos were eliminated as separate ethnicities.

What attracted Spaniards to Chihuahua? The principal lure was silver. The impressive discoveries in Zacatecas just before mid-century spurred explorations farther north. After founding Durango and several other mining towns (*reales*), Francisco de Ibarra directed the establishment of a mining camp in southeastern Chihuahua in the 1560s. This settlement, Santa Bárbara, and the nearby agricultural district of Valle de San Bartolomé (today Valle de Allende) became the northernmost outposts of the new province of Nueva Vizcaya and the axis of subsequent colonization to the north.[9] Silver continued to be the impetus for settlement in Chihuahua, with the next stage occurring in the environs of Parral after silver was discovered there in 1631. Later in the century silver drew prospectors into Tarahumara country surrounding Cusihuiriáchic, and after 1702 Chihuahua became the preeminent locus of silver production in the eighteenth century.

What other patterns characterize these stages? Colonization was not a steadily advancing process from south to north since it tended to occur around silver mines and labor sources. Silver mines became towns and villas, which drew upon the same organizational and administrative practices of church and state already employed in more settled areas to the south. A highly stratified society developed, with a marked distinction between elites—Spanish miners, landowners, and merchants—and Indian and *casta* (mixed-blood) laborers. On the Chihuahua frontier, military service was an important requirement for obtaining elite status in the early years of any Spanish settlement, and it continued to confer status somewhat longer than was true for areas to the south. Nonetheless, the continued arrival of Spanish immigrants, many of them merchants, was also a key to elite composition. Agricultural development and commerce followed mining, and a variety of social and familial ties linked miners, landowners, and merchants. A shortage of mining and agricultural labor continued to foster forced-labor procurement, indigenous resistance, and a subservient but surly multiethnic labor force. The ever-present threat of hostilities from indigenous groups not yet dominated by Spaniards encouraged elite practices that mixed coercive and appeasing behaviors in dealing with subordinates. Introduction of Spanish ideals was partial at best, although some scholars have argued that the Spanish ethos of patriarchy, which stressed the importance of the father's dominance in the family and depreciated women's status, did acquire wide acceptance.[10] The following historical sketch will elucidate these patterns and their demographic underpinnings.

From their sixteenth-century base in southeastern Chihuahua, Spaniards sought to establish a silver-mining economy. Royal officials extended considerable leeway in this endeavor, especially in allowing or overlooking coercive labor practices. Following well-established patterns of Spanish conquest in Mexico, conquistadors quickly seized local Indians, either through outright slavery or grants of *encomienda* (which distributed the labor of specified numbers of Indians to a Spanish *encomendero*), to supplement small retinues of workers (black slaves, Indians, and mixed-race mestizos and mulattos) brought from settled areas.

The deployment of encomienda faced obstacles in Chihuahua where neither band nor ranchería groups were accustomed to systems that compelled

them to provide tribute to overlords. Spaniards sought to overcome this impediment by using brute force, where their numbers permitted, and by establishing a system of missions designed to instill Spanish ways among indigenous
peoples. Nearby Conchos and, to a lesser extent, Tepehuanes and natives
captured from various band groups were brought in chain gangs to work in
mines and farms around Santa Bárbara. The establishment of mission pueblos
in the late sixteenth and early seventeenth centuries, first by Franciscans among
Conchos and then by Jesuits in Tepehuán territory, created an Indian labor
pool that facilitated the use of *repartimiento,* which gradually replaced encomienda. In this system of forced labor, work crews were drafted from villages
and given fixed-term assignments in Spanish enterprises for which they were
meagerly paid in kind. In Chihuahua, repartimiento was used primarily for
seasonal agricultural tasks, but it also commonly provided labor for mining
activities in the seventeenth century. Although laws that limited the numbers
and duration of repartimientos were often ignored, this system was still insufficient to meet labor demands, which grew as Spanish colonization increased
and as the Indian population declined due to epidemic disease. Spanish enterprises adapted to changing circumstances by using a variety of methods of
labor recruitment, ranging from Indian and black slavery to repartimiento, to
private contract labor (used mainly for more specialized tasks in mining or
stock-raising).[11]

Silver deposits were never substantial around Santa Bárbara, and its early
years proved to be unstable as Indians resisted labor drafts and Spaniards
sometimes used the town as a center of recruitment for further exploration (for
example, Juan de Oñate's 1598 expedition to New Mexico drained off a substantial portion of settlers and Indian allies). Santa Bárbara survived primarily
because its early settlers obtained land grants in nearby Valle de San Bartolomé,
the main breadbasket for the entire northern province of Nueva Vizcaya
(whose capital was located to the south, in Durango).

While the Spanish and casta population grew slowly, if at all, during the first
fifty years (never more than a few hundred), native numbers plummeted.
Epidemics of smallpox and measles in 1577, during the 1590s, and in the
succeeding two decades reduced Conchos, Tepehuanes, and other Indians
drawn into Santa Bárbara's orbit by well over half.[12] Warfare and flight also
contributed to the decline of native populations, as Conchos, Chisos, Tepehuanes, and some eastern Tarahumaras intermittently fled or attacked missions
and Spanish settlements. Indian resistance tended to be piecemeal until the
Tepehuán rebellion of 1616, which mobilized thousands of Tepehuán warriors
and allies from surrounding areas, severely disrupting Spanish economic activities in all of Nueva Vizcaya for more than two years.[13] Conchos, some of

whom had rebelled earlier, for the most part showed allegiance to Spaniards, and many actually served as auxiliary troops to Spanish forces in crushing the Tepehuán rebellion. Since Conchos were less united in bands and geographically dispersed than Tepehuanes, there tended to be wide variability in their responses to Spanish intrusion.

The Tepehuán revolt was led by messianic leaders responding to catastrophic population loss and the dismantling of their social institutions. The mission system forced Indians to live in villages, to produce agricultural surpluses, and to provide labor for Spaniards. Christian doctrine called for the suppression of native ritual activity aimed at ensuring harmony, and insisted on monogamous marriages. Linking the arrival of Christianity to plague and calamity, Tepehuán leaders desperately sought to wipe out the intruders, predicting a utopian future in which even cactus would bear corn. Several hundred Spaniards and castas lost their lives, including Jesuit and Franciscan missionaries who were forced to witness the desecration of churches and religious ornamentation before they were murdered. The rebellion, suppressed brutally but with great difficulty by informally recruited militias, was testimony to the fragility of the Spanish presence.

The next silver cycle, which began in 1631 with discoveries at nearby San José de Parral, proved to be more sustaining for the Spaniards of southern Chihuahua. The Tepehuán rebellion had convinced Spanish officials of the need to expand the mission program and to provide more effective means of military defense, including the establishment of a presidio in northern Durango at Tepehuanes. Parral grew rapidly, drawing several thousand prospectors, merchants, and laborers within a decade.[14] Although Durango remained the official provincial capital, governors resided in Parral, which became the hub of commercial activity for the rest of the seventeenth century.

The labor force was assembled haphazardly, comprising the same mix of free and unfree labor noted above for Santa Bárbara. Not by coincidence, Jesuits and Franciscans pushed farther north into Tarahumara and Concho territory, establishing several new missions in the 1630s and 1640s. In addition to Conchos, Tepehuanes, and Tarahumaras, Indians were brought from central Mexico, Sinaloa, and Sonora to work in the mines. Local repartimientos supplied some of the labor, but many workers were lured by the practice that allowed them to retain a part of the ore they mined (*pepena* or *partido*) and by the promise of credit advances. Black slaves, mestizos, and mulattos also toiled in mines.[15]

Parral's steady economic development fueled further agricultural production in the Valle de San Bartolomé, a related rise in labor drafts from Concho, Tepehuán, and Tarahumara missions, and renewed expeditions to capture Indian slaves in the Bolsón de Mapimí and New Mexico. Competition for scarce labor escalated among Spanish entrepreneurs in the next few decades.[16] The attendant pressures on Indian populations were made worse by epidemics in 1636, 1645–47, and 1650–52, and several years of drought beginning in 1645. Rebellion erupted once again, first in Concho territory in 1644, then in the Tarahumara, where Jesuit efforts to expand the mission frontier into the Papigochic river valley met with revolts in 1648, 1650, and 1652, effectively halting Jesuit expansion among the Rarámuri for the next twenty years. At the same time, Tobosos and other nomadic groups operating out of the Bolsón de Mapimí stepped up attacks on ranches along the Conchos and Florido rivers and on mule trains moving along the royal road.[17]

The following sad tale offers an idea of the chaos and uncertainty that plagued the times. In one of many similar incidents occurring in 1645, a band of Salinero Indians attacked a mule train carrying provisions from Mapimí to Parras. These Salineros had been resettled in the Jesuit mission of Tizonazo along with other bands and some Tepehuanes, but they had fled (perhaps because Tizonazo converts were being heavily recruited in repartimiento). Their leader had taken the name of Gerónimo Moranta, a Jesuit slain in the Tepehuán rebellion. The practice of assuming the names and titles of Spanish authorities as a way of taking on their power was common to many of the indigenous groups of the region.[18]

Traveling with the mule train were the wife and children of Antonio Pérez de Molina, a Portuguese immigrant and petty trader. After killing the Spanish freighters and seizing items of clothing and food, the Salineros carried off Doña Antonia Tremeño, her daughter, and three sons. The terrified woman was forced to watch as the Indians killed two of her sons. The remaining son and the fifteen-year-old daughter were handed over to two of the warriors. Doña Antonia became the slave of the leader, Moranta, and was ordered to carry water, gather firewood, and grind corn. With her hair cut short and dressed in deerskins, she was traded from owner to owner, eventually coming into the hands of a group of Tobosos. Meanwhile the daughter, now pregnant, was eventually released by her captor and made her way to the hacienda of Diego de Ontíveros on the Nazas River.

Many of the native raiders were reported by the missionaries to be relapsed converts, who preferred a life of freedom (which to Spaniards meant irresponsibility and moral laxity) to "honest" work as servants of the colonizers. Spanish soldiers who considered Indian tactics of war to be completely barbarous and fiendish nonetheless retaliated in kind, summarily executing captured Indians, including women. By the fall of 1645, Indian rebels and raiders had killed or robbed several thousand head of cattle in southern Chihuahua, but Spanish militias had succeeded in confining the Tobosos to the arid basin lands east of the Valle de San Bartolomé, where they were running out of food. Their desert survival skills, which often astonished and repelled Spaniards who claimed they even ate their own excrement, were hard-pressed by drought. Several of the Toboso and Salinero leaders entreated for peace in October and, in return for supplies of flour and beef, promised to settle in the Franciscan mission of Atotonilco and to serve as Spanish allies. In the peace negotiations, the Spanish captain bartered for the return of Doña Antonia, but the Toboso chief reported that she had been set free earlier. Skeptical Spaniards surmised that she had been killed just before the peace negotiations concluded in order to keep her from testifying about rebel misdeeds. For Spaniard and Indian alike, the Chihuahua frontier offered a precarious existence, but women faced particularly harrowing perils.[19]

Sporadic hostilities continued throughout the 1660s while epidemics flared in 1662 and 1667, followed by another extended drought in 1667–68. Nonetheless, Parral's mines continued to operate, since silver mining received the highest priority from colonial officials; and because most local officials were directly involved in the mining economy. Labor coercion was at its height in the middle third of the seventeenth century as the last of the encomenderos battled with recipients of repartimientos, Nueva Vizcayan governors cooperated in the enslavement of Indians, and working conditions were extremely harsh. Not surprisingly, the ruthless tactics of Spanish officials contributed to the violence which exploded in the 1650s and 1660s: the tyranny of Spanish rule in Parral contrasted starkly with the disrespect shown to Spanish person and property outside urban or fortified areas. After persistent rebukes and threats of punishment from the Spanish crown, local officials ceased their direct participation in the slave trade and began to impose sanctions on employers who severely abused their workers.[20]

These measures seem to have contributed to the easing of tensions in the 1670s. Furthermore, mining operations began to be seriously curtailed by problems of flooding early in the decade, reducing the demand for labor. Jesuits and Franciscans renewed their efforts in the western Tarahumara area, establishing a score of new missions while arguing over their respective jurisdictions.[21] The first detailed count of Nueva Vizcaya's Jesuit mission population was made in 1678 by Father Juan Ortiz Zapata.[22] When compared with contact-population estimates, it shows steep decline in the areas penetrated earliest by Spaniards. And although Chihuahua's non-Indian population was still relatively small, less than 5 percent of the total population, it was growing and it was ethnically diverse.

The mobility of the population as a whole is striking. Although it would be impossible to assess population movements with precision, several factors contributed to mobility and contact among nonelite ethnic groups. The potential for profit on a mining frontier sparsely populated by Spaniards attracted Spanish immigrants. This also served as a motive for mixed-blood groups, for example for mestizos who might be able to "pass" as Spanish. Other castas fled to these remote regions in order to escape obligations or prosecution for criminal activities. And still others, including central Mexican Indians, went in search of paid labor. Once arrived in Parral, they found an established elite and an institutional structure that protected local notables.

Chief among the region's dignitaries was Valerio Cortés del Rey, who had arrived in Parral from Spain as a young man and assumed the post of royal assayer, the official who determined the quality of silver ores and tax valuations. Taking advantage of his position, he was able to accumulate a silver fortune of his own. Much of this wealth was invested in land, and by the 1660s he was the largest landowner in Chihuahua. On his holdings, which stretched for more than a hundred miles along the Río Conchos, Cortés del Rey raised thousands of sheep and cattle. His influence bought him favor with provincial governors and *audiencia* (high court) officials in Guadalajara, prompting him to boast that he was the key to the kingdom of Nueva Vizcaya.[23] In 1674, the Spanish crown granted him the right to found a *mayorazgo,* the only one to be established in the north.[24] Mayorazgos were large entailed estates that could not be subdivided or sold, but passed intact from the oldest son of one generation to the next, thus ensuring the family's social and economic prominence.

The power and wealth of Cortés del Rey presents many contrasts to the situation of Indian and other lower-status groups who worked for him and other landowners and miners. In many cases, elites' access to judicial officials allowed them to expand landholdings into areas claimed by Tepehuanes, Tarahumaras, and Conchos.[25] This process was helped by the decline in numbers of Indians, as Spanish hacendados could lay claim to lands they alleged were no longer in use by the indigenous population. Even when Indian lands were protected by titles registered and defended by missionaries, stock raisers presented a threat to unfenced boundaries. For example, in the mid-1660s, several Franciscan and Jesuit missions had croplands trampled by the expanding herds of Cortés del Rey. Although he was ordered to remove his cattle from Indian lands, other testimony charging him with extreme cruelty in "disciplining" Indians was ignored, and the loss of crops was irreversible.[26]

In rare cases, indigenous or Spanish middlemen were able to take Indian grievances to the high court in Guadalajara and obtain favorable judgments. This was the case in 1670, when complaints from Concho Indians served as the stimulus that led to the final abolition of encomienda in the north.[27] But the primary means of avoiding Spanish abuses continued to be flight—a recourse aided by long distances between settlements and empty spaces as well as labor shortages that facilitated geographic mobility and access to new jobs. Employers were loathe to ask many questions when a prospective laborer turned up; such a situation actually encouraged fugitivism and protected outlaws of all social categories.

The mix and volatility of social relationships among subordinate peoples is illustrated by a series of incidents that came to the attention of the Mexican Inquisition in 1673.[28] The local inquisitorial official, a priest in Parral, charged Nicolás de Guzmán, a mestizo who worked for a landowner near the Jesuit mission of Satevó, with the practice of witchcraft. The forty-seven-year-old Guzmán was arrested as he was walking along the road from his home on his way to work and charged with casting a spell on Mateo de Medrano, the mulatto-slave husband of Guzmán's niece Petrona, an Indian. The spell had made Medrano ill, and conventional remedies had not produced a cure. Mateo and Petrona were herders on the sheep holdings of Cortés del Rey. The charge of witchcraft had been presented to the Spanish overseer of the property, Alonso de Irigoyen, by two Indians, one from Sinaloa and the other a Tarahumara. They alleged that Petrona had asked her uncle to cast the spell on Mateo to punish him for his dalliance with María, a black slave who worked on a neighboring hacienda. Martín from Sinaloa claimed to have found the errant couple after they had been tied up by Guzmán, when he performed the act of inserting a small stone into Mateo's hip without breaking the skin. Such occurrences were commonly reported in Inquisition cases, and were accepted as plausible by Spanish priests who used prayer or exorcism to extract demonic objects and substances from the body as well as by many indigenous peoples who practiced sucking rituals to remove foreign objects from the body.[29]

Deciding that the matter merited investigation, Irigoyen took Guzmán into custody with the aid of two of the ranch's cowboys, both mulatto slaves. In the course of the investigation, Guzmán, a native of Analco in Nueva Galicia who admitted that he had once broken the arm of a friar who attempted to discipline him, denied that he had ever practiced witchcraft. To the contrary, he alleged that one of his accusers, Martín from Sinaloa, was actually the culprit who had employed magic in attempting to cure Mateo. Several witnesses testified that Martín had in fact extracted foreign objects including hairs, a small piece of cloth, and a small snake from Mateo's body. Martín did admit to recognizing the signs that a spell had been cast, but he maintained that his role was merely to try to remove the spell or offending objects. Claiming to have special grace from God, Martín testified that he always knew when he was needed because a little bird would appear, accompanied by a voice directing him what to use for a cure.

When Mateo gave his version of events, he said that both Guzmán and Martín had attempted to cure him of what had begun as a case of typhus, but had mutated into a pain localized in his back where he could feel things moving under his skin. As the testimony unfolded, Nicolás Guzmán and Martín turned out to be only two in a parade of healers that also included a Spaniard, an unconverted Tarahumara, and an Indian from Sonora. Among the curing techniques mentioned in various testimonies were herbal potions to be swallowed, poultices applied to the back, sucking the wound through a hollow cane, attempts to induce sweating, and bleeding. The case, apparently not deemed worthy of further investigation from Mexico City, offers a picturesque glimpse into the multiethnic and often turbulent relationships and contacts that evolved in areas newly claimed by Spaniards.

The relative calm of the 1670s gave way to new troubles in the 1680s. News of the Pueblo rebellion in New Mexico reached groups to the south, certainly prompting Spanish fears that unrest might spread among them. Spanish authorities were also preoccupied by French incursions into Texas, near Matagorda Bay.[30] Whether or not they were encouraged by Spanish indecisiveness about retaking New Mexico, groups of Conchos and other bands went on the offensive in 1684, attacking Spanish settlements and silver shipments. In 1685, the crown reacted by establishing several new presidios along the royal road in eastern Durango and Chihuahua.[31] Although these measures helped to quell the raids, a new disturbance followed silver strikes at Coyáchic and Cusihuiriáchic in the mid-1680s. Jesuit missions in the upper Tarahumara area, barely a decade old, were a tempting source of labor, but once again Tarahumaras resisted coercion. Although some Tarahumaras had voluntarily traded corn and sold their labor in Spanish enterprises, others were determined to keep Spaniards from full-scale occupation of their lands. In 1690, Tarahumaras in almost all of the recently established missions joined unconverted Tarahumaras, who had been migrating northwest into rugged areas of the Sierra Madre, in rebellion. The presidial captain at Conchos, Juan Fernández de Retana, was able to quell the revolt (also joined by eastern Pimas and other serrano groups), but only after most of the new churches had been destroyed and two Jesuits killed.[32]

Severe epidemics of smallpox and measles in 1692 and 1693 also put a damper on native unrest, as an estimated one-third of Nueva Vizcaya's Indian population succumbed. When drought and famine followed in 1693–94, Spanish mining operations in the Tarahumara were severely threatened.[33] In desperation and incited by millenarian prophecies, Rarámuri warriors seized the moment in 1696 to try one more time to drive out the Spaniards. Tarahumaras were particularly troubled over Jesuit attempts to reorganize their social structure by insisting upon Christian marriage, imposing a governing hierarchy, and obstructing rituals of cooperative work that were followed by celebrations (*tesguinadas*) incorporating the uninhibited consumption of maize beer and dancing. This second rebellion was brutally suppressed by Spanish soldiers and militiamen who forced a surrender by burning Indian corn fields and then hanged hundreds of rebels.[34]

At the turn of the eighteenth century, the Spanish presence was uneven, still concentrated in the southeastern portion of present-day Chihuahua. To the northwest, mining continued at Cusihuiriáchic and Jesuit missionaries renewed their efforts among the Tarahumara. Some of the latter returned to reconstructed missions, but others retreated farther into the Sierra Madre Occidental, intensifying a pattern already begun. Choosing remote mountain canyons and pastures, they avoided the Spanish orbit while paradoxically helping to assure their subsistence by raising Spanish sheep. Adopting a strategy similar to other groups like Pimas on the Sonoran side of the sierra and Tepehuanes in southwestern Chihuahua and northwestern Durango, they fashioned a blend of sheep raising, horticulture, hunting, gathering, and occasional raids that allowed them to resist incorporation until well after the end of the colonial period. The remaining Conchos, whose population was now much depleted, were reorganized in missions along the Conchos River and in the north . . . While the non-Indian population of all of Nueva Vizcaya had grown to approximately one-half that of the Indian by 1700, in Chihuahua Spaniards and castas still constituted less than a tenth of the total.[35] The eighteenth century would see a shift with the non-Indian population finally exceeding that of the natives by 1800. That story begins with the exploitation of silver near the present-day city of Chihuahua.

Although some attempts had been made earlier to mine silver there, and a few Spaniards had established cattle herds along the Sacramento and Chuvíscar rivers, Indian unrest inhibited Spanish exploitation of the area. Silver mining became more promising after Conchos and Tarahumaras were resettled nearby at the end of the seventeenth century, and when the new presidios provided more protection against raids by eastern bands. In the first decade of the eighteenth century, Spanish miners began to exploit the silver deposits at Santa Eulalia. Because this site lacked a sufficient water source, in 1708 the Spanish settlement was moved to its present location, where it attained the status of villa in 1718 with the name of San Felipe el Real de Chihuahua.[36]

Chihuahua's mines quickly superseded production at Cusihuiriáchic, producing about a fourth of New Spain's silver for the next three decades.[37] The promise of riches followed earlier patterns in attracting Spanish miners and merchants from Cusihuiriáchic, Parral, and farther south. Officers from the new presidios also took advantage of the new bonanza. Work crews were assembled haphazardly, encompassing an ethnic and geographic mix that included Tarahumaras, Yaquis, Apaches, mulatto slaves, and mestizos. Some were forced to work, but many came voluntarily, attracted by the pepena—at least until one of the wealthiest miners, Manuel San Juan y Santa Cruz (who had served as governor of Nueva Vizcaya from 1714 to 1720), began a campaign in 1730 to end this practice. In what was perhaps northern Mexico's first labor strike, hundreds of workers stopped work and threatened to storm the city unless the pepena was restored. Although authorities backed down temporarily, in the end the practice was curtailed, and employers found other means of procuring labor. Force continued to be used, but credit advances became the most common way to attract laborers. Where employers were more in need of laborers, workers were sometimes able to negotiate substantial advances even though salaries tended to be low. Compared with Mexico City, the relative buying power of workers in the north, where grain prices were normally double those of Mexico City, was low.[38]

The population of the new mining area may have climbed over twenty thousand by the 1730s. After the richer surface ores became more depleted around 1740, mining declined and the population dropped, but probably not much below ten thousand.[39] Chihuahua remained an important commercial center controlling the supply of goods to New Mexico until the nineteenth century, although there were frequent disputes between officials of Chihuahua and Parral over the regulation of grain sales in the periodically drought-stricken region. Leading miners were usually merchants as well, and their ranks were reinforced by Spaniards who continued to immigrate throughout the century. These elites monopolized local government and kept the potentially unruly labor force in check, although Chihuahua's Indians and castas were not as servile as their employers would have liked, taking advantage of religious holidays to indulge in their favorite secular pastimes of cockfighting, gambling, drinking and dancing.[40]

In the eighteenth century, except in the western Tarahumara area, Indian mission pueblos, which had supplied laborers to Parral, Chihuahua, other mining centers, and the farms and ranches of the Valle de San Bartolomé, became transformed. Some of their inhabitants chose to live permanently in their workplaces while outsiders moved into the missions, building houses and renting Indian lands that had not been lost already to expanding haciendas. Widespread drought in the 1730s and a severe epidemic of *matlazáhuatl* (probably typhus) in 1738–39 further eroded numbers of Indians and means of subsistence in the missions. In recognition of these demographic and economic changes, in the 1740s Jesuits relinquished their missions in southeastern

Chihuahua to the diocesan clergy. The transition from mission to parish was an acknowledgment of the lack of Indianness and the erosion of indigenous communal solidarity in these villages.[41] By 1750, the non-Indian population had overtaken Indian numbers, by about four to one, in all but the western Tarahumara, where the situation was almost exactly the reverse. Jesuits claimed more than ten thousand Tarahumara and other serrano converts, but few actually lived permanently in the missions, preferring to choose between rancheria locations, where they could practice a variety of subsistence activities.[42]

The unevenness of Spanish control remained the problem that the Marqués de Altamira contemplated at mid-century. The high degree of geographical mobility that has been noted for late eighteenth-century Nueva Vizcaya had always been the case in Chihuahua, but its proportions were particularly disturbing to officials who were more intent than ever on controlling behavior, at least in the areas of Spanish settlement.[43] Royal officials attributed a growing incidence of raiding, livestock theft, and highway robbery to the ease with which Indians could leave their villages. Repeated attempts to regulate travel by Indians and to prevent them from occupying unauthorized settlements failed.[44]

Volatility on the Chihuahua frontier was certainly not a novelty, however, and officials might have begun to breathe easier since most of the eastern raiding groups had been eliminated or remnants of their bands incorporated into villages. But at mid-eighteenth century, another threat emerged. Apaches, having been pushed south and west since the seventeenth century by displacements of Plains Indians, now penetrated even farther into Nueva Vizcaya. When Comanches usurped their role as the primary traders of buffalo products and deerskins to Pueblos and Spaniards in New Mexico, various southern Apache bands resorted to another subsistence strategy. With their access to buffalo ranges blocked by Comanches, Apaches needed something to trade for buffalo meat, hides, and European goods. They found it in the livestock ranches of central and southern Chihuahua and northern Durango. From the late 1740s until the last decade of the eighteenth century, Apache bands entered this region through the Sierra Madre Occidental, from Paso del Norte and from the eastern deserts whose presidios had been closed down at mid-century, carrying out raids on Spanish haciendas and ranchos. Although they did take cattle at times, their primary objects were horses and mules, more easily moved to areas of refuge where they could be traded in a high-demand market. As the raids escalated, thousands of animals were stolen, many haciendas and ranchos were abandoned, and scores of people (predominantly herders and cowhands) were killed each year. Reprisals (including the taking of Apache captives who were virtually enslaved) from Spanish soldiers at newly established presidios in northwestern Chihuahua had the effect of escalating the violence, as retaliation continued on both sides. Although Spaniards continued to use Indian allies to fight Apaches, a growing number of Indians who had once been sedentarized in missions or villages joined or imitated Apaches in raiding. The majority of these were Tarahumaras from former Jesuit missions, either those secularized in the 1740s or others that had come under Franciscan or diocesan control after the Jesuits were expelled in 1767.[45]

The removal of the Jesuits from Spain's empire was only one of several so-called reform measures implemented by the Bourbon kings in the late eighteenth century to enhance royal control over colonial resources. Another was the creation in 1776 of a new administrative jurisdiction for northern Mexico, the Comandancia General de las Provincias Internas, designed to deal more effectively with foreign challenges to Spain in North America and to establish peace and security in the face of Indian hostilities. Chihuahua was the capital of the Provincias Internas for much of its existence; its administrative dominance was paralleled by the expansion of commerce. Although mining output had declined in the 1740s, Chihuahua's miner-merchant elites continued to profit, especially as they came to control trade with New Mexico. Chihuahua merchants charged high prices for goods (including tools, arms, clothing, sugar, tobacco, chocolate, liquor, and other items) imported from central Mexico and Spain and then exported to New Mexico.[46]

Apache hostilities may have inhibited the growth of Chihuahua, especially during the 1760s and 1770s, when they were at their peak, but during the last decade of the eighteenth century new policies providing commodity subsidies to Apaches in return for promises of peace did succeed in reducing raids. The last three decades of colonial rule witnessed relative peace and prosperity for Spaniards, as mining revived slightly in Parral and Cusihuiriáchic, agricultural production increased, commerce grew, and the non-Indian population expanded through immigration, surpassing the total number of Indians by 1800.[47]

By the time of Mexican independence in 1821, Chihuahua's population was approaching 100,000.[48] The Indian population was less than half of the total and increasingly isolated in the rugged mountain canyons of western Chihuahua, where it was more possible to avoid Spanish demands. These were primarily Tarahumaras, but also included a variety of smaller serrano groups and some Tepehuanes in the southwestern corner of the present state of Chihuahua. Franciscans took over the Jesuits' missions in the western Tarahumara after 1767, but very few natives resided in them year round. Even fewer Tarahumaras still dwelled in their old eastern homelands, now administered by Franciscans or parish priests, but much of their land had been acquired by Spaniards, either through subterfuge, purchase, or rent.[49]

Chihuahua on the eve of Mexican independence looked a bit more like the social composite the Marqués de Altamira had fancied three-quarters of a century earlier. In several populous towns, elite Spanish men controlled political, economic, and cultural life through institutions of the Spanish state and church. They owned the productive mines, haciendas, and commercial enterprises with ties in Mexico City and Guadalajara, and occupied important local offices of government. Although they could not completely control the behaviors of ethnic and economic subordinates, they effected and conserved a general stability. Male-female relations tended to follow Spanish patriarchal codes that demanded female submissiveness to fathers and husbands; these were accepted by and large across class and ethnic lines. Yet a substantial number of women headed households and engaged in economic activities to support their families.[50] Located in what was still a frontier province where indigenous peoples were incompletely incorporated, Chihuahua's urban officials and businessmen struggled to attain a level of civility that would command respect from the core areas to the south. Yet, in order to maintain control in often precarious frontier conditions, they had to be willing to negotiate with their social inferiors and to accommodate their aspirations to varying degrees.[51] In some cases, this situation abetted social mobility, as in the example of the military colonists who continued to fight Apaches in northwestern Chihuahua. These mixed-race peoples were "whitened" by virtue of their marked differentiation from "barbarous" Apaches.[52]

The countryside was less regulated than the towns. Haciendas expanded, sometimes incorporating ranches and remnants of former Jesuit missions. Other rural villages provided laborers and produce for urban areas. Where Indian government and communal solidarity had existed in former mission villages of central and southern Chihuahua, it was now a thing of the past. Elites were poised to accumulate and consolidate large landholdings in that region. Most of Chihuahua's original native groups had disappeared through warfare, disease, and racial mixing. Only Tarahumaras survived in substantial numbers, while a smaller number of Tepehuanes straddled the Chihuahua-Durango border. For a while, they would be left alone in their mountain and canyon homes, eschewing outsiders. Not until the late nineteenth century did Chihuahua's elites move to appropriate the timber and metal resources of the sierra. More interested in commercial opportunities opened up by U.S. westward expansion, they moved northward into the Chihuahua desert, only to confront reinvigorated Apache raiding societies after Mexican independence in 1821. For the next half-century, Chihuahua was virtually segregated in three distinct parts with little interaction. Only the force of the Porfirian state would integrate them at the turn of the twentieth century, at the same time dealing a decisive blow to indigenous autonomy.

TABLE 1.1

Population Shifts in Colonial Chihuahua

	1550	1600	1650	1700	1750	1800
Non-Indians		400	2,100	5,800	30,300	42,500
All Indians	175,000	163,500	139,500	74,000	46,300	39,100
Tepehuanes & Tarahumaras	120,000	109,500	95,000	55,000	34,350	29,500

SOURCE: Estimates adapted from Peter Gerhard, *The North Frontier of New Spain,* rev. ed. (Norman: University of Oklahoma Press, 1993), 170–200, and various estimates and censuses located in the Archivo General de la Nacíon (Mexico City); Archivo Histórico de Hacienda, Temporalidades, legs. 279, 1126, 2009; Archivo de Hidalgo de Parral (microfilm), reels Durango, Varios, Año 1749; and *Documentos para la Historia de México* (Mexico, 1853–57), 4th series, vol. 3, 301–419.

NOTES

1. Altamira's advice to the viceroy is found in various reports from 1747 to 1749 in Archivo General de la Nación, Mexico City (hereafter cited as AGN), Archivo Histórico de Hacienda, Temporalidades, leg. 278, exp. 40; and Archivo General de Indias, Sevilla (hereafter cited as AGI), Audiencia de Guadalajara, leg. 191. See also María del Carmen Velázquez, *El Marqués de Altamira y las provincias internas de Nueva España* (Mexico City, 1976).

2. Viceroy to Council of the Indies, July 27, 1749, AGI, Guadalajara 301.

3. Peter Gerhard's total in *The North Frontier of New Spain,* rev. ed. (Norman, 1993), from the jurisdictions which make up modern-day Chihuahua, is just over 175,000; 170–71. Gerhard's estimates of contact population tend to be conservative, as noted in Chantal Cramaussel, *La provincia de Santa Bárbara en Nueva Vizcaya, 1563–1631* (Cd. Juárez, 1990), 86–88; and compared with estimates in Daniel T. Reff, *Disease, Depopulation and Culture Change in Northwestern New Spain, 1518–1764* (Salt Lake City, 1991).

4. Rancherías were dispersed settlements of a few to a hundred dwellings. Often located along water sources, their inhabitants practiced agriculture and engaged in hunting and gathering activities. Edward H. Spicer, *Cycles of Conquest: The Impact of Spain, Mexico and the United States on the Indians of the Southwest, 1533–1960* (Tucson, 1962), 12–13.

5. William B. Griffen, *Culture Change and Shifting Populations in Central Northern Mexico* (Tucson, 1969).

6. Thomas D. Hall, *Social Change in the Southwest, 1350–1880* (Lawrence, 1989), 50–109; Nancy P. Hickerson, *The Jumanos: Hunters and Traders of the South Plains* (Austin, 1994).

7. Some Tepehuanes may have lived in more stratified villages before the seventeenth century. George P. Hammond and Agapito Rey, eds., *Obregón's History of the Sixteenth Century Exploration in Western America* (Los Angeles, 1928).

8. Susan M. Deeds, "Legacies of Resistance, Adaptation and Tenacity: History of the Native Peoples of Northwest Mexico," in *Cambridge History of Native Peoples of the Americas,* forthcoming.

9. Cramaussel, *La provincia de Santa Bárbara,* passim.

10. This idea is argued, in different ways, in Cheryl E. Martin, *Governance and Society in Colonial Mexico: Chihuahua in the Eighteenth Century* (Stanford, 1996), and Ana María Alonso, Thread of Blood: Colonialism, Revolution, and Gender on Mexico's Northern Frontier (Tucson, 1995).

11. Labor practices are outlined in Susan M. Deeds, "Rural Work in Nueva Vizcaya: Forms of Labor Coercion on the Periphery," *Hispanic American Historical Review* 69:3 (1989), 425–49; and Chantal Cramaussel, "Encomiendas, repartimientos y conquista en Nueva Vizcaya," in *Actas del Segundo Congreso de Historia Regional Comparada* (Cd. Juárez, 1990), 139–60.

12. Gerhard, *North Frontier,* 170–71; Cramaussel, *La Provincia de Santa Bárbara,* 86–87; Jesuit cartas ánuas in AGN, Historia, vol. 19.

13. Susan M. Deeds, "Las rebeliones de los tepehuanes y tarahumaras durante el siglo

XVII en la Nueva Vizcaya," in Ysla Campbell, ed., *El contacto entre los españoles e indígenas en el norte de la Nueva España* (Cd. Juárez, 1992).

14. Robert C. West, *The Mining Community in Northern New Spain: The Parral Mining District* (Berkeley, 1947).

15. Ignacio del Río, "Sobre la aparición y desarrollo del trabajo libre asalariado en el norte de Nueva España (siglos xvi y xvii)," in Elsa Cecilia Frost Michael Meyer, and Josefina Zoraida Vázquez, compilers, *El trabajo y los trabajadores en la historia de México* (Tucson, 1979), 92–111. For earlier use of the pepena in the north, see Andrés Pérez de Ribas, *Historia de los triunfos de nuestra santa fe entre las gentes más bárbaras del nuevo orbe* [1645] (Mexico City, 1992), book 8, chap. 3.

16. Deeds, "Rural Work," 435–38; Viceroy to Audiencia of Guadalajara, Apr. 25, 1659, Biblioteca Pública del Estado de Jalisco, Archivo Judicial de la Audiencia de Nueva Galicia (hereafter cited as BPEJ, AJANG), Civil, C–4–1 (39).

17. Series of reports on Indian depredations in AGN, Historia, vol. 19, fols. 121–166; relación de Diego de Medrano, Aug. 31, 1654, AGI, Guadalajara 68.

18. Relación de la guerra de los tepehuanes, P. Francisco Arista, Dec. 1617, AGN, Historia, vol. 311.

19. Information on these series of events can be found in a report of the Jesuit priest at San Miguel de las Bocas, Padre Nicolás de Zepeda, to the Jesuit provincial head, Apr. 18, 1645, AGN, Historia, vol. 19, fols. 136–166; and in military reports of the Spanish captain, Francisco Montaño de la Cueva, Oct. 1645, in Archivo de Hidalgo de Parral (hereafter cited as AHP), microfilm copy in University of Arizona Library, reel 1645a, frames 230–243.

20. Governor Antonio Oca de Sarmiento to Viceroy, Mar. 12, 1667, in Charles Hackett, *Historical Documents relating to New Mexico, Nueva Vizcaya, and approaches thereto, to 1773*, 3 vols. (Washington, 1923–37), 2:188–95; testimony on labor conditions in Nueva Vizcaya, 1670, BPEJ, AJANG, Civil, caja 12, exp. 2 (157).

21. Report of P. Tomás de Guadalajara, Matachic, Jul. 20, 1677, AGN, Misiones 26, fols. 237–8; F. Antonio de Valdés to P. Com. Gen., Parral, Jun. 17, 1677, Biblioteca Nacional (Mexico City), Archivo Franciscano (hereafter cited as BN, AF), Caja 12, 195–2.

22. AGN, Misiones 26, fols. 241–269.

23. Various reports in Hackett, *Historical Documents*, 2:188–95.

24. Francisco de Almada, *Resumen de historia del estado de Chihuahua* (Chihuahua, 1986), 72–79.

25. Susan M. Deeds, "Mission Villages and Agrarian Patterns in a Nueva Vizcayan Heartland, 1600–1750," *Journal of the Southwest* 33:3 (Autumn 1991), 345–65.

26. Testimony before Gov. Antonio de Oca Sarmiento, Satevó, Feb. 21, 1667, AHP, reel 1667 B, fr. 738–743.

27. Series of autos, 1670–71, in BPE, AJANG, Civil, C–12, exp. 2 (157).

28. Denuncia by Comisario del Santo Oficio Felipe de la Cueva Montaño Villamayor, Parral, Sept. 9, 1673, AGN, Inquisición, vol. 516, fols. 405–431.

29. Causa criminal . . . por indicios de hechicero, Mar. 1703, AHP, reel 1703, fr. 973–982.

30. Various autos, 1688–89, in Hackett, *Historical Documents*, 2:234–89.

31. Thomas H. Naylor and Charles W. Polzer, S.J., eds., *The Presidio and Militia on the Northern Frontier of New Spain, 1570–1700* (Tucson, 1986), 548–67.

32. Joseph Neumann, *Historia de las rebeliones de la sierra tarahumara, 1626–1724*, ed. Luis González Rodríguez (Chihuahua, 1991); Deeds, "Las rebeliones de los tepehuanes y los tarahumaras."

33. Report of Gov. Joseph Marín to Viceroy, Parral, Sept. 30, 1693, AGI, Guadalajara, leg. 120; testimony regarding grain shortages, Sept. 1694, AHP, reel 1694A, fr. 48–125.

34. Documents on the Tarahumara rebellions in AGI, Patronato, leg. 236; and AGI, Audiencia de Guadalajara, leg. 156.

35. Gerhard, *North Frontier*, 24, 170–71.

36. Martin, *Governance and Society*, 18–28; Philip L. Hadley, *Minería y sociedad en el centro minero de Santa Eulalia, Chihuahua, 1709–1750* (Mexico City, 1979).

37. Hadley, *Minería y sociedad*, 27–28.

38. Martin, Governance and Society, 47–73.

39. José Antonio Villaseñor y Sánchez, Theatro americano: descripción general de los reynos, y provincias de la Nueva España y sus jurisdicciones (Mexico City, 1952), 2: 352–63.

40. Cheryl E. Martin, "Public Celebrations, Popular Culture, and Labor Discipline in Eighteenth-Century Chihuahua," in William H. Beezley, Cheryl E. Martin, and William S. French, eds., *Rituals of Rule, Ritual of Resistance: Public Celebrations and Popular Culture in Mexico* (Wilmington, Del., 1994), 95–114.

41. Susan M. Deeds, "Rendering unto Caesar: The Secularization of Jesuit Missions in Durango," (Ph.D. diss., University of Arizona, 1981), passim; report of Corregidor de Chihuahua, July 1, 1759, AGN, Alcaldías Mayores, vol. 6, fols. 184–189.

42. Reports of Jesuits in Tarahumara missions, 1757–8, AGN, Jesuitas, II–7, exps. 16–24.

43. Michael Swann, "Tierra Adentro": Settlement and Society in Colonial Durango (Boulder, 1982), 171–207.

44. Order of Governor Ignacio Francisco de Barrutia, June 18, 1729, marriage registers, Santiago Papasquiaro, LDS microfilm 658011; P. Juan Antonio Balthasar to Viceroy, n.d. 1754, W. B. Stephens Collections, no. 1719, University of Texas Nettie Lee Benson Library.

45. William B. Griffen, *Apaches at War and Peace: The Janos Presidio, 1750–1858* (Albuquerque, 1988), 1–36; William L. Merrill, "Cultural Creativity and Raiding Bands in Eighteenth-Century Northern New Spain," in William B. Taylor and Franklin Pease G. Y., eds., *Violence, Resistance, and Survival in the Americas* (Washington, D.C., 1994), 124–52.

46. Oakah Jones, *Nueva Vizcaya: Heartland of the Spanish Frontier* (Albuquerque, 1988), 186–88; David J. Weber, *The Spanish Frontier in North America* (New Haven, 1992), 196–98.

47. Luis Aboites, *Breve historia de Chihuahua* (Mexico City, 1994), 69–73.

48. Padrones of 1804–6 and 1820 in AGN, AHH, Consulado, 917–2, and Biblioteca Nacional, AF, Caja 18/387, respectively.

49. Padrón de Santiago de Babonoyahua, 1778, BN, AF, caja 16, exp. 328.

50. Martin, Governance and Society, 149–83.

51. Ibid.,Martin, *Governance and Society*, 184–195.

52. Alonso, *Thread of Blood*, 21–71.

CHAPTER TWO

DEMOGRAPHIC, SOCIAL, AND ECONOMIC CHANGE IN NEW MEXICO

ROSS FRANK

INTRODUCTION

In many respects the province of New Mexico serves as a pivotal example in the Spanish colonization of the northern Borderlands. The earliest explorations of the areas by Fray Marcos de Niza and Vásquez de Coronado took place within the context of the first wave of Spanish conquest. Following a sixteenth-century pattern already established in central Mexico, Spanish interest in New Mexico included the mass conversion of Native Americans, mission building, and the exploitation of mineral resources and native labor. When Fray Marcos de Niza returned from his expedition in search of the "Cities of Cibola" in 1539, he spread the story that he had seen the golden cities of great wealth from a distance. In fact, he had most likely fled before reaching one of the villages that made up Zuni Pueblo, where his more experienced black guide, Estéban, had been killed shortly before.

In response to the reports of Fray Niza, the governor of Nueva Galicia, Vásquez de Coronado, traveled throughout the Pueblo region beginning in 1540, and then as far as central Kansas, in search of the elusive cities of gold or mines that could produce precious metals. The failure of these early expeditions to New Mexico to find any wealthy Native American states with lucrative resources and precious minerals, along the lines of the discoveries in central Mexico or Peru, delayed settlement until the very end of the sixteenth century. Don Juan de Oñate, a wealthy mine owner from Zacatecas, received a license in 1598 from Phillip II to found a settlement in New Mexico. Even after he had established the first Spanish town near San Juan Pueblo, Oñate dispatched a series of exploratory parties to look for signs of precious metals and to scout out promising locations for mines. Only after failing once again to find any quick means to wealth and fame did the Oñate expedition settle for the occupation of New Mexico for the primary purpose of converting the Pueblo Indians and establishing a permanent agricultural settlement. The decision to colonize New Mexico, despite its lack of fabulous wealth, presaged other seventeenth-century provinces on the peripheries of New Spain settled expressly to take advantage of land for agriculture and ranching. In the case of the province of New Mexico, the roots of Spanish settlement in the era of the conquistadors created difficulties that destroyed the first New Mexican colony within a century.

The success of the Pueblo revolt of 1680 in driving the Spanish colonists out of New Mexico fundamentally altered the tone of relations between the Spanish and the Pueblos after the reconquest twelve years later. During the eighteenth century New Mexico again performed a pivotal role in the development of the northernmost provinces of New Spain. Due to the distant location of New Mexico and hostilities with Apache and Comanche bands that bordered the areas of settlement, the Spanish population grew only slowly during the first half of the 1700s. At the same time, settlement in New Mexico began early in comparison to that of Texas or Alta California, and a system of coexistence with the Pueblo Indians developed after the reconquest, encouraged by the need for a common defense.

When government authorities in charge of New Spain decided to take action in the 1770s, in response to the continuous raids on Spanish settlements and missions, they decided upon a strategy calculated to isolate and make peace with the Comanche in order to use them against the Apache. New Mexico proved central to the strategy because of its geographic position between Apache groups to the west and south and the Comanche divisions to the north and east. Bourbon officials recognized that within New Mexico Spanish population growth and harmonious social relations had produced a sizable Pueblo and vecino[1] militia. This force could supplement soldiers from the presidio of Santa Fe in the execution of the new strategy of warfare and diplomacy. The success of Governor de Anza, in 1779, against a major band of the western Comanche led to a peace and alliance, negotiated in 1785, between the Spanish and Comanche.

The Comanche peace, after the drain from a generation of raids and campaigns, freed the energies of New Mexicans for other productive endeavors. At the same time, the Comanche-Spanish alliance against the Apache reopened routes for trade between the province and other markets in Nueva Vizcaya and Sonora. The vecino population found itself well positioned to take charge of these new opportunities. Rapid economic growth in New Mexico began in the late 1780s and lasted into the second decade of the nineteenth century. In taking advantage of the economic developments, vecinos created a society of comparative wealth, and one that increasingly defined itself by socially sub-jugating and economically exploiting the Pueblo Indians. Economic growth, demographic expansion, and the changing dynamic of Pueblo-vecino relations combined to produce a vigorous, self-confidant vecino society at the turn of the nineteenth century. Just as the province had straddled the conquistador legacy and the colonist beginnings in the late sixteenth century, New Mexico's burst of economic and cultural activity two centuries later indicated one pos-sibility for the future of other northern provinces—one that remained unre-alized elsewhere along the northern periphery of New Spain.

I. THE INDIAN POPULATION

A. Estimates of contact size

The Pueblo world that the Spanish described in the 1500s had been shaped by large-scale migrations into the area of the Río Grande from the San Juan River drainage, to the northwest of the present concentration of Pueblo peoples. The people that began to build new villages along the Río Grande and its tributaries came from those that had occupied the great cities built into cliffs, such as at Mesa Verde in southwestern Colorado. The Navajo, who later occupied the river bottoms of the canyons housing ruins of Anasazi cliff dwellings at Canyon de Chelly in northeastern Arizona, named these people Anasazi, meaning "enemy ancestors." A generation of drought in the last quarter of the thirteenth century contributed to the movement of as many as thirty thousand people from the Anasazi homelands.[2] A large portion of these mingled with migrants from the Chaco culture area and other groups already well established on the Pajarito Plateau, just west of the Río Grande, and in the Río Grande area itself. Together, these peoples formed the core population that created a dynamic new phase of Pueblo development.

From the early 1300s to the time of the first Spanish explorations to New Mexico, Pueblo Indians established dozens of settlements in the Río Grande area. One study found that during this period at least seventy villages, each consisting of more than four hundred rooms, occupied the area north of present-day Albuquerque alone.[3] Some settlements had two and even three thousand rooms. When Fray Alonso de Benevides arrived in New Mexico, he estimated in his enthusiasm that, all told, the Indian pueblos held half a million inhabitants. In his revised report on New Mexico written in 1634, Benevides gave his reconsidered opinion that the province had contained eighty thousand Indians living in ninety pueblos when the Franciscan missionaries first arrived with Oñate. Benevides's estimate can be taken as a reasonable upper limit of the population of the Pueblos at the time of the Spanish occupation and settlement (see Table 2.1), although there may have been as many as 150 Pueblo Indian villages. Although as *custos* of the New Mexican missions from 1626 to 1629 Benevides held a good position from which to judge the number of the Puebloans, other estimates of the Pueblo population at the time of Spanish occupation have ranged as low as 40,000.[4]

B. Degree and manifestations of demographic collapse

At the time of the first contact with the Spanish in 1540 the people in each Indian pueblo that made up the eventual province of New Mexico spoke one of three distinct language groups: Tanoan, Keres, or Zuni. Members of the Tanoan pueblos spoke one of at least six distinct and mutually unintelligible dialects that had developed much earlier from a common ancestral tongue. The geographic distribution of these different language groups indicates the complexity of the Pueblo world that faced Spanish colonizers (see Map 2). Tanoan speakers lived on a north-south axis roughly centered on the Río Grande Valley. The northernmost Pueblos of Taos and Picurís spoke Tiwa. Further south a group of pueblos along the Río Grande and its Río Chama tributary spoke Tewa. Next came the Tano-speaking pueblos in the Santa Fe area, including Galisteo Pueblo. Towa speakers flanked this region on both sides; Jemez to the west, and Pecos on the eastern side. Proceeding to the south, the large province of Tiguex spoke a southern version of Tiwa, and stretched from just north of present-day Albuquerque to Socorro in the south. The pueblos of Sandía and Isleta form the modern representatives of Tiguex. Farther south and east lived groups of Piro and Tompiro villages, distantly but still related to the other Tanoan-speaking groups.

In addition to the complex movement of peoples that the distribution of the Tanoan villages suggests, the Keres group of pueblos settled on an east-west axis that met the Tanoan progression at the Río Grande, between present-day Santa Fe and Albuquerque. These people descended from the earlier groups that built and occupied the sophisticated settlements of Chaco Canyon. Acoma formed the center of the western Keres villages (which later included Laguna Pueblo), and the eastern Keres pueblos of San Felipe, Santa Ana, Zia, Santo Domingo, and Cochití. To the west of Acoma, the Zuni villages (the original "Cities of Cibola") spoke a language unrelated to any in the region, and represent another story of migration and resettlement. Further west still, the Shoshone-speaking Hopi people settled in a group of villages in north-eastern Arizona.

The complicated religious and social bonds that knit settlements into vibrant communities mirrored the geographic and linguistic relationships among the Pueblos. Together, these socioreligious structures tied the Native American peoples of the Río Grande region loosely together within a "Pueblo worldview." The internal organization of each pueblo reflected not just a method of ordering social and political relations, but expressed a complex religious system that maintained the harmonious function and balance of natural forces upon which the Puebloans relied to survive.[5] Today, through the many changes over five centuries, nineteen Río Grande pueblos in New Mexico and the group of Hopi pueblos in northeastern Arizona continue a way of life based upon these ancient traditions.

The group of western pueblos, encompassing Acoma, Laguna, Zuni, and the Hopi villages, had a similar internal social structure based upon clans—that is, a group of families related through the mother's line. Besides forming matrilineal clans, the western Pueblo households were exogamous and matrilocal; persons who came from different clans could marry, and the life of the new family centered primarily around the wife's relatives. Each clan took its name from an important actor in the religious mythology of the Pueblo. For example, Zuni Pueblo has Eagle, Badger, Corn, and Crane clans, among others, each with its own subdivisions. Some pueblos remained small enough that the members of a clan consisted of a web of families all related to a common female ancestor. Larger pueblos had clans that contained a number of different family lineages. Such an arrangement emphasized the importance of the clan system in organizing Pueblo social relations. In the western pueblos the clan system incorporated households into a framework of reciprocal relations and also served as a corporate repository of ceremonial information.[6]

Just as the clan performed the central task of social organization among the western pueblos, the eastern pueblos divided into halves, or moieties, that served to pattern social and ceremonial relations. For the Tewa and Tiwa pueblos,[7] the moieties represented Summer People and Winter People. Within these divisions, households participated in the social-religious life of the pueblo through kiva societies, associations dedicated to performing the ceremonial functions centered around special structures (kivas) in which religious instruction and observance took place. Kinship ties in the Tiwa and Tewa pueblos proceeded bilaterally—that is, families traced their lineage through the relatives of both the mother and father.

In the case of the Tanoan-speaking and northeast Keres pueblos, each group has borrowed some traits of the other over centuries of coexistence. The Tewa and Tiwa pueblos have structures that some anthropologists have labeled clans, but these do not serve to regulate marriage or to organize households into groups connected by kinship. The weak connection of the clan groupings to the organizations that drive social relations and religious ceremonies suggest that the Tanoan clanlike groupings grew out of influence from Keresan neighbors. Similarly, the eastern Keres pueblos have borrowed moieties from the Tewa. Turquoise and Squash (or Pumpkin) People correspond to the Tanoan Winter and Summer divisions within the pueblo. The eastern Keres have matrilineal clans and have also incorporated other religious associations such as medicine societies. The relationship between close proximity and cultural borrowing becomes equally clear in the development of the Towa-speaking Jemez people, who organize kinship within exogamous, matrilineal clans clearly borrowed from the Keres.

Overlaying the social organization of each of the pueblos, the *Kachina* (or *Katsina*) cult provided the religious focus for the Pueblo world. Kachinas are supernatural beings who can bless the Pueblos and humankind with rain, fertile crops, good hunting, and general well-being. Religious ceremonies and public dances provide the Pueblo people with opportunities to call on the Kachinas to continue the natural cycle of life. A number of Pueblo myths identify Kachinas with the Anasazi people making, in essence, gods out of ancestral spirits. From the evidence of mural paintings on the interior kiva walls of pueblos occupied before the Spanish conquest, the Kachina cult reached the Río Grande in the early to mid-fourteenth century. Kivas are ceremonial chambers whose function relates specifically to Kachina rituals. The early Spanish chroniclers described kivas as well as the masked dancers (also called Kachinas), which in colorful costumes impersonate the Kachinas in dance ceremonies. Specialists disagree about the exact path that the Kachina ceremonial complex took before spreading across the Pueblo area, but the masked gods and rites of impersonation clearly link the southwestern Kachina cult to religious practices in central and western Mexico.[8] Perhaps the arrival of the new religious cult during a period of migration into the Pueblo region facilitated the connection between the Anasazi and the Kachina.

Depending on the historical development of a particular Pueblo, either the clans or the kiva societies organized by moiety held the esoteric ceremonial information required for participation in the inner workings of the Kachina cult and other religious associations. In the case of the western pueblos (Zuni, Acoma, and Laguna), and to a lesser extent the eastern Keres pueblos and Jemez, clans connected (and connect) religious ceremony to kinship networks and in this manner served to organize the social and cultural fabric of whole villages. In the other pueblos of Tanoan descent, the dual division of the pueblos provided by the moiety system alongside the kiva societies expressed a network of relationships that the Kachina religion also held together and invigorated.[9] The Kachina cult not only connected and ordered complex webs of kinship, family, and other social groupings within pueblos; it also engaged all of the peoples in the region in a conscious religious observance in common that kept the world in balance and in a productive relationship with humankind.

The importance of the religious life of the Pueblos and its interconnections into all realms of social, cultural, and economic activity goes a long way toward explaining why the Pueblos survived the intrusion of the Spanish adventurers and colonists. Although the warfare brought by Coronado and the illegal expeditions later in the sixteenth century did disrupt Pueblo life, they did not initially cause the massive depopulation that preceded or followed them elsewhere in northern Mexico. During his two years in New Mexico, Coronado's men attacked Hawikuh, one of the towns of Zuni Pueblo, and commandeered the Tiguex pueblo of Coorfor as a headquarters during the winter of 1540. When the Tiguex people began to resist Spanish requisitions of food and clothes in preparation for winter, Coronado destroyed Arenal, another Tiguex pueblo. This event marked the beginning of a period of warfare that resulted in the looting and destruction of most of the Tiguex pueblos. From that time until the Spanish left the Río Grande area in the summer of 1542, the inhabitants of the Tiguex villages repeatedly fled to find temporary shelter in the mountains, fearing further demands or retaliation.

The disruption of Pueblo life that the Coronado expedition caused cannot easily be estimated. From Spanish accounts of the expedition, somewhere between five hundred and one thousand Pueblo people died directly as a result of the sporadic warfare that broke out in opposition to the Coronado occupation. We can guess that many more suffered from the privations that followed and that some Puebloans died of starvation due to the burden of feeding the Spanish, particularly during the two winter-spring periods. The effects of the displacement of so many Pueblo people and the social disruption that followed the Spanish action probably took a gradual but more serious toll on the Pueblo population. According to one estimate, the Pueblo population may have declined by 20 percent by the middle of the sixteenth century.[10]

Although the events of the 1540s slowed or reversed the rate of population growth in the Pueblo area for a time, they did not signal the start of massive or prolonged depopulation, as had the Spanish entrance into other parts of Mexico, such as Sonora.[11] Neither the accounts of the period nor archaeological research have yielded any evidence of epidemic diseases preceding or arriving with the Spanish invaders.[12] After Coronado's departure, the Tiguex slowly returned to their lands and began the task of rebuilding their pueblos and way of life. The next Spanish visits to the region in the 1580s reported more Tiguex villages than Coronado had seen four decades earlier.

For the Río Grande Pueblos, the real demographic disaster took place in the seventeenth century. Epidemic diseases did play a role in the precipitous population decline from sixty thousand to eighty thousand inhabitants to around seventeen thousand on the eve of the Pueblo revolt. Smallpox killed as many as a third of the Pueblo population when it broke out in 1636, and four years later another epidemic struck. By the 1630s other factors, described more fully below, had combined to make the Puebloans more susceptible to disease. Attacks by Apache groups on the Zuni and the Piro and Tompiro Pueblos also did damage to the available acreage that the Indians could safely work. Due to loss of population from disease, prolonged drought, and their inability to stave off raids by Apache raiders, by the 1670s the Tompiro had abandoned their pueblos south and east of present-day Albuquerque.[13] The onslaught of Franciscan missionaries on Pueblo institutions in order to convert the Indians to Christianity and the labor and tribute demanded by Spanish officials and colonists provided the deciding factor in the seventeenth-century loss in Pueblo population. Together, these events triggered the decline of the Pueblo population by 70 to 80 percent during the first century of Spanish occupation and settlement.

The twelve-year period of freedom from Spanish rule did not reverse the decline of the Pueblo population. Continued drought, famine, and fighting between pueblos and with the Apache and Utes did not allow the region time to recover from the previous decades of Spanish occupation. The population of the Piro pueblos in the southern portion of the Río Grande area fled with the Spanish settlers during the 1680 revolt. When the Spanish began probing the region in preparation for a reconquest, they found the rest of the Piro villages sacked and abandoned. In 1692 and 1693, when they reentered New Mexico under the leadership of Diego de Vargas, the Spanish found that many of the pueblos had merged or moved to defensive locations in order to better protect their people from the violence and instability that had persisted after the revolt.

The reconquest itself was not a bloodless reoccupation of the province, as de Vargas claimed, although some of the Keres Pueblos did help the Spanish retake the region.[14] A second wave of pueblo abandonment and consolidation took place during the early years of the reconquest and subsequent uprisings that signaled Pueblo readjustment to the second Spanish regime in New Mexico. The Tewa left the pueblos of Jacoma and Cuyemungue for good. Southern Tiwas, and Tano from San Cristóbal and San Lázaro, fled to the Hopi people to avoid living under the Spanish once again. The Tano refugees settled the town of Hano on First Mesa in return for the promise to defend the mesa against enemies of the Hopi. The Picurís reestablished old links with Apache bands, as had the Jemez before them. The Apache-Picurís connection particularly worried the Spanish until the Picurís asked for an escort back to their pueblo in 1706. The Spanish estimated in the same year that fewer than nine thousand Indians lived in the twenty-three pueblos that remained (see Table 2.2). Clearly, some of the depopulation represented temporary refugees and the larger groups that left the Pueblo region for good. Bands of refugees continued to drift back over more than a generation. In the 1740s groups of refugees from Hopi country resettled in Sandía, Isleta, and Jemez Pueblos.[15]

Pueblo population fluctuated within a range of between eighty-five hundred and about twelve thousand people during the eighteenth century. Over the long run, the Pueblo region sustained itself demographically, in contrast to other Native American populations in Texas and California living under Spanish mission systems. On the other hand, a look at the population figure in Table 2.2 shows that the Pueblos did not permanently recover from their disastrous losses of the previous century.

No single factor can account for the stagnant number of Pueblo inhabitants during the eighteenth century. One is tempted to argue that the Pueblo population did increase during the first half of the century, despite the erratic and inconsistent techniques used to count population in that period. From 1750 to about 1790, the raids of Apache, Comanche, and other non-Pueblo peoples clearly limited the growth of the Pueblo population. Disease also affected Pueblo population growth during the eighteenth century. A severe smallpox epidemic reached New Mexico in the spring of 1780 and by the following February had killed 20 to 25 percent of the New Mexican population. Although the epidemic struck Pueblo and vecino alike, the baptism and burial registers from the Río Grande missions show that the Pueblo population rebounded far more slowly than did the vecinos after the smallpox had subsided. The Pueblos most likely felt the effects of smaller recurrences of the disease more keenly until Spanish officials in 1805 undertook a program of vaccination in the province.[16]

At the same time, the common defense of the province against raids brought the Pueblo and vecino populations closer together than at any time previously. Not surprisingly, the cooperation and mutual dependence encouraged by war with the Plains Indian groups facilitated intermarriage between Puebloans and vecinos. In most cases, the Pueblo wives left their pueblo to live in a vecino community, even in those Pueblos that had matrilocal traditions. Some Pueblos expelled both women and men who had cohabited with outsiders. In spite of such instances, the exigencies that allowed for increased intermarriage resulted in the movement of Pueblo people into vecino communities, and clearly expressed the imbalance of power in favor of vecino society.[17] The continual drain of Puebloans into vecino communities helps to account for the lack of Pueblo population growth before 1790.

Colonial New Mexican court records provide examples of the manner in which Pueblo people became marginalized and absorbed into vecino society. In one instance, Antonio Beitia lived in Santa Clara Pueblo until 1784, when Governor Juan Bautista de Anza ordered his banishment for committing an act of sedition.[18] In punishment, Beitia was forbidden visits to Santa Clara in order to attend any of the pueblo meetings or ceremonies. Beitia moved to live in a vecino village near the Pueblo named Plaza de San Rafael. The Spanish authorities sought to sever from Pueblo society those like Beitia who were identified as troublemakers. Like other Indians banished from their pueblos by Indian or Spanish officials, or joined with non-Pueblo mates to live in vecino communities, Beitia no longer appeared in censuses listed as a Pueblo Indian.

In this case the attempt at discipline did not work. Nine years later, Antonio Beitia was identified as one of the participants in an alleged plan among the Tewa Pueblos to work with one of the Comanche, Navajo, Ute, or Hopi to overthrow Spanish rule in New Mexico once again.[19] He had attended a meeting at San Ildefonso, and one at his former pueblo, Santa Clara, in which Spanish officials feared that the Indians had discussed a plan for revolt. Although Governor Francisco de la Concha felt that he never got to the bottom of the matter, Beitia received a harsh sentence of labor and a large fine because he had disregarded his previous banishment. One can see in a case like that of Antonio Beitia how the actions of people tended to blur the attempts of authorities to sharpen the lines between ethnic groups. Census surveys represented one of the customary tools that colonial officials used to establish and assert ethnic boundaries.

C. Indians and the missions

Two very different mission systems functioned in New Mexico before and after the Pueblo revolt and the subsequent Reconquest. In the first Spanish colony, Franciscan missionaries undertook a program of religious and social conversion calculated to undermine native institutions and sources of cultural strength in order to make the Pueblo people into Catholics and Spaniards. After the reconquest, the Franciscans gave up their pretensions of wielding power within the Pueblos as the price for returning their missions to the Pueblos. At the end of the seventeenth century, the mission system lay in ruins and with it ended the first Spanish colony in New Mexico. Twenty-one Franciscan missionaries and at least four hundred settlers died at the beginning of the revolt, and afterward the Kachinas returned to the Pueblos. The Spanish received reports that Popé, the San Juan leader of the revolt, and his captains encouraged the Pueblos to dismantle and destroy all reminders of the missions and abandon everything that the Franciscans had taught. In contrast, at the close of the nineteenth century the twenty Río Grande pueblos had accepted a layer of Christianity and anchored it firmly alongside the practice of their traditional religion.

The mission system that the Franciscans built after the initial conquest of the Pueblos had to confront the powerful integration of religious and social structures that opposed their program of conversion. With Pueblo labor, the Franciscans rapidly built a chapel or a larger mission complex in each Indian pueblo. After 1616, a head missionary who lived at the mission in Santo Domingo Pueblo coordinated the mission system. Within the protective walls of the mission, missionaries offered to teach their converts the fruits of civilized life. Large numbers of Indians worked to run the community. The missions had workshops where Franciscan fathers trained blacksmiths, leather workers, weavers (on European looms), and imparted other skills. The fathers organized Pueblo workers to prepare maize and wheat fields for cultivation and to tend vegetable gardens. Pueblo herders took care of mission livestock.

Each missionary sought to encourage or coerce the Puebloans to give up visible aspects of their way of life that appeared to contradict the practice of Christianity. For example, the Franciscans objected to the Pueblo practice of dissolving marriages by mutual consent among younger couples, and allowing senior men to have more than one wife as a way of increasing wealth and influence within the community. To rectify the situation, the missionaries stepped into the midst of Pueblo society and appropriated from the households and related clans or moieties the power to regulate marriage.

At every turn the Franciscans tried to impose a Spanish, patriarchal social system in Pueblos that accorded important spheres of influence to women. In Pueblo households the women took charge of preparing the maize fields and guarding each year's seed. The house and sacred fetishes that guarded the household belonged to the matriarch of the family. The missionaries expected Pueblo males to farm and, to help accomplish that end, introduced domesticated sources of meat that took away their role as hunters. The reversal of the traditional sexual division of labor served to help destabilize the normal locations of authority inside the Pueblos. Fray Benevides noted that "if we compel any man to work on building house, the women laugh at him . . . and he runs away." Women made adobe bricks of mud and built houses with them, just as men wove cloth for everyday and ceremonial use. The reversal of roles imposed by the mission fathers represented an attack on the deeper linkage of social and religious structures that gave the Pueblo culture strength.[20]

The first decade of the New Mexican missions did not prove very successful in making Pueblo converts. Beginning in 1607, Franciscan missionaries reported converts by the thousands, accelerating at a rapid pace throughout the 1630s. External changes brought upon the Pueblo world by the Spanish helped to encourage these conversions. The tribute required by Spanish settlers and officials (see below) placed a serious burden on Pueblo labor and maize supplies. The Spanish reorientation of Pueblo Indian production to the missions and settler households hobbled the trade relationship between the Apache and the Pueblos. The Apache responded with increasing attacks on New Mexican livestock and stores of grain. The promise of the Franciscan missionaries to protect converts from Apache raids as well as against unreasonable demands of the settlers facilitated the Pueblo acceptance of the Franciscan missions and their religious message.[21]

The Franciscans projected their authority inside the Pueblos in direct ways as well. In order to more easily deal with Pueblos that had no previous form of secular government that the Spanish could understand or control, Oñate had each Pueblo elect a governor and supporting officials. The Franciscan missionaries soon controlled the election process inside the Pueblos, despite a royal decree of 1620 that called for elections within the Pueblos without any outside supervision. Using the political control of the Spanish-imposed system of Pueblo officials, and help from Spanish soldiers when necessary, Franciscans began a determined assault on the kivas and Kachina religion. Experiences elsewhere in Mexico had taught the missionaries the dangers of religious syncretism if the Pueblos were allowed to mix their religious practices with those of Christianity. For the Pueblos, the periodic campaigns of the Franciscans against the Kachina and the kivas turned religious conversion into a conflict for cultural survival.

Today the Río Grande Pueblos point to the 1680 revolt as the event that saved Pueblo culture. The revolt did fundamentally alter the terms upon which the Pueblos accepted the return of the Franciscan missionaries. After the reconquest the Franciscans had to give up any attempt to dominate the internal Pueblo social and political order. Puebloans rebuilt the missions, but not on the scale of the first mission system. This arrangement represented a compromise between the domination and authority of the Spanish governors and Pueblo resistance to renewed oppression. In Hopi, where reasserted Spanish control projected only weakly, the Franciscans failed to reinstate the missions. When the Hopi of Awátowi allowed the Franciscans to begin construction on a new mission, the other villages gathered together and destroyed the pueblo, razing it and dividing the Awátowi inhabitants among themselves.[22]

During the eighteenth century, Franciscan use of Pueblo labor to run the missions was sharply curtailed. Catholic observance within the Pueblos ran alongside the kiva ceremonies and Kachina dances, but the missionaries seldom had the power to interfere. Instead of serving as a tool for Franciscan control, Pueblo religious leaders used the Indian elected officials to shield them from interference by the Spanish governor and his officials. The Pueblo caciques and the clans or kiva societies also kept elements of Christianity from entering the sphere of Pueblo religion. The resulting cultural adaptation and integration of Christianity was described by anthropologists Edward H. Spicer and Edward P. Dozier (the latter of Santa Clara Pueblo descent) in the 1950s and early 1960s as "compartmentalization."[23]

II. SETTLERS

A. Size of settler population

From the point of view of the Spanish colony, New Mexico did not attract a large number of settlers during the seventeenth century. Of the 129 soldier-settlers and their families that accompanied Oñate in the initial occupation of New Mexico, only about 25 remained when the king took over the province in 1609 and appointed a new governor. The settlers who abandoned the province, often in the face of possible judicial punishment, expressed their dismay at the lack of food and clothing, and the environment of hostility they faced.[24]

The new governor, Pedro de Peralta, established Santa Fe as the new capital and reorganized the Spanish settlement. Placed on a more stable economy based on extracting Pueblo tribute and labor, the population of Santa Fe grew to around 250 in 1630 and the total population of the province grew to approximately 1,000 (see Table 2.1). The population continued to grow, mostly due to natural increase, until the Pueblo revolt drove the Spanish and more acculturated Pueblo Indians out of the province and into the El Paso area. The estimates of 1630 and 1680 shown in Table 2.1 include Indians who chose to leave their pueblos and live in Spanish communities.

With the reestablishment of the colony by Diego de Vargas in 1693, New Mexican population growth took a different trajectory. Fundamental changes in the makeup of the province assured a marked increase in non-Pueblo numbers, even during times of little or no immigration from other parts of Mexico. The new farming communities that began to spread out along the Río Grande could support themselves. In addition, because of the foundation of Chihuahua in 1703 and the subsequent growth of numerous settlements in Nueva Vizcaya, New Mexico became less isolated from the rest of northern New Spain during the eighteenth century.

The rate of population growth for the period from 1730 to 1821 averaged about 1 percent per year. The relatively strong rate of growth masks periods of slow growth or losses in population that do not necessarily register in the New Mexican censuses. Table 2.1 suggests slower growth of the vecino population during the intense hostilities with Comanche and Apache raiders between 1760 and 1779. On the other hand, the censuses of 1779 and 1782 do not adequately account for population losses from the 1780–81 smallpox epidemic. The mission baptismal records show a 20 to 25 percent rate of mortality among vecino communities, and although the recovery of the population proceeded quickly, it could not have rebounded to the levels shown for 1782. These problems occur because we are comparing very different types of census data. The missionaries or local officials who took the census in colonial New Mexico used inconsistent criteria to assign ethnicity, and in general the census system did not account for the movement of people between the Pueblos, the vecino settlements, and Plains Indian groups. In any case, by 1821 the non-Pueblo population of New Mexico revealed far greater numbers than did the other northernmost provinces (Texas, Florida, and the Californias) put together.

B. *Settlement types and settlement patterns*

In the seventeenth century the Spanish population lived in one of three types of settlements. Santa Fe represented the one legally founded civil settlement, and by 1680 it held a large number, perhaps a quarter, of the population. The loss of the Spanish records from the first colony during the Pueblo revolt makes reconstruction of the capital difficult.

Another group of the soldier-settlers received *encomiendas* from Governor Oñate in return for their part in the conquest. The grantee or *encomendero* received the tribute from a defined group of Pueblo Indians. Each Pueblo household owed one *fanega* of maize (about 1.6 bushels) and a cotton woven blanket or tanned hide from a buffalo or deer. As the Pueblo population declined during the century, the relative burden of the annual tribute on each household increased.

Encomenderos often did not hesitate to extract much more from their encomienda. Some obtained grants of arable land next to the Pueblos they held in encomienda, and forced the Puebloans to till, plant, and harvest wheat or maize. Some disobeyed laws that prohibited encomenderos from living on

Indian lands, manufacturing their own grants through their encroachment on Pueblo fields. Encomenderos often required Pueblo men and women to work as household servants. For the first few decades after the conquest, a soldier that served at his own expense could apply for an encomienda and settle as a hidalgo (a title of the lesser nobility). As settlements, the encomiendas functioned as haciendas or extended ranches near a Pueblo, often far away from other settlers.[25]

Settlers who could not afford to give five years of service to the crown, or arrived too late to apply for an encomienda (after about 1640), could petition for grants of land. The governor gave land to individuals and to groups of households without land or to those who wanted to better their lot. As a result, scattered ranches and small communities formed by a cluster of families spread over areas of good farmland along the Río Grande and its tributaries. During the Pueblo revolt these settlers were overwhelmed, or joined others in Santa Fe or La Isleta (in the southern part of the province) before fleeing the province altogether.

After the reconquest, the expanding Spanish population established two new villas to supplement Santa Fe. In 1685 Governor de Vargas granted settlers permission to move to Santa Cruz de la Cañada, located in the Tewa basin north of Santa Fe and a few miles southeast of San Juan Pueblo. New settlers formally laid out the villa of Albuquerque in 1706, at the center of the old Tiguex region of settlement extending from Santo Domingo Pueblo south to Socorro. As the population grew, colonists who wanted more or better croplands petitioned for a grant to found a new community. The governor reviewed the request and sent the *alcalde mayor*[26] to investigate the area for its suitability for growing crops and for mounting a defense against raids. The alcalde mayor also made sure that the proposed grant did not encroach upon other grants or Pueblo lands. If no impediments existed, the alcalde proceeded to conduct a granting ceremony with the settlers, who began to lay out their village along a central plaza.

In spite of the attempt to regulate new settlements and ensure their viability, settlers proceeded to build their houses far from the village plaza in order to live near their fields. Since the most fertile land normally stretched in a thin line that ran along streams and small valleys, small ranches and scattered houses spread haphazardly over a large area. Fray Juan Agustín Morfí described the inhabitants of Albuquerque in 1779: "As if fleeing from the company of their brothers, they withdraw their habitations from one another, stringing them out in a line as fast as they can build them."[27] What could have been an orderly, compact settlement stretched some thirty miles along the Río Grande. During the intense Comanche and Apache raids of the 1750–1780s, many outlying areas of settlement disappeared as their owners fled to larger villages such as Santa Fe or lost their lives. As Morfí put it, "they dare not go out and work, or if they do, they become victims of their own folly, since the enemy sweeps through the communities with perfect liberty, on account of their disorderly layout."

Firm action by Governors Pedro Fermín de Mendinueta (1767–1778) and Juan Bautista de Anza (1778–1789), coupled with the effect of raids and limited markets for vecino produce, helped to control this pattern of settlement somewhat. With the conclusion of the Comanche attacks in 1786, vecinos rapidly sought out agricultural and grazing lands previously too dangerous to inhabit, and the pattern of scattered settlement reasserted itself with a vengeance. By 1821, Spanish settlers had built new communities that significantly extended the inhabited boundaries of the province in every direction.[28]

C. Social structure

The small size of the non-Pueblo population of New Mexico during the seventeenth century and the paucity of documentation makes a discussion of Spanish social structure difficult before the revolt. The economic privileges granted the encomenderos also carried with them the social status of hidalgo. At the same time, only thirteen of the soldiers that entered New Mexico with Oñate brought wives, and very few women from Spain or New Spain joined the early group of settlers. In the same generation that the New Mexican "conquistadores" acquired their Spanish lineage by achieving the title of hidalgo, they sexually used Pueblo and Plains Indian women and black female slaves, with whom they established families. Some of these women became legal wives, and many others remained mistresses or concubines.

Although the Pueblo revolt arrested the evolution of Spanish society in New Mexico, its eighteenth-century development probably represented more continuity than disjunction. The soldier-settlers that undertook the reconquest of New Mexico claimed for themselves a social position equivalent to that which the encomenderos possessed, but they received a modest salary from the crown rather than Pueblo tribute. The governor, his alcaldes, and wealthy landowners or merchants occupied the top rung in New Mexican society. These people considered themselves *españoles*, regardless of their actual racial composition.

Eighteenth-century New Mexican society could and did distinguish between new generations of racially or ethnically mixed persons. New Mexicans used labels common elsewhere in New Spain for the issue of a mixed union (for example, mulatto, mestizo, *casta*) and some with particular provincial significance. Vecinos referred to the children of Pueblo or Plains Indian slave women as *coyotes* or *lobos*. Lobo also could refer to the children of a Pueblo-Plains Indian union. New Mexicans typically purchased or ransomed *genízaros*, Indians captured by the Comanche or other non-Pueblo Indians from the other nomadic tribes within a large region of the Southwest and Southern Plains. The Spanish brought genízaros into their houses in servitude, baptized them and their offspring, and proceeded to assimilate them into vecino society. A contemporary source describes genízaros as "Indians of all nations of gentiles that surround us, but all who had been, or were [at the time,] servants of the vecinos. They had been purchased from the gentiles, and these speak no other language than Spanish."[29]

Colonial records describe a clear social hierarchy that placed españoles at the top, with the various mixed groups below, in a category often referred to as castas (castes). The Pueblo Indians occupied a separate social status, somewhat apart from the normal hierarchy, that mirrored their protected legal status under Spanish law. Toward the end of the colonial period, vecinos began to push Pueblo social status to the bottom level of the dominant society.

In contrast, the position of genízaros changed for the better. Because they entered vecino society in servitude, genízaros began as social outcasts. Little information exists about how genízaros left vecino households, but in the 1740s genízaro families began to successfully petition for land on which to build their own villages. To the south of Albuquerque, genízaros settled Belén in 1740; and Abiquiú and Ojo Caliente, to the northwest of Santa Fe, received grants in 1754. New Mexican governors consciously placed genízaro settlements on the frontiers of the province, expecting them to provide added defense against raids, and they performed with distinction.[30] Despite the lower social standing initially accorded to them, intermarriage and proven loyalty began to erase racial boundaries in genízaro communities. By the turn of the nineteenth century, documents commonly classified genízaros as castas or even as españoles.

During their lifetimes, vecinos and Indians continuously negotiated the rigid categories of race and ethnicity that form most pictures of social organization in colonial New Mexico. The life of Juana Hurtado provides one example. Navajo raiders captured Juana from her father's encomienda just before the Pueblo revolt.[31] Her mother came from Zia Pueblo and probably worked in the Hurtado hacienda as a domestic servant. Juana came into the world a coyote. Juana appears in Spanish records again in 1696 as one of the captives ransomed after the reconquest of New Mexico. She petitioned for a land grant and received it near San Ysidro, just northwest of Zia Pueblo.

Juana Hurtado Galván died in 1753 a relatively wealthy women. She owned three houses and numerous livestock she had raised on her grant lands. A good deal of her wealth had come from using her mixed cultural position and linguistic skills to facilitate Pueblo, Spanish, and Navajo commerce at her rancho. Although she never married, Juana had four children with a married Zia man named Galván. Only a protest from Zia Pueblo prevented the Franciscans, in 1727, from placing Juana in the stocks to punish her for her sexual transgressions.

Juana "La Galvana" used her connection with the pre-revolt encomendero Hurtado family, her knowledge of the Navajo, and her matrilineal and kinship links to Zia Pueblo to carve a prosperous existence and gain a respected position. In doing so, she demonstrated the ways in which the new colonial social order could prove surprisingly malleable. She also conferred her carefully negotiated position within Spanish society on at least one of her illegitimate sons. When she died, Juan Galván held the post of *teniente*[32] of the Keres jurisdiction.

New Mexican society changed rapidly at the end of the eighteenth century, as a result of economic changes discussed below. Increased wealth entered at the top of the social ladder and widened the gap between rich and poor. More frequent commerce and communication between New Mexico and other parts of Mexico served to bring social behavior among the *ricos* in line with prevailing norms in Mexico City or Puebla. Ramón Gutiérrez has shown how the change in vecino attitudes affected interethnic marriage. Vecinos and Pueblo Indians were more likely to intermarry during the period from the 1760s through the 1780s than previously, but after 1790 vecinos chose fewer Puebloans as spouses.[33] The hardening of the New Mexico social structure that accompanied economic growth made stories such as that of Juana Hurtado rare by the end of the Spanish colonial era.

D. Indian-settler relations

Spanish settlers entered New Mexico bent on the complete domination of the Pueblo population. During the Oñate expedition, the first sign of resistance met with a deadly reaction. In early December 1598, Vicente de Zaldívar, an officer and Oñate's nephew, approached Acoma pueblo to requisition supplies. Zaldívar planned to meet Oñate at Zuni Pueblo and accompany him on a search for a harbor to the west. Oñate's force had read the *requerimiento* in Spanish to each pueblo during the previous October. A legal document, the "Act of Obedience and Homage," explained that the Pueblos must submit to the king of Spain as his vassal, and if they refused they faced enslavement or death and their lands would be taken from them. The Acoma may have decided to resist from the outset; they gave maize and wood only grudgingly, and told Zaldívar to return in three days to give them time to grind more maize. The actions of one soldier, who stole two sacred turkeys and raped an Acoma maiden, did not help the situation upon their return. The Acoma responded by attacking the Spaniards as they made their way up the mesa on which Acoma Pueblo still stands. Zaldívar and twelve of the soldiers who accompanied him died in short order.

Oñate took swift and decisive action to set an example for the benefit of the other pueblos. Don Vicente de Zaldívar, the dead officer's brother, marched to Acoma with seventy soldiers and demanded surrender. Acoma fell after two or three days of fighting and five to eight hundred Pueblo casualties. Zaldívar razed the pueblo and took eighty men and five hundred women and children prisoners of war to await trial and punishment. The following February, the Acoma received their sentences: men and women over twelve were placed in the servitude of Spanish officers and soldiers for twenty years; and males were also to have one foot cut off. The Spanish carried out the amputation of twenty-four Acoma men. Oñate's men also distributed boys and girls under twelve to monasteries in Mexico for conversion, and placed the elderly in the care of a Plains Indian group.[34]

In many ways, the events at Acoma in the early years of the Spanish occupation set the tone for relations between the Puebloans and settlers until 1680. At the same time as the missionary effort attacked the intertwined social and religious structures within the Pueblos, Spanish governors and colonists fashioned an economic system based on the exploitation of Pueblo labor and production. The tribute required by encomiendas and drafts of labor used to raise crops, complete public works, and weave blankets for the gain of the governor and his officials all contributed to the pressure placed on Pueblo institutions.

The only respite afforded to the Pueblos by those in charge of provincial government came as a result of the series of furious and often violent conflicts fought between the governor and Franciscans over control of the Pueblos. At times, one side or the other rose to the defense of the Pueblos against the alleged abuses of the opposite party. During the 1660s the church-state conflict allowed the Kachina religion to resurface in the Pueblos, and proved instrumental in bringing them together in revolt a few years later.

During the first half of the eighteenth century, the reestablished vecino villages and ranchos interspersed between areas of Pueblo habitation searched for a mode of coexistence based upon much greater respect for Pueblo lands and prerogatives. The new settlers needed fields and water for crops and pasturage, but until the vecino population rose dramatically in the 1780s the competition over resources did not become intense. The Pueblos won most legal cases decided by the governor concerning vecino encroachment on

Pueblo lands until the late 1770s. In one case that came before the Governor Tomás Velez de Cachupín in 1763, the Indians of San Ildefonso charged that vecino families had illegally farmed or settled on Pueblo land in four separate locations. One of these involved Marcos Lucero of Ojo Caliente, who had purchased land for a house from a San Ildefonso Indian. The Pueblo had protested this sale in 1760 to the previous governor and had won their case. The governor ordered the Pueblo to pay back Lucero and reversed the transaction. San Ildefonso now complained to Governor Cachupín that, although they had repaid the purchase price, Lucero had still not given up the property. Although when Cachupín investigated the various claims he sided with the Pueblo, the compromises that he attempted to impose in order to mollify some of the vecino parties kept the matter open until Governor de Anza settled it, again in favor of the Pueblo, twenty-three years later.[35]

A fair degree of cultural accommodation developed during the course of the eighteenth century. At trading fairs in Taos, Pecos, and Galisteo, Pueblo Indians, vecinos, and the governor and alcaldes mayores bartered alongside each other with the Comanche, Ute, Apache, or Navajo visitors. Soldiers from the presidio of Santa Fe routinely fought defensive engagements, chased raiding parties, or mounted offensive campaigns alongside Pueblo auxiliaries and vecino militia. Close interaction continued away from the hostilities. Due to the severity of Comanche raids in the 1770s, vecinos around Taos and Picurís abandoned their settlements and moved into compounds they built within the Pueblo walls. Spanish regulations strictly forbade non-Indians from living on Pueblo lands, but the settlers felt that they had little choice.[36]

The close interaction between Pueblo, Spanish, and Southern Plains people that took place in New Mexico toward the end of the eighteenth century created some interesting and unintended consequences. One night in early November 1795, the intendant of the provincial town of Valladolid (Morelia), now in the state of Michoacán, was called to deal with a vagabond in the streets. After warning the man to retire to his own house, he saw that the man did not understand and was making signs that he wanted to be baptized. The intendant brought him to the sanctuary and left him in the care of a priest, Doctor Don Juan José de Michelena. At the time, the man apparently could not say more than "Concha, Chihuahua, and Nuevo Mexico, making signs of being very far away."[37]

The intendant and priest took him to be Comanche, in part because Fernando de la Concha had retired in 1794 as governor of New Mexico, and because of the frequency of joint Spanish, Comanche, and Pueblo auxiliary expeditions against the Apache after 1786.[38] A short while later, the man added that he was Comanche, that he had entered New Mexico with General José

Antonio Rangel as an "ambassador of my people," and had shed his blood in defense of the crown. When he asked again for baptism, Michelena proceeded with his catechism and baptized him Juan de Díos and the new covert added the surname Michelena.

Five years later, in an unguarded moment, Juan de Díos Michelena revealed that he had made up his identity because it had seemed convenient at the time. He said that he was a Comanche born in Tarca, at the seashore below the Río Grande. He had held the title "Captain of Spies" among his people, who had named him "*Zapato Bordado* [Embroidered Shoe]." The information passed quickly to the *comandante general* of the Provincias Internas,[39] and Zapato Bordado, alias Juan de Díos Michelena, found himself in the Valladolid jail.

At this point, officials in charge of the case wrote to the governor of New Mexico to attempt to verify the prisoner's identity. At the same time, Comandante General Pedro de Nava and other important officials tried to determine whether to send Michelena to Havana to spend the rest his days laboring on the Spanish fortress and harbor, "like the others of his Nation." Having given up hope of an answer from New Mexico, Pedro de Nava told the intendant of Valladolid that he could use his own judgment of Michelena's character to decide whether to free him or condemn him to servitude. By December 1800, Michelena had been transferred to a jail in Mexico City, in preparation for his journey to San Juan de Ulúa near Veracruz, and from there to Havana.

Finally, in March 1801 the current governor of New Mexico sent a response to the inquiry of the comandante general. He pointed out that in a frontier country, such as New Mexico, people came in contact with all sorts of different Native American groups, which made it impossible to verify the Indian's claim to be a Comanche. He had not heard of Tarca, but as for the name Zapato Bordado, that referred to the practice of decorating the shoes or *teguas* commonly given to the "gentile" Indians. Chacón feared that Zapato Bordado represented yet another alias, and he might really be Juan de Díos Rodríguez, "of the genízaro caste." Rodríguez married and had one daughter before he left the province in 1791, in the service of Fernando de la Concha, the previous governor. He disappeared for good when the contingent got to Chihuahua, which, Chacón thought, might explain his first words to the intendant of Valladolid.

In light of the information of Governor Chacón, the matter received the consideration of the *fiscal* (royal attorney) of civil justice, who concluded that it would be impossible to certify that Michelena and Rodríguez were the same. Here the documentary record ends, but one cannot escape the presumption that Michelena spent the rest of his life a prisoner in Havana.

The examples of Antonio Beitia, Juana Hurtado, and Juan de Díos illustrate different aspects of the transformation of a provincial society, with ramifications for relations across all racial and ethnic groups in late colonial New Mexico. As a part of its growth over the eighteenth century, New Mexico matured into a society increasingly dominated and directed by a newly emerging vecino culture. In the middle of the century, Juana Hurtado could move between areas staked out by Pueblo, Navajo, and Spanish societies on a cultural and geographical terrain negotiated and contested by many peoples. Antonio Beitia and Juan de Díos, each in their own way, found that the old rules no longer functioned. Neither man could manipulate his ambivalent status in order to negotiate his own path. Ethnicity, social status, and economic position became more tightly controlled as vecino society began to define itself, encouraged by greater numbers and an era of economic growth. A vigorous and dynamic vecino population had its most telling effect on the Río Grande Pueblos.

Anthropologists have long noted differences between Pueblo groupings that suggest the influence of the Spanish toward assimilation. Unlike the western pueblos, among the Tewa pueblos only a weak Kachina cult survived the nineteenth century, and the northern Tiwa pueblos of Taos and Picurís do not perform masked Kachina dances. Instead of the matrilineal and matrilocal clans of the western Keres and Zuni, the Tanoan-speaking pueblos in general have bilateral descent groups.[40] The eastern Keres pueblos fall somewhere in between, with weakened clan systems and medicine societies that take on some the functions of the Tewa and Tiwa kiva societies.[41]

Put another way, the erasure of masked Kachina rituals, the substitution of bilateral for matrilineal descent, and the truncation of the eastern Keresan clan system's involvement in kiva activities can all be explained as cultural adaptations in the face of the coercive actions of Spanish colonizers at some point in the past.[42] At which point in the past? Any attempt to explain these changes within the Pueblos as primarily the result of the pre-revolt period has the problem of documented Kachina revival and persistence during the eighteenth century. Nor did the twin forces of religious and civil authority appear to apply tremendous pressure for social transformation during the early eighteenth century.

The answer to this puzzle more likely lies in pressure suddenly placed on the Pueblos by a vecino society experiencing rapid growth in population, economic production, and new areas of settlement. A boom in trade between New Mexico and Chihauhua (see below) created a powerful economic incentive to appropriate Pueblo resources. A number of Pueblo cases brought to the governor's attention after 1810 show that incidents of vecino encroachment on Pueblo lands increased in the 1780–1810 period, sometimes with the complicity of local officials. Pressure to produce more exports led to the forced distribution of goods on credit among the Pueblos. In payment, the Pueblos produced pottery, sheep, and wool for export, as well as foodstuffs for internal markets.[43] The practice, known as *repartimiento de efectos*,[44] had long existed in other parts of New Spain, but appeared suddenly in New Mexico. Economic coercion in the context of increasing vecino domination and social differentiation may explain the internal changes in the social structure of the Pueblos in closest contact with vecino settlements.

III. ECONOMIC DEVELOPMENT

A. Contribution of missions

A summary of economic development in New Mexico helps to shed further light on social and cultural changes taking place during the late colonial period. Despite the best intentions of Spanish administrators, the seventeenth-century missions in New Mexico did not act as supply sources for mining regions or settlements farther south. Until the peopling of Nueva Vizcaya during the next century reduced the distance between New Mexico and other settlements, exporting foodstuffs and livestock did not prove practical. In fact, the missions depended on a caravan of imported goods every three years to supply the missions. The governors did send illegal shipments of hides and woven goods collected from the Pueblos south to sell on their own account, but the same factors of distance and lack of markets limited such commerce.[45] Perhaps if the settlement of the Chihuahua region had occurred a generation earlier economic links with New Mexico would have affected the success of the Pueblo revolt.

B. Mining (if applicable)

No mining occurred until a little copper exploration was conducted at Santa Rita late in colonial period.

C. Ranching and agriculture

The eighteenth-century New Mexican farming and pastoral economy grew slowly until the 1780s. Until then, Apache and Comanche raiding parties limited access to cropland and stole or destroyed sheep and cattle. Vecinos grew wheat, maize, beans, squash, chili, onions, and *punche* (a regional substitute for tobacco). Farms and ranches supplied sheep, cattle, horses, mules, and a few goats and oxen. With relative peace from raids in the mid-1780s, and spurred by rapid population growth, vecinos began to prepare new lands for farming and livestock that had previously been too dangerous to utilize. Colonial documents describe increasing production from farms and ranchos. An analysis of the New Mexican tithe records confirms that vecino households produced more per capita beginning in the 1780s until about 1815.[46] By that time economic disruptions caused by insurrections farther south began to disrupt the regional economy.

D. *Trade and regional markets*

Soon after its foundation, Chihuahua became the principal market for New Mexican goods, and for supplying imported items that could not be obtained elsewhere to soldiers, missionaries, and settlers. Chihuahua also represented the shipping and transportation hub that linked the regional market to Durango, the presidios in Nueva Vizcaya and Sonora, and other areas of New Spain to the south. New Mexicans brought their produce to Chihuahua in a large convoy that departed from Santa Fe once a year. By the last quarter of the eighteenth century, the *cordón* operated on a relatively fixed schedule, leaving for Chihuahua in November or late October, and returning the following January. The 750-mile trek normally took forty days in one direction. Part of the journey passed through a difficult 80-mile stretch of desert located between Albuquerque and El Paso.

The first eighteenth century long-distance trade system, enduring into the 1770s, principally supplied deerskins and buffalo hides obtained in trade from the Plains Indians at annual trade fairs at Taos and Pecos pueblos.[47] Some blankets and other woven goods went south, as did a small amount of livestock. In spite of the protection offered by the detachment of soldiers that accompanied the cordón, Apache or Comanche bands could attack at any time, or the threat of likely raids could delay or cancel the journey. The paucity of money in circulation, and the related scarcity of credit, limited commerce within New Mexico and hampered trade with outside merchants.

Just as the Comanche-Spanish peace and alliance allowed vecinos to expand their settlements and farmlands, the end of hostilities rejuvenated long-distance trade and significantly quickened economic activity within the province. By the mid-1780s a boom in long-distance trade brought with it an expansion of the range of items exported from New Mexico. The market for New Mexican woolen textiles and finished blankets and clothing expanded along with the population of the urban centers of Nueva Viscaya and the establishment of new presidios in Nueva Vizcaya and Sonora in the 1770s.

Sheep and their by-product, wool, became the export engine of the late New Mexican colonial economy. Vecinos began to produce woven goods for trade in the south. Cattle, horses, small amounts of grain, punche, and the traditional export of hides completed a group of products that, in the 1790s, looked much closer to the produce of other areas of Nueva Viscaya.

With increasing export trade, New Mexican products became far better integrated into the regional economy of Nueva Viscaya. New Mexican textiles and wool show up in the 1780s in records of Chihuahuan merchants, the town council, and the municipal *obraje* (textile workshop) of Chihuahua.[48] *Frasadas* (woolen blankets) from New Mexico appear in the inventory of the major house of commerce in Durango.[49] The obraje in Chihuahua contracted a year in advance for wool from New Mexico to be delivered in 1794; a huge herd of New Mexican livestock figured prominently in a partnership, entered into in 1795, between Fernando de la Concha, at that time the departing governor of New Mexico, a prominent Chihuahua merchant, and the administrator of the Hacienda de Encinillas (near Chihuahua), in order to supply the Chihuahua market.[50]

E. Conclusion

The economic and demographic developments that shaped New Mexico during the last decades of Spanish colonial rule directed and deepened social and cultural change. A renewed export trade and increasing vecino productivity created new wealth, especially for some segments of society. Population growth and commercial expansion in the province between 1780 and 1820 created a mature and self-confident vecino society. Vecinos had emerged in the province as the dominant population, the vigorous export trade provided a strong incentive to increase production, and new contacts with outside elites influenced views of race and ethnicity at home. Economic prosperity at the end of the colonial period fueled a flowering of vecino culture even as it provoked a process of self-definition. As a result, in economic relations and in marriage, vecino society increasingly defined itself in contrast to the Pueblo Indians.

TABLE 2.1

Population of New Mexico in Selected Years, 1598–1821

Year	Settlers	Pueblos
1598	—	80,000
1626	350	34,650
1680	2,379	17,000
1706	3,300	8,840
1746	4,355	11,357
1800	14,849	9,432
1821	29,390	8,852

SOURCES: 1598–1680—Ramón Gutiérrez, *When Jesus Came, the Corn Mothers Went Away: Marriage, Sexuality, and Power in New Mexico, 1500–1846* (Stanford, 1991), 92, Table 2.1.;1706–1821—Ross Frank, "From Settler to Citizen: Economic Development and Cultural Change in Late Colonial New Mexico, 1750–1820" (Ph.D. diss., University of California, Berkeley, 1992), 413–32, Table 1.

Pueblo Indian Population of New Mexico for Selected Years, 1598–1821

Pueblo Population	1598	1626	1638	1680	1706	1730	1746	1750	1760	c. 1765	1776	1779
Rio Arriba Pueblos:												
Taos:					700	730	541	540	505	506	427	624
Picurís:					300		322	400	328	288	223	474
San Juan:					340	300	404	500	316	674	201	1,014
Santa Clara:					210	279	272	272	257	252	229	279
San Ildefonso:					300	296	354	354	484	309	387	484
Nambé:					300	440	350	350	204	223	183	204
Pojoaque:								130	99	157	98	99
Tesuque:					500		507	171	232		194	186
Santa Fe (Indios):							570	570			164	
Galisteo:					150	180	350	350	255	235	152	198
Pecos:					1,000	521	1,000	1,000	344	532	269	84
Rio Arriba — Total:					3,800	2,746	4,670	4,637	3,024	3,176	2,527	3,646
Rio Abajo Pueblos:												
Cochití:					520	372	400	521	450	181	486	441
Santo Domingo:					240	281	300	300	424	267	528	296
San Felipe:					500	234	400	400	458	411	406	236
Santa Ana:					340	209	606	600	404	408	384	426
Zía:					500	318	606	600	578	479	416	331
Jemez:					300	307	574	574	373	309	345	502
Sandia:							400	440	196	205	275	217
Albuquerque (Indios):					50							
Isleta:					330	400	250	250	304	375	454	352
Laguna:					760	600	401	528	600	534	699	441
Acoma:					1,500	800	750	960	1,502	1,184	530	1,034
Zuñi:							2,000	2,000	664	1,593	1,617	1,387
Rio Abajo — Total:					5,040	3,521	6,687	7,173	5,953	5,946	6,140	5,663
Pueblo — Total:	80,000	34,650	40,000	17,000	8,840	6,267	11,357	11,810	8,977	9,122	8,667	9,309

SOURCES: 1598–1680—Ramón Gutiérrez, *When Jesus Came, the Corn Mothers Went Away: Marriage, Sexuality, and Power in New Mexico, 1500–1846* (Stanford, 1991), 92, Table 2.1; 1706–1821—Ross Frank, "From Settler to Citizen: Economic Development and Cultural Change in Late Colonial New Mexico, 1750–1820" (Ph.D. diss., University of California, Berkeley, 1992), 413–32, Table 1.

NOTES

1. The Spanish word *vecino* used here refers to the non-Indian settlers of New Mexico. The term, literally meaning "neighbor," took on a meaning that included a sense of belonging to the province in late colonial New Mexican documents. Settlers were commonly referred to by Franciscans or provincial officials as "vecinos," signifying a particular type of neighbor, in distinction to the "*indios*," the inhabitants of the Pueblos.

2. L. Carroll Riley, *Rio del Norte: People of the Upper Rio Grande From Earliest Times to the Pueblo Revolt* (Salt Lake City, 1995), 91.

3. Ibid., 95, citing Paul F. Reed, "A Spatial Analysis of the Northern Rio Grande Region," in S. Upham and B. D. Stalet, eds., *Economy and Polity in Late Rio Grande Prehistory* (Las Cruces, 1990), 1–89.

4. Fray Alonso de Benevides, *Fray Alonso de Benevides' Revised Memorial of 1634* (Albuquerque, 1945), 1:34. See also Ramón Gutiérrez, *When Jesus Came, the Corn Mothers Went Away: Marriage, Sexuality, and Power in New Mexico, 1500–1846* (Stanford, 1991), 92–93 and 113; and Edward P. Dozier, *The Pueblo Indians of North America (New York, 1970),* 125. In 1602, Juan de Montoya gives a figure of sixty thousand Pueblo Indians; see Juan de Montoya, *New Mexico in 1602: Juan de Montoya's Relation of the Discovery of New Mexico* (Albuquerque, 1938), 8:39. The figure of forty thousand comes from Riley, Rio del Norte, 224 and 250.

5. Joe S. Sando, Pueblo Nations: Eight Centuries of Pueblo Indian History (Santa Fe, 1992), 30.

6. Fred Eggan, *Social Organization of the Western Pueblos* (Chicago, 1950), 284–87, 291–321; and Dozier, *Pueblo Indians*, 133–76.

7. Historic and contemporary Tewa pueblos: San Juan, Santa Clara, San Ildefonso, Nambé, Tesuque, and Pojoaque; Tiwa pueblos: Taos and Picurís, Sandía, and Isleta.

8. See Dozier, *Pueblo Indians*, 155–57; E. Charles Adams, "The Katsina Cult: A Western Pueblo Perspective," in Polly Schaafsma, ed., *Kachinas in the Pueblo World* (Albuquerque, 1994), 35–46; Polly Schaafsma, "The Prehistoric Kachina Cult and Its Origins as Suggested by Southwestern Rock Art," in Schaafsma, *Kachinas in the Pueblo World*, 63–80.

9. Even though the Taos and Picurís have not had masked Kachina ceremonies in the recent past, it can still be said that the northern Tiwa pueblos participated historically in the cult. The southern Tiwa villages, Isleta and Sandía, do have Kachina rituals, but in both cases their historical association with refugees returning from the western or Hopi pueblos complicates the situation.

10. Riley, *Rio del Norte*, 224.

11. See Daniel T. *Reff, Disease, Depopulation, and Culture Change in Northwestern New Spain, 1518–1764* (Salt Lake City, 1991).

12. Riley, *Rio del Norte*, 221–24. For an alternative view, see Andrew L. Knaut, *The Pueblo Revolt of 1680* (Albuquerque, 1995), 154–55.

13. See Albert H. Schroeder, "Shifting for Survival in the Spanish Southwest," in David J. Weber, ed., *New Spain's Far Northern Frontier: Essays on Spain in the American West, 1540–1821* (Albuquerque, 1979), 244.

14. Gutiérrez, *When Jesus Came*, 139; and ibid. 246–47, and 250; Marc Simmons, "History of Pueblo-Spanish Relations to 1821," in Alfonso Ortiz, ed., *Handbook of North American Indians: Southwest*, vol. 9 of *Handbook of North American Indians* (Washington, D.C., 1979), 9:185–87.

15. Charles W. Hackett, *Historical Documents Relating to New Mexico and Nueva Viscaya, and Approaches Thereto, to 1773* (Washington D.C., 1937), 3:388–90, 411, 464, and 472.

16. See Ross Frank, "From Settler to Citizen: Economic Development and Cultural Change in Late Colonial New Mexico, 1750–1820" (Ph.D. diss., University of California, Berkeley, 1992), 64–74.

17. Oakah L. Jones, *Pueblo Warriors and Spanish Conquest* (Norman, 1966), 131–69; Gutiérrez, *When Jesus Came*, 284–92 and 174.

18. Commandant General Felipe de Nava to Governor Juan Bautista de Anza, Chihuahua, January 24, 1784. Spanish Archives of New Mexico, New Mexico State Records Center and Archives, Santa Fe (hereafter cited as SANM II), roll 10:623–624, Twitchell (hereafter cited as TW) no. 876.

19. The case appears in SANM II 13:237–240, and 13:241–326, TW no. 1237 and 1237a.

20. See Gutiérrez, *When Jesus Came*, 12–14, 76–77, and Benevides, *Fray Alonso de Benavides' Revised Memorial of 1634*, quotation from 1:76; Dozier, *Pueblo Indians*, 48–50.

21. Gutiérrez, When Jesus Came, 92–94; Knaut, Pueblo Revolt, 61–72.

22. Dozier, *Pueblo Indians*, 70.

23. Edward H. Spicer, "Spanish-Indian Acculturation in the Southwest," *American Anthropologist* 56 (1954), 663–84; Edward P. Dozier, "Spanish-Catholic Influences on Rio Grande Pueblo Religion," *American Anthropologist* 60:3 (1958), 445–47.

24. Knaut, *Pueblo Revolt*, 132 and 48–49; Gutiérrez, *When Jesus Came*, 54–55.

25. David Weber, *The Spanish Frontier in North America* (New Haven, 1992), 124–25; Gutiérrez, *When Jesus Came*, 102–6; Oakah L. Jones, *Los Paisanos: Spanish Settlers on the Northern Frontier of New Spain* (Norman, 1979), 110; and Dozier, *Pueblo Indians*, 54–55.

26. In eighteenth-century New Mexico, an official appointed by the governor with civil jurisdiction over one of the eight districts of the province.

27. See Marc Simmons, "Settlement Patterns in Colonial New Mexico," *Journal of the West* 8:1 (1969), 7–21. Quotation from Fray Augustín de Morfí, "Account of Disorders, 1778," in Marc Simmons, ed., *Coronado's Land: Essays on Daily Life in Colonial New Mexico* (Albuquerque, 1991), 130–33.

28. Frank, "From Settler to Citizen," 198–203; Richard L. Nostrand, "The Century of Hispano Expansion," *New Mexico Historical Review* 64:4 (1987), 361–86.

29. Noticias de las misiones que ocupan los Religiosos de la regular observancia de N. S. P. S. Francisco . . . en los años 1793, 1794 . . . , SANM II, 21:538, B. M.. Read Collection. See also Gutiérrez, *When Jesus Came*, 194–97; Jones, *Los Paisanos*, 132.

30. Frances Leon Swadesh, *Los Primeros Pobladores* (Notre Dame, 1974), 39–46; and Gutiérrez, *When Jesus Came*, 178–79 and 305–6.

31. The story of Juana Hurtado comes from James F. Brooks, "'This Evil Extends Especially to the Feminine Sex': Captivity and Identity in New Mexico, 1700–1846," manuscript in the possession of the author.

32. Assistant to the alcalde mayor. A teniente often administered a partido, a portion of the alcade's jurisdiction.

33. Gutiérrez, *When Jesus Came,* 287–92.

34. Riley, *Rio del Norte,* 250–51; Knaut, *Pueblo Revolt,* 36–46; Gutiérrez, When Jesus Came, 52–54.

35. Myra Ellen Jenkins, "Spanish Land Grants in the Tewa Area," *New Mexico Historical Review* 47:2 (1972), 124–29.

36. Taos: Fray Atanasio Domínguez, *The Missions of New Mexico, 1776,* in Eleanor B. Adams and Fray Angelico Chavez, eds., *The Missions of New Mexico, 1776* (Albuquerque, 1956), 111–13; Picurís: Governor Mendinueta to Viceroy Bucareli, Santa Fe, July 23, 1773, Archivo General de la Nación, Mexico City, Provincias Internas (hereafter cited as AGN:PI), 103:1, 232V.

37. The following case appears in AGN:PI 204, 458R–483V. Morelia, Michoacán (Valladolid) is located about sixteen hundred miles from Santa Fe, New Mexico.

38. See Jones, *Pueblo Warriors,* 160–64.

39. The administrative unit for the northern provinces of the Californias, New Mexico, Texas, Coahuila, Nueva Viscaya, and Sonora, set up in 1776 in order to provide centralized military authority separate from the viceroy.

40. As noted above, the Tanoan, Towa-speaking Jemez Pueblo adapted its institutions influenced by close contact with the Keresan pueblos.

41. Dozier, *Pueblo Indians,* 144–76, provides a good summary of the salient "sociocultural" differences. See also Alfonso Ortiz, *The Tewa World* (Chicago, 1969).

42. See Eggan, Social Organization of the Western Pueblos, 304–21, esp. 310–13.

43. Ross Frank, "Changing Pueblo Indian Pottery Tradition: The Underside of Economic Development in Late Colonial New Mexico, 1750–1820," *Journal of the Southwest* 33:3 (1991), 312–15.

44. Literally, "distribution of goods."

45. Max L. Moorhead, *New Mexico's Royal Road* (Norman, 1958), 28–36.

46. See Frank, "From Settler to Citizen," 167–210.

47. Proceedings regarding debt owed to the estate of Juan Reaño, Santa Fe, 29 VI–13 VIII 1761. SANM II 9:386–400, TW no. 559. In lieu of a list of documents, reference to a few of the published documents suffices to describe the trade south: Report of the Father Provincial, Fray Pedro Serrano to the Viceroy, Marquis of Cruillas . . . , 1761, in Hackett, *Historical Documents,* 3:486–87; Morfí, "Account of Disorders," 133; Domínguez, *Missions,* 244–45, 254–55, 272, 322–23.

48. Pagos a soldados a si como los raciones y generos . . . , 1778, Archivo Palacio Municipal, Chihuahua (hereafter cited as CPM), Hacienda (hereafter cited as HA), caja 45, expediencia 6, 4R–95R; CPM:HA, caja 46, 17:8R–10R; the obraje records appear in CPM:NO (Notaria) 5, caja 46 7:1R (Haviendo tratado la Junta Municipal . . . con don Miguel Ortiz, vecino de la Villa de Santa Fe de nuevo Mexico), and expediencia 11 (Cuenta de Hacienda y Tesoreria del Ayuntamiento de Chihuahua).

49. Nota de lo que he comprado a don Antonio Ondarza . . . , Juan José Zambrano, Palacio Gobierno, Durango (DUR:PG), cajón 29, 3:52V.

50. Contract between don Francisco de Elguea, don Phelipe Gonzales de Cosio, and Coronel don Fernando de la Concha, Registro de Propriedades, Archivo Historico, Chihuahua (CHI:RG), libro 34 11R–15R.

CHAPTER THREE

NORTHWESTERN NEW SPAIN
The Pimeria Alta and the Californias

ROBERT H. JACKSON

This chapter documents the evolution of frontier colonial societies in three regions located in northwestern New Spain: the Pimeria Alta region of northern Sonora, and Baja and Alta California. Spanish colonization of Sonora began after 1620 as Jesuits established missions among various ethnic groups, including the southern Pima and Opata Eudeve. Spanish frontiersmen discovered mines, which stimulated the settlement of Sonora and the development of a regional market economy in the seventeenth and eighteenth centuries. Jesuit missionary Eusebio Kino established the first mission in the Pimeria Alta (the lands occupied by northern Pimas) in 1687, and Jesuit and later Franciscan missionaries administered missions in the area until the 1820s and 1830s. Spanish explorers first visited Baja California in the 1530s, but the aridity of the peninsula and initial hostility of the native peoples delayed colonization until 1697, when Jesuit missionaries established the first permanent mission at Loreto. The Franciscans replaced the Jesuits following the expulsion of the order in 1768, and were followed in 1774 by Dominicans. The expulsion of the Jesuits enabled the government to rethink its frontier policy. José de Gálvez, a high-ranking Spanish official sent by King Carlos III to evaluate and, if necessary, change colonial policies in Mexico, took a direct interest in the frontier. Gálvez spent considerable time in Baja California, and organized the colonization of Alta California in 1769, in response to rumors of Russian and English activities in the Pacific Basin. Gálvez used the Baja California missions both as a base for the expedition that colonized Alta California and as a source of supplies. In all three regions, missions were an important colonial institution, but different settlement patterns emerged.

PATTERNS OF INDIAN POPULATION DECLINE

Several generations of scholars have debated contact Indian-population size, and the scale of demographic collapse from the sixteenth through the nineteenth centuries. The size of Indian populations prior to the arrival of the Spanish will never be known with any precision, since native societies never compiled anything like censuses. The hierarchical states in Mesoamerica and the Andes kept tribute records, which scholars have analyzed in an effort to convert the category of tributary into total population. However, tribute records do not even survive or never existed for the less stratified societies in the Borderlands region. Nevertheless, scholars have teased information from available sources to infer contact populations. It should be pointed out, though, that these estimates are nothing more than educated guesses.

A number of distinct ethnic groups lived in Sonora during the colonial period, including the southern and northern Pima and Opata-Eudeve. These groups were sedentary village-dwelling agriculturalists. The northern Pima, the group occupying northernmost Sonora and modern Arizona south of the Gila River, lived in locally dispersed *rancherías* and practiced seasonal agriculture in the late seventeenth century when the first missions were established in the region. In a recent book, anthropologist Daniel Reff suggested that waves of epidemics in the sixteenth and seventeenth centuries devastated the Indian population of Sonora, and led to a degree of social disintegration and a shift in settlement patterns from nucleated villages to the more dispersed ranchería.[1] Elements of Reff's argument are plausible. In the Gila River region, near modern Phoenix, are the remains of Hohokam villages characterized by intensive agriculture based upon an extensive irrigation system. According to the conventional chronology, the Hohokam culture declined prior to the Europeans, but it is equally possible that sixteenth-century epidemics may have accelerated the decline. At any rate, scholars will be debating Reff's hypothesis for some time in the future.

Jesuit missionaries who visited northern Sonora in the late seventeenth century recorded the number and size of the villages they encountered. These reports provide the basis for estimates of the population organized into mission villages, but not for the population prior to the arrival of the Spaniards in Mexico in 1519. Considerable controversy surrounds the interpretation of the consequences for native populations of the Spanish conquest of Mexico and subsequent exploration and settlement of the north. Reff, among others, contends that lethal epidemics rapidly spread along established trade routes, causing thousands of deaths. The fundamental assumption underlying this line of analysis is that native populations in 1519 were large, and experienced large losses due to disease and other factors. Reff estimates that the northern Pima (northern Sonora and modern Arizona south of the Gila River) population numbered some fifty thousand prior to the first Spanish incursion into Mexico.[2]

Detailed demographic studies of Sonoran mission populations based upon the analysis of parish registers and other sources shows that, at least in the eighteenth century, causes of Indian demographic collapse in the missions were more complex than suggested by scholars who focus almost solely on epidemics as the cause for population decline.[3] Periodic epidemics certainly were traumatic episodes that, in the short term, killed large numbers of people, generally those born or brought to live at the missions since the previous epidemic outbreak. But equally important was the failure of the Indian populations living in the missions to rebound or experience long-term recovery through natural reproduction in the years following epidemics. Birthrates in the missions were moderate to high, but infant and child mortality was also chronically high and average life expectancy at birth was low. At San José de Tumacacori Mission, for example, mean life expectancy at birth averaged a mere 15.2 years between 1775 and 1825. Moreover, death rates were consistently higher than birthrates. Epidemics certainly contributed to the decline of the population of Tumacacori, but other factors, such as endemic disease, poor child care, and environmental factors like unsanitary water supply, were also important.

Several factors contributed to shifts in the population of the Pimeria Alta missions. Chronically high death rates caused attrition in the population, but Jesuit and, later, Franciscan missionaries made efforts to repopulate the missions by resettling non-Christian converts from outside the missions. Missionaries took advantage of a seasonal pattern of migration that brought Pimans from the more arid areas in the region to the main river valleys where the missions were located to recruit new converts. Missionaries frequently accompanied by soldiers also went on short expeditions to look for new recruits. Fluctuations in the populations of individual missions reflect these recruitment efforts, but throughout the eighteenth century the Pima population in the missions declined, and in response to the population decline the missionaries reduced the number of mission communities and reduced the surviving population to a smaller number of villages. In 1761, for example, 4,088 converts lived in twenty-two mission communities. By 1820, the numbers had dropped to 1,127 living in only fourteen communities.[4] The pattern of rapid demographic collapse in the missions, however, does not reflect changes among the northern Pima groups that did not live in mission communities.

The Indians brought to live in the Baja California and Alta California missions experienced similar patterns of chronically high mortality caused by epidemic and endemic ailments, living conditions in the missions, and environmental conditions such as polluted water. Records also show that the venereal disease syphilis was also a serious problem. In the Alta California establishments, one measure employed to maintain social control also endangered the health of Indian converts. The Franciscans maintained dormitories for single girls and the wives of male fugitives from the missions. According to descriptions, the dormitories were badly crowded, cool, damp, and fetid.[5]

Baja California supported only a small Indian population that rapidly disappeared following the establishment of the first Jesuit missions after 1697 and the introduction of disease. Estimates of the population of the peninsula range from around forty thousand to sixty thousand.[6] Jesuit, Franciscan, and Dominican missionaries established missions throughout the peninsula, where thousands of Indians lived and died. In 1768, following the expulsion of the Jesuits from the peninsula, 7,149 converts lived in fifteen missions. The numbers dropped precipitously following a series of devastating epidemics between 1768 and 1782, brought to the peninsula by soldiers and new missionaries sent to replace the Jesuits. In 1782 3,056 converts lived in sixteen missions, and 3,156 inhabited eighteen missions in 1804. The average population per mission dropped from 477 in 1768 to 191 in 1782, and 156 in 1804. The collapse of the Indian population of Comondu Mission (established in 1708) was typical. Following decline in the first decades after the establishment of the mission, the population experienced a short period of recovery and growth through natural reproduction in the late 1730s. The population of two other Baja California missions, San Francisco Xavier and Guadalupe, rebounded and grew for several decades prior to the expulsion of the Jesuits from the peninsula. However, in the years after 1740 death rates were consistently higher than birthrates, and the Indian population dropped.[7]

Demographic patterns in the Alta California missions were distinct in some respects from patterns observed in the northern Pima and Baja California missions. Fewer epidemics reached Alta California, and the deadliest outbreaks occurred after 1800. In contrast, data from extant parish registers of burials shows that epidemics broke out more frequently in Sonora and Baja California. Death rates fluctuated in the Alta California missions, but were chronically high and consistently higher than was documented for many of the northern Pima and Baja California missions. Despite the differences, the Indian populations in all three regions were condemned to gradual extinction, as evidenced by imbalanced age and gender structures. In the 1820s in the Alta California missions, for example, women and young children made up a disproportionately small percentage of the total population.[8]

Scholars have debated the size of the pre-Hispanic Indian population, and generally estimate the population of all of the land that makes up the modern state of California. The figure most commonly cited is Cook's estimate of some 300,000 for the entire state. More relevant to the study of Spanish colonization is a figure for the population of the coastal zone occupied by the Spanish after 1769. Cook estimates the population of the coastal zone to have been around 64,500.[9] Gerhard provides an estimate of 59,700 for the same area.[10]

Death rates in all of the Alta California missions were chronically high, and were consistently higher than birthrates. Therefore, growth in the size of the mission populations largely resulted from recruitment of non-Christian Indians first from the coastal area where the missions were established, and later from the interior valleys. As the Franciscans attempted to resettle converts from greater distances from the missions, more and more coercive force had to be employed. After about 1800, tribelets from the interior valleys, especially the San Joaquín Valley, began raiding the horse herds of the missions and pueblos. Indians who had run away from the missions frequently led the bands of horse raiders. Spanish and, after 1821, Mexican officials in California organized military expeditions to return fugitives to the missions and punish horse raiders, and forcibly relocated hundreds of Indians to the missions.[11]

The population of the missions fluctuated from year to year with the ebb and flow of relocation of Indian converts to the missions, but generally increased until the early 1820s. In 1790 7,711 converts lived in eleven missions, 13,628 in eighteen missions in 1800, and 21,063 in twenty missions in 1820. Over the next fifteen years the population of the missions rapidly dropped, and in 1834 15,225 Indians lived in twenty-one missions. The rapid decline in numbers primarily resulted from growing resistance by interior tribelets to Mexican military expeditions to the interior, and a decline in the number of converts being brought to live in the missions. Another factor was the legal emancipation of hundreds of Indians in the late 1820s and early 1830s, and their leaving the missions since they were now considered to be free Mexican citizens.[12]

INDIANS, MISSIONS, AND SETTLERS

The basic goal of the Jesuit, Franciscan, and Dominican missionaries was to radically alter the religious beliefs and the cultural, social, and economic organization of the Indian converts who settled or were settled in the missions. A very important element of mission history is the wide range of Indian responses to the mission acculturation programs.

Anthropologist Daniel Reff recently suggested that Sonora natives readily accepted Jesuit missionaries in the seventeenth century because the Jesuits served as a point of reference for social reorganization following a century of drastic demographic decline and social disintegration due to epidemics and other factors. Reff points out that the early descriptions of the social and political organization of many Sonora Indian groups do not concur with the seventeenth-century missionary accounts. Sixteenth-century accounts in many instances describe strong chiefs who dominated large nucleated villages. In the seventeenth century, on the other hand, many Sonora groups, including the northern Pima who inhabited the region later known as the Pimería Alta, lived in dispersed settlements known as rancherías, a pattern that would help blunt the impact of epidemics. Moreover, many traditional Indian leaders and ruling lineages died out during the epidemics.[13]

Reff's hypothesis helps explain Indian responses to the mission acculturation program in the Pimería Alta in the late seventeenth and eighteenth centuries. Resistance to the missions and Spanish colonization did occur. In 1695 and 1751 northern Pimans revolted against Spanish domination, and apostate northern Pima joined Apache and Seri bands to raid the missions and other settlements in the region. However, in relative terms, the weight of the mission system was lighter in the Pimería Alta missions than in the Baja and Alta California establishments, especially in the missions located in modern Arizona, which did not even have resident missionaries for long periods of time. Missionaries demanded less labor for communal mission projects, and left converts with more time to work on the subsistence plots that the missionaries assigned to each Indian family. Missionaries sold surplus communal produce in the local market, but the Spanish colonial regime in Sonora did not rely on mission production to help cover the costs of colonization, as was the case in Alta California. Indian converts living in the missions had greater freedom to leave the missions and look for work in the mines and other settlements that developed in the province, but were also liable for labor drafts to the mines.

In general terms, Indian–settler relations were symbiotic. Individual natives benefited from voluntary participation in the local market through the sale of surplus produce from their own subsistence plots, and the sale of their labor in the developing labor market in the mines. The missionaries, however, condemned what they considered to have been the corrupting influence of settlers on Indians living in the missions, although such attitudes may have been caused, in part, by the resentment of the missionaries over the loss of control over their charges. There was also a downside to Indian–settler relations. The growth of the local market, for example, created considerable demand for high-quality irrigated lands that were at a premium in the Sonora Desert. Settlers placed considerable pressure on and in a number of instances usurped Indian lands.[14]

In contrast, the missionaries stationed in the Baja and California missions attempted to more radically transform the culture, social organization, and economy of the Indians, who were hunters and gatherers rather than the semisedentary agriculturalists living in northern Sonora. Because of this and other factors, the mission acculturation program in the Californias relied more heavily on coercion and threats of coercion, in addition to persuasion. The missionaries brought Indian converts to newly created communities where the Indians were to be transformed into sedentary farmers. Indian resistance to the missions and Spanish colonization consisted of rebellion, large-scale flight, and even the murder of missionaries. Major Indian revolts occurred in southern Baja California in the 1730s and 1740s, and in Alta California in 1774 and 1824. There were numerous instances of raids on mission communities by hostile Indians, and instances of flight from the missions by small and large groups of converts.[15]

Missionaries employed a number of strategies to persuade Indians. One strategy was to discredit traditional religious leaders and shamans called *hechiceros* by the missionaries. In order to persuade adults to move to the missions, the Alta California establishments used dormitories to house single girls and women, the wives of men absent from the missions, and in some instances single men. Indians who broke mission rules regarding sexual behavior, labor, and compliance with church attendance were punished. Missionaries commonly gave soldiers and/or Indian collaborators responsibility for enforcing punishment—primarily corporal punishment—and then might intervene to reduce punishment. Francisco Clavigero, S.J., described the use of this strategy in northern Baja California against a group of Indians who had raided one of the missions.

Led to Adac in triumph, they [the hostile Indians] were imprisoned in the soldiers' house, whose corporal, acting as judge, informed the criminals that he had condemned them only to the punishment of floggings. This punishment was applied only to the twelve most culpable ones, with the same preparation exercised before in a similar case in the Mission of San Ignacio and by availing themselves of the same subtlety which Fathers Sistiaga and Luyando had used so successfully. Scarcely had eight or ten lashes been applied to each one of the criminals when Father Link came out and begged the judge to have the punishment stopped; and he agreed (informing the criminal) that if it were not for the mediation of that saintly Father, he would have been treated with greater severity.

Clavigero went on to describe how the same tactic was used on all twelve Indians over a number of days until their resistance to the missions broke down.[16]

In Alta California patterns of Indian resistance threatened to undermine Spanish/Mexican colonization. Converts ran away to the San Joaquín Valley, and helped organize bands that stole horses from the herds of the missions, presidios, and pueblos. Interior tribelets adopted use of the horse both to provide greater mobility, as a source of food, and as a trade item. In the 1820s, 1830s, and 1840s, Indian raids and Mexican punitive military expeditions led to escalating levels of violence, and as noted above significantly reduced the ability of the Franciscan missionaries to recruit new converts to the missions. The interior tribelets who practiced hit-and-run raids enjoyed the advantage until large numbers of Anglo–Americans began to settle in the Sacramento and San Joaquín valleys.

Most information on the missions comes from documents written by the colonizers, the missionaries who staffed the missions or civil-military officials sent to administer and protect the frontier of northwestern New Spain. Very few Indians became literate in Spanish, and generally there are no sources that provide an Indian perspective. One exception is a handful of oral histories recorded in the late nineteenth century by researchers working for H. H. Bancroft. One such account was given by Lorenzo Asisara, an Indian born at Santa Cruz Mission in Alta California in 1820. The Asisara account provides a rare glimpse into the life of Indians living in the missions, a view that is very different from the church self-history that dominated the early writing of frontier-mission history. Asisara provides details of his own life and events in California, corroborated by information from Spanish documents.

Born on August 10, 1820, Lorenzo was the son of a local Indian brought to live at Santa Cruz Mission in 1793, and a woman only recently brought to the mission. Following the secularization of the mission, Lorenzo did not receive any lands or sections of mission buildings, which indicates that he was not a part of the privileged inner circle of converts favored by the missionaries. In the 1840s Lorenzo lived in Yerba Buena (San Francisco) and San José, and was back at Santa Cruz in the 1860s. In 1877, when he was fifty-seven years of age, Lorenzo dictated his account of mission life to Thomas Savage. At that time Lorenzo was a ranch hand living at Whiskey Hill (modern-day Freedom) in the Pajaro Valley south of Santa Cruz.[17]

The Asisara-account records detail the methods of social control employed by the Franciscan missionaries, as well as the measures taken to ensure against the practice of abortion and infanticide. Asisara recounts the results of an encounter between Father Ramón Olbes, stationed at Santa Cruz Mission between 1818 and 1821, and a married Indian woman who faced a problem of fertility. Olbes examined the sexual organs of both the woman and her husband, and, according to Asisara,

Then the Father [Olbes] had them placed in a room together, so they would perform coitus in his presence. The Indian refused, but they forced him to show them his penis in order to affirm if he had it in good order. The Father next brought the wife and placed her in the room. The husband he sent to the guardhouse with a pair of shackles. Then, he [Olbes] asked her again why she didn't bear children like the rest of the women. Padre Olbes asked her if her husband slept with her, and she answered that yes. The Padre repeated his question, "Why don't you bear children?" "Who knows," answered the Indian. He had her enter another room in order to examine her reproductive parts. She resisted him and grabbed the Father's cord. There was a strong and long struggle between the two that were alone in the room. She tried to bury her teeth in his arm, but only grabbed his habit. Padre Olbes cried out, and the interpreter and the *alcalde* entered to help him. Then Olbes ordered that they take her and give her 50 lashes. After the 50 lashes, he ordered that she be shackled and locked in the nunnery [women's dormitory]. Finishing this, Padre Olbes order that a wooden doll be made, like a recently born child. He took the doll to the whipped woman and ordered her to take that doll for her child, and to carry it in front of all the people for nine days. He obligated her to present herself in front of the temple with that [doll] as if it were her child for nine days.[18]

Manuel Rojo, a Mexican government official assigned to Baja California in the 1840s, recorded the stories of a handful of Indians who had lived in the missions in the northernmost section of Baja California. Rojo recorded the account of the recruitment of an Indian named Janitin to San Miguel Mission. According to Janitin,

I and two relatives of mine came down from the Neji Mountains to Rosarito Beach to catch clams. While we were doing this, we saw two men on horses racing toward where we were; my relatives, of course, were afraid and began to run away as fast as they could. When I saw that I was alone, I became afraid of those men too, and I ran toward the forest to join my companions, but it was too late, because just then they caught and lassoed me and dragged me a long way. After this, they tied me up with my arms behind me and took me to the mission of San Miguel. When we arrived at the mission, they shut me up in a room for a week; the father would make me go to his room and would talk to me through an interpreter, telling me to become a Christian and Cunur (that was the interpreters' name) advised me to do as the father told me, because they weren't going to let me go and it would go very badly for me if I didn't consent to it. One day they threw water on my head and gave me salt to eat, and with this the interpreter told me that now I was a Christian. On the day following my baptism they took me out to work with the rest of the Indians. In the afternoon they whipped me because I didn't finish my job, and on the following day the same thing happened to me as happened the day before; every day they whipped me unjustly because I didn't do what I didn't know how to do[.][19]

PATTERNS OF NON-INDIAN SETTLEMENT IN NORTHWESTERN NEW SPAIN

Sonora developed a complex frontier society characterized by the evolution of a market economy and diverse settlement patterns. In addition to the mission communities established by Jesuit missionaries in the seventeenth and eighteenth centuries, there were mining camps, farming hamlets, and cattle and sheep ranches. At the same time, the population of the Sonora frontier was unstable, fluid, and highly mobile. A population of professional miners and fortune hunters tested their luck in a series of mining strikes throughout the province, both placer and hard-rock deposits of gold and silver. News of a mining strike set hundreds or thousands of people in motion, drawn to the prospect of quick wealth in the new mining districts, often depopulating older communities. The mobility of the population challenged the colonial objective of the development of stable populations on the frontier, and created a problem conceptualized by royal officials as vagabondage. The mobility of the Sonora population also posed problems for the Jesuit and later the Franciscan missionaries, who attempted to slowly bring their charges into Spanish society without being contaminated by what they considered to be the vices of a racially mixed population that could not be made to stay in one place or be prevented from establishing contact with the Indian converts living in the missions.[20]

In a recent study, historical geographer Michael Swann argued that the reform measures implemented in the late eighteenth century in New Spain led to economic growth in the northern frontier of New Spain that "set off a surge of mobility."[21] Although the Bourbon reforms did stimulate an expansion of mining in some regions in the north, the expansion of mining itself did not stimulate the mobility of a population that had been on the move for several centuries. The history of the settlement of Sonora in the seventeenth and eighteenth centuries was characterized by a series of boom-and-bust mining cycles, and the mobility of a small population of miners who tried their luck with each new gold and silver discovery. What differentiated the pattern of migration in the late eighteenth century from the earlier period was not the mobility of people living in the northern frontier, but the scale. What Swann ignores when he discusses patterns of migration in the late eighteenth century was population growth during the late seventeenth and eighteenth centuries, and the growing pattern of land consolidation in central and northern Mexico, often at the expense of indigenous corporate communities and frontier missions.[22] The expansion of internal markets led to an intensification of commercial agriculture, and growth of the populations of the corporate indigenous communities placed greater pressure on a limited land base. The frontier population experienced growth through short- and long-distance migration and natural reproduction, and a relatively larger number of people were on the move when compared to the previous century.

The number of people attracted to newly discovered mineral deposits increased during the course of the eighteenth century, and by the last third of the century involved thousands of people. The example of the La Cieneguilla mining district located in the southern Pimeria Alta is a case in point. A military patrol discovered placer gold deposits at La Cieneguilla in 1771, and news of the richness of the deposits soon attracted large numbers of fortune hunters. By January of 1773, some seven thousand people reportedly lived in the La Cieneguilla mining district. Moreover, a sizable number of Yaqui and other Sonoran Indians came to work in the mines on a seasonal basis. From the 1770s until the 1840s the population of the mining district fluctuated as a consequence of the exhaustion of known deposits and the discovery of new placers, until the last settlement in the district was abandoned as a result of raids by hostile Indians and forty-niners on their way to the California gold fields. In 1778, the population of the mining district was down to 775, but grew to 5,000 people in the first years of the nineteenth century, only to decline again to 838 at the end of 1816.[23]

The growing number of mining strikes in Sonora contributed to the growth of a dynamic local market economy in produce, livestock, and leather products, as well as a labor market. The establishment of military garrisons in central and northern Sonora created secondary markets for goods produced locally. Farming and ranching communities developed in response to the growth in the local market, and directly led to an accelerated rate of usurpation of mission lands. Moreover, settlers moved into the mission communities in the Pimeria Alta and other parts of Sonora, and marginalized or completely displaced the Indian populations. In 1801, for example, a large number of settlers lived in the San Ignacio mission district, and had completely displaced the northern Pima who previously lived at Ymuris.[24] Large numbers of settlers also lived in communities formed around the presidios (military garrisons) established in northern Sonora, seeking protection from hostile Indians and markets for surplus agricultural production.

Presidios were also important centers of settlement in Sonora, because they offered greater protection to settlers from raids by hostile Indians and potential markets for surplus agricultural production. In the 1770s Comandante General Teodore de Croix instituted a plan that promoted civilian settlement at presidios in order to replace expensive military garrisons with settler militias. In Croix's planned communities, settlers received land grants and modest government financial support, but also had to abide by rules set up by the government. For example, settlers receiving land were prohibited from subdividing or selling their parcels for a period of ten years, and after the ten-year grace period land transactions could take place only with proper authorization. Settlers were also expected to remain at the planned communities, keep their houses in good repair, and serve in the militia when called upon by the presidio commander. In 1780, Croix ordered Horcasitas Presidio transferred to Pitic (the modern site of Hermosillo), and the establishment of a planned community. The detailed plans included the preparation of a plat map by a military engineer, the construction of an irrigation system, and the allocation of sufficient lands, including both house lots and irrigated parcels, to each settler. Land titles were granted conditionally to settlers initiating improvements, which included planting fruit trees along the edge of the parcels, within three months of taking possession, and construction of a house. The new town was established late in 1782.[25]

In contrast to the Pimeria Alta, the aridity of much of Baja California limited the development of conventional European agriculture and, as a consequence, non-Indian settlement in most of the peninsula. With the exception of several oases in the southern third of Baja California, most of the peninsula was inhospitable to settlers. The non-Indian population clustered around the few mission sites with arable land and water, and gradually displaced the Indian populations living in the missions from the best lands.[26]

With the exception of small detachments of troops stationed in the central and northern missions, the majority of the settler population in Baja California lived in the southern Cape district bounded on the north by La Paz, and in a community surrounding Loreto Presidio, the administrative and military center of the peninsula. In 1808, for example, 528 soldiers and settlers lived at Loreto Presidio, and another 994 soldiers and settlers in three communities in the Cape district. The population of Loreto and the three communities in the Cape district grew at moderate rates at the end of the eighteenth century and during the first decade of the nineteenth century.[27]

Several factors contributed to the growth of the settler population of the southern Cape district. Several marginally profitable silver mines operated in the San Antonio–Santa Ana mining district, and were brought under crown control in 1768. Todos Santos, a former mission community with abundant arable land and water for irrigation, developed as an important farming center following the distribution of land titles in 1768 and 1769, on the orders of José de Gálvez as an incentive to attract settlers. A military detachment stationed at San José del Cabo protected the Cape district, which had been the site of several major Indian uprisings in the 1730s and 1740s.[28] Following the collapse of the mission system in the 1830s, La Paz emerged as the largest settlement in both the Cape district and the entire peninsula as a result of its growing importance as an administrative center and the growth of pearl fishing in the waters surrounding the town. According to one estimate, La Paz had a population of some thirteen hundred in 1857.[29]

Although Alta California was an isolated region located at the extreme northern edge of the Spanish empire in North America, the greater availability of arable land and water when compared to Baja California allowed for the settlement of larger numbers of people by the Spanish government. Moreover, the mission economies flourished, and produced large surpluses that eliminated the precariousness of the food supply which was such a problem in Baja California. However, the long distance from the population centers of central Mexico greatly restricted the potential number of settlers to the region. In the last years of the eighteenth century, royal officials in Mexico City expressed considerable concern over the weakness of Spain's hold on Alta California and the rest of the northern frontier, especially the sparseness of the settler population. Royal officials encountered considerable difficulty in finding colonists to send to Alta California and ended up recruiting settlers from among convicts condemned for what today would be considered social crimes such as concubinage.[30]

The colonization of Alta California was controlled and planned to a higher degree than in the other frontier areas of northern New Spain. The missions organized and administered by the Franciscans controlled much of the arable land and labor force, so potential sites to place settlers were limited. Moreover, the missionaries had an unusually strong voice in the implementation of colonial policy in the region, and were able in some instances to limit settlement. Finally, contrary to the uncritical view presented by some historians, an important symbiosis existed between missionary, soldier, and settler.[31]

Two settlement types developed in Alta California: the presidio (military garrison), and the pueblo or farming–ranching community. The royal government established four military garrisons in the region: San Diego in 1769,

Monterey in 1770, San Francisco in 1776, and Santa Barbara in 1782. All four garrisons developed into communities populated by soldiers and their families, the families of retired soldiers who elected to remain at the presidios, and settlers brought to the province. Monterey eventually became one of the largest urban centers in the province, and the center both of administration and the clandestine trade with foreign merchants that grew in importance after about 1810.

The government established three farming–ranching villages in an effort to populate the region: San José in 1777, Los Angeles in 1781, and the Villa de Branciforte in 1797. Although granted farming and grazing lands and water rights, the incipient economies of the pueblos stagnated until the development of the hide and tallow trade in the early nineteenth century. The only potential market for surplus produce, the presidios, was dominated by the missionaries, and there was little opportunity to move out from the community land grants to develop alternative economic activities. For example, in the first decade of the nineteenth century Branciforte resident and retired soldier Marcelino Bravo proposed resettling from Branciforte to Corralitos about fifteen miles south of Branciforte in the Pajaro Valley, to exploit rich pasture and agricultural lands. The Franciscan missionaries stationed at nearby Santa Cruz Mission vetoed the proposal. With the lack of economic opportunity and the limited amount of land available to settlers in the pueblo grants, many settlers left the pueblos to join the military or settle near the presidios. In the case of the Villa de Branciforte, the population did not grow until after the secularization of the missions in the 1830s that led to the granting of former mission lands to settlers, and the migration of Indian converts from the missions to work on the ranches being carved out of former mission lands.[32]

Whereas Sonora and Baja California remained a part of Mexico, American forces occupied Alta California during the Mexican–American War (1846–1848). The gold rush beginning in 1848–1849 and Anglo–American settlement in California significantly modified land-tenure patterns that evolved in the 1830s. Actual foreign settlement in Alta California began in the 1820s and 1830s, led by merchants and sailors who elected to remain in the province and generally integrated into local society, and migrants who came to California overland and often formed an hostile presence. In the jurisdiction of the Villa de Branciforte, for example, Isaac Graham was the de facto head of a community of illegal Anglo-American settlers engaged in the extraction of lumber and periodically became a part of local political struggles.[33] Anglo-American settlers brought with them the tradition of the yeoman farmer and small-holder agricultural economy that clashed with the pattern of land tenure rapidly developing in Mexican California in the decade following the secularization of the missions. Moreover, the gold rush stimulated migration to California by thousands of Anglo-Americans, who quickly outnumbered the Hispanic settler population. The United States introduced new land laws and a cumbersome and expensive system to validate the hundreds of land grants made by the Mexican government in the 1830s and 1840s, which in the long run swept aside the large Mexican landowners.[34] The bulk of Mexican settlers in California experienced marginalization, whereas the large landowners sought acceptance in Anglo-American society by claiming to be "Spanish."

The size of the settler population in northern Sonora and the Californias was small in the eighteenth and nineteenth century, which proved to be a major source of concern for the government and led to efforts at different times to develop a comprehensive colonization policy.[35] In hindsight, this policy largely failed because Mexico still lost roughly half of its national territory to the United States as a result of the Texas revolution (1836) and the Mexican-American War (1846–1848). In the case of Texas, colonization policy at the end of the period of Spanish rule, as well as local initiatives and the Mexican colonization laws of 1822 and 1824, led to the organization and later expansion of the *empresario* system that brought Anglo-American families to Texas. Anglo-American culture and political traditions clashed in Texas, and these clashes were one of the causes of the Texas revolution of 1836. Similarly, clashes between Anglo-American and Mexican settlers in California created tensions, especially with the overland migrants such as Isaac Graham and the loggers living in the vicinity of Branciforte who refused to accommodate to Mexican cultural and political norms.

One aspect of the cultural clash was the differing interpretation of the role of Indians in society. The thrust of Spanish frontier policy was to incorporate Indians into colonial society, albeit in a subservient position. Anglo–American settlers coming to California brought preconceived notions about Indians. The new settlers either saw the Indian population as a potential source of labor, or else as an impediment to development and tried to force them off the land. In the early 1850s the United States Senate refused to ratify treaties that would have created Indian reservations on some of the best-quality agricultural lands in California, and the newly created state government sanctioned genocidal attacks on Indian communities masked under the rubric of Indian wars.[36]

Throughout the Spanish colonial period, northern Sonora and the Californias remained a sparsely settled frontier. The settler population of Sonora grew slowly in the seventeenth century, and then experienced rapid growth in the eighteenth. In 1600, some six hundred settlers lived in the province, growing to fifteen thousand a century later, and seventy thousand in 1800. In the modern state of Arizona, in the Santa Cruz River Valley, there were some one thousand to two thousand soldiers and settlers in the early nineteenth century. Baja

California never had a large settler population, and in the early nineteenth century no more than one thousand to two thousand soldiers and settlers lived on the peninsula. The record for Alta California is more complete. The population of the presidios and pueblos totaled 906 in 1790, 2,062 in 1810, and 4,506 in 1834, excluding foreigners residing illegally in the province. For example, in 1845 there were 56 illegal foreigners living within the jurisdiction of the Villa de Branciforte, listed in a census prepared that year under a separate category distinct from the population of the villa. Similarly, an 1829 census listed all foreigners residing in the Monterey jurisdiction.[37]

The society of northwestern New Spain was stratified, but was also fluid. The race/caste system that evolved in central Mexico also existed on the frontier, but was not as rigid as in central Mexico. Censuses and parish registers record the standard racial terms that appear in similar records in central Mexico, although the use of these terms was more common in Sonora. The registration of racial terms, however, is misleading, since the racial terms do not necessarily reflect social or cultural realities. Racial terms frequently reflect the subjective idiosyncracies of the priest or official recording the racial identity of an individual. For example, a cursory examination of fifty years of baptisms recorded at Sahuaripa in central Sonora indicates differential growths in the number of people identified as mestizos, *mulatos, coyotes*. A closer examination reveals that different priests stationed at Sahuaripa used specific racial terms more commonly than others.[38] Moreover, in the registration of racial identity in families with parents of mixed ancestry, census takers routinely assigned the racial status of the father to the children. Therefore, within the logic of the caste system, a child who might otherwise be categorized as mestizo would appear in censuses as Pima, an Indian group in northern Sonora.[39] Missionaries stationed at different communities in Sonora used different racial terms to identify the population of the communities. In 1814, for example, the population of Ures was categorized as *Español Europeo, Español Americano,* and *Pardo,* while the population of Baserac, administered by a different missionary, was categorized as *Español, Negro, mulato,* and mestizo.[40] Finally, the caste system could also be manipulated by the humble folk who lived on the frontier to improve their social status, and their mobility as a people moving from community to community facilitated this process. People moving to a community where they were not known could and did claim a higher status. In 1797, officials in Mexico City shipped a group of petty criminals to Alta California as settlers. On arriving in Monterey, the majority of the heads of household claimed to be "Spanish," although in the minds of Spanish–born missionaries and soldiers stationed in California they clearly were not.[41]

Social differentiation outside the hierarchical military establishment and royal bureaucracy had already begun in northern Sonora by the early eighteenth century as a market economy evolved. Acquisition of land was one means of social mobility, and ranchers did enjoy some local social prestige. As noted above, a number of ranches were established in the 1720s and 1730s in northern Sonora, in the Santa Cruz River Valley. Owners of the ranches, such as Diego Romero who owned Santa Bárbara, frequently served as godparents for both Indian and settler children. The most influential local landowners claimed the status of "Spaniards," which was distinct from the category of "European" or "European Spaniard" reserved for European–born Spaniards, which also appeared in late eighteenth century censuses.[42] Ranch owners faced the same hazards of death from hostile Indians or economic ruin resulting from depredations against herds of livestock, but also presided over a dependent workforce made up of both Indians and settlers.[43]

The degree of social differentiation in Sonora becomes evident through a discussion of a meeting held in 1722 at the Real de San Juan Bautista. Rafael Zevallos, *alcalde mayor* of the mining camp, called the meeting to discuss closing the Sonora missions and the distribution of mission lands to settlers. In addition, the settlers wanted more Indian labor, especially for the mines. The miners, merchants, and hacienda owners presented a petition to the viceroy, and elected two representatives to negotiate on their behalf. One representative came from the group of miners present, and the second from the merchants.[44] The miners, merchants, and hacienda owners who were identified as *españoles* had shared interests, and sufficient local prestige to be consulted on an issue of such importance.

Further evidence of social differentiation comes from a 1773 census of the La Cieneguilla mining district located in the Pimeria Alta. The census did not record race/caste categories, but did identify a handful of men by the term *Don*, which implies high social status. Moreover, the majority of miners living at La Cieneguilla were unmarried, or if married did not have their families with them at the mining camp. In contrast, high-status men identified as "Don" had families, and in several instances also had extended households that included servants.[44]

The majority of settlers in northern Sonora were humble folk who scratched out a living as subsistence farmers, ranch hands, miners, petty traders, or soldiers. Social distinctions that existed were based both on wealth and status, but not in the same sense as in a modern class society. An individual gained status through birth, and one's background could help or hinder the accumulation of wealth. For example, whites born in Spain frequently enjoyed a higher status than did whites born in the Americas regardless of wealth, and recent migrants from Spain could use their place of birth to marry into wealthy

Creole families. Moreover, Spanish–born españoles were given preference in the appointment to lucrative government posts. *Castas* and Indians had a lower status, based on their racial identity and not on ability or personal qualities. This having been said, frontier society was also fluid and provided for some social mobility. The case of the group of settlers sent to Alta California in 1797 is illustrative. They claimed a higher caste status when they arrived in Monterey, but certainly did not fool the Spanish–born missionaries and officials who governed the province and who wrote of the settlers in condescending terms. Finally, in contrast to frontier regions of English North America and later the United States, Spanish frontier policy in northwestern New Spain did not promote or retard the development of a large class of small family farmers similar to the yeoman farmers that Thomas Jefferson believed to be the backbone of the new American republic.

Although in many senses frontier society was fluid with opportunities for social climbing, there was also a degree of control exercised by the Spanish colonial regime that in some instances also stifled development. The experience of one settler in Alta California, a retired soldier named Marcelino Bravo, typifies the ways in which government policy hindered development. Bravo, an *invalido* settled at the Villa de Branciforte as a part of a government colonization scheme in 1797, clearly recognized the limited potential for the development of Branciforte. In violation of colonial legislation, the governor of California, Diego de Borica (1794–1800), established Branciforte at a site close to Santa Cruz Mission. Branciforte had insufficient lands for farming and grazing livestock, and, because the community was surrounded by mission lands, had limited opportunity to obtain new lands. In 1803, Bravo made a proposal to take a group of settlers from Branciforte to establish a new community at a site in the Pajaro Valley, located between Monterey and the Villa de Branciforte. Despite reports that presented compelling evidence of the problems faced by settlers living at Branciforte, Bravo's plan was ultimately turned down. The proposal languished for three years at different levels in the colonial bureaucracy, and Bravo died before any decision was made. The intransigence of colonial officials condemned Branciforte to economic stagnation, and outmigration by residents of the villa ignored regulations that stipulated they could not leave the villa.[46]

ECONOMIC DEVELOPMENT

Sonora, including the Pimeria Alta, developed the only true market economy in northwestern New Spain, driven by mining and farming and ranching that provided food and leather goods for the mines. As noted above, Sonoran mining in the eighteenth century was characterized by the exploitation of placer deposits, which led to boom-and-bust cycles, but hard-rock mines also were exploited, which created more stable mining camps such as Alamos, a major population center in southern Sonora.[47] The Sonora missions also actively participated in the regional economy. Jesuit and, later, Franciscan missionaries sold livestock, leather goods, and grain, produced with the labor of Indian converts, to the mining camps and local military garrisons. Indians living in the missions also took advantage of the local market to sell surpluses produced on their own plots, and to work on a seasonal basis in the mining camps.[48]

The organization of mining camps, farms, and villages in Sonora also led to disputes between the growing settler population and the missionaries over land and Indian labor. In the early 1720s, for example, prominent Sonora settlers and government officials pushed to have the Jesuit missions closed, a measure proposed to increase access to Indian labor and mission lands. The growth of the local economy apparently outstripped the supply of Indian labor supplied to miners and others through a government-run labor draft, and profits could be made through farming and ranching. The Jesuit missionaries responded to the challenge from the settlers, in a detailed report sent to the viceroy, and successfully blocked the effort to close the missions. However, tensions continued to exist between settlers and missionaries.[49]

Until the development of the so-called hide and tallow trade in the 1820s, Baja and Alta California were not a part of the economy of New Spain/Mexico. The aridity of the Baja California peninsula retarded the development of farming and ranching, and only several marginal silver mines were developed beginning in the late 1740s. Alta California is a different story. Geographically isolated until American merchant ships began visiting in the early nineteenth century, the economy of Alta California supplied the basic subsistence needs of the missions, military garrisons, and a small number of settlers. The province never found profitable exports until American merchants began buying cattle hides for the shoe factories of New England and tallow for the production of soap and candles. In the early nineteenth century, American and Russian hunters came to the coast of both Californias in search of sea otters and fur seals, but the missionaries and settlers participated only marginally in the fur trade.

The Franciscan missionaries who staffed the Alta California missions contributed to the colonization of the region by exploiting Indian labor to produce large agricultural surpluses and large herds of livestock used to subsidize the cost to the government of maintaining military garrisons in the region. The Franciscans supplied food, leather goods, and clothing to the presidios at a cost that was significantly lower than the cost of supplying the presidios from central Mexico via the port of San Blas in Sinaloa. When the first mission was established in San Diego in 1769, the Franciscans had a mandate from Visitor-General José de Gálvez to colonize Alta California, but the mandate did not include Franciscan control over mission temporalities (Indian labor and all economic activity in the missions). The Franciscans were not given control over mission temporalities, but assumed control over the Baja California missions from the recently expelled Jesuits, and occupied Alta California under the same conditions. In 1773 Junipero Serra, O.F.M., father-president and architect of the Alta California missions, signed an agreement with the viceregal government in Mexico City. Under the terms of the agreement, the government granted the Franciscans control over mission temporalities in exchange for selling food and other goods to the military garrisons, at rates set in an official price list put together by the governor of the province. Over the next sixty years the Franciscans supplied food, clothing, and leather goods to the military.[50] However, in granting the missions a monopoly over the supply of the military, the government contributed to the economic stagnation of the three pueblos established in the province. The settlers fully participated in the economic development of Alta California only after 1834, when the missions closed and mission lands and livestock were distributed to prominent settlers and local politicians through hundreds of land grants.[51]

TABLE 3.1

Population of the La Cieneguilla Mining District in Selected Years

Month/Year	Population
May 1771	2,000
May 1772	5,000
Oct. 1772	4,000
Jan. 1773	7,000
Dec. 1773	786 + 1,500–2,000 Indians
1778	775
1803	5,000
Dec. 1816	838

SOURCE: Peter Stern and Robert H. Jackson, "Vagabundaje and Settlement Patterns in Colonial Northern Sonora," *The Americas* 44 (1988), 466–69.

TABLE 3.2

The Population of the Principal Non-Indian Settlements in Baja California in the Late Eighteenth and Early Nineteenth Centuries

Community Population In:	1798	1799	1800	1808
Loreto Presidio	375	372	401	528
Santa Ana & Todos Santos		615		627
San José del Cabo		239		367

SOURCE: Biennial Reports, Archivo General de la Nación, México, D.F.

TABLE 3.3

Population of the Non-Mission Settlements in Alta California in Selected Years

	Presidios				Pueblos		
Year	San Diego	Monterey	San Francisco	Santa Barbara	San Jose	Los Angeles	Branciforte
1790	197	178	128	213	66	124	N.A.
1800	158	344	223	369	161	305	66
1810	328	465	319	446	110	354	40
1820	515	562	320	623	244	612	83
1830	439	978	238	645	540	764	148
1834	743	997	360	740	542	923	201

SOURCE: Ms. Mission Statistics, The Bancroft Library, University of California, Berkeley.

NOTES

1. Daniel Reff, *Disease, Depopulation, and Culture Change in Northwestern New Spain, 1518–1764* (Salt Lake City, 1991).

2. Ibid., 226.

3. See Robert H. Jackson, "The Dynamic of Indian Demographic Collapse in the Mission Communities of Northwestern New Spain: A Comparative Approach with Implications for Popular Interpretations of Mission History," in Virginia Guedea and Jaime Rodríguez, eds., *Five Centuries of Mexican History/Cinco Siglos de Historia de México,* 2 vols. (México, D.F., 1992), 1:139–56.

4. Ibid., 153; Robert H. Jackson, *Indian Population Decline: The Missions of Northwestern New Spain, 1687–1840* (Albuquerque, 1994).

5. Ibid.

6. Sherburne Cook, "The Extent and Significance of Disease among the Indians of Baja California from 1697 to 1773," *Ibero-Americana* 12 (1937), 18; Robert H. Jackson, "Epidemic Disease and Population Decline in the Baja California Missions, 1697–1834," *Southern California Quarterly* 63:4 (1981), 310.

7. Jackson, "Dynamic of Indian Demographic Collapse," 152–53.

8. Ibid.

9. Sherburne Cook, *The Population of the California Indians 1769–1970* (Berkeley and Los Angeles, 1976), 42–43.

10. Peter Gerhard, *The North Frontier of New Spain* (Princeton, 1982), 309.

11. See George Phillips, *Indians and Intruders in Central California, 1769–1849* (Norman, 1993).

12. Jackson, "Dynamic of Indian Demographic Collapse," 152; Robert H. Jackson, "Post-Secularization Dispersion of the Alta California Mission Populations, 1834–1846," *RMCLAS Proceedings* (1991), 27–44.

13. Reff, Disease, Depopulation, and Culture Change.

14. General observations on Indians in the Pimeria Alta missions are based on John Kessell, *Mission of Sorrows: Jesuit Guevavi and the Pimas, 1691–1767* (Tucson, 1970); John Kessell, *Friars, Soldiers, and Reformers: Hispanic Arizona and the Sonora Mission Frontier 1767–1856* (Tucson, 1976); Henry Dobyns, *Spanish Colonial Tucson: A Demographic History* (Tucson, 1976); Cynthia Radding, "Las estructuras socioeconomicas de las misiones de la Pimeria Alta, 1768–1850," *Noroeste de México* 3 (1979); Cynthia Radding, "La acumulación originaria de capital agrario en Sonora," Noroeste de México 5 (1981), 15–46; María Arbelaez, "The Sonora Missions and Indian Raids of the Eighteenth Century," *Journal of the Southwest* 33:3 (1991), 366–386.

15. Observations on the Baja and Alta California missions are based on Miguel del Barco, S.J., *Historia natural y cronica de la antigua California,* ed. Miguel León Portilla (México, D.F., 1973); Francisco Javier Clavigero, S.J., *The History of California,* trans. and ed. Sara Lake and A. Gray (Stanford, 1937); Peter Dunne, S.J., *Black Robes in Lower California* (Berkeley and Los Angeles, 1952); Zephyrin Engelhardt, O.F.M., *The Missions and Missionaries of California,* 4 vols. (San Francisco, 1908–1915); Peveril Meigs, *The Dominican Mission*

Frontier of Lower California (Berkeley, 1935); Homer Aschmann, *The Central Desert of Baja California: Demography and Ecology*, repr. ed. (Riverside, 1971); Luis Sales, O.P., *Observations on California, 1774–1790*, trans. and ed. Charles Rudkin (Los Angeles, 1956); Sherburne Cook, *The Conflict between the California Indian and White Civilization*, repr. ed. (Berkeley and Los Angeles, 1976); Robert H. Jackson, ed., *The Spanish Missions of Baja California* (New York, 1991); Phillips, *Indians and Intruders in Central California*; Jackson, *Indian Population Decline: The Missions of Northwestern New Spain, 1687–1840*; Edward Castillo, "The Native Response to the Colonization of Alta California," in David Thomas, ed., *Columbian Consequences: Archaeological and Historical Perspectives on the Spanish Borderlands West* (Washington, D.C., 1989), 377–94; Robert H. Jackson and Edward Castillo, *Indians, Franciscans, and Spanish Colonization: The Impact of the Mission System on California Indians*, (Albuquerque, 1995).

16. Clavigero, *History of California*, 343.

17. Edward Castillo, trans. and ed., "An Indian Account of the Decline and Collapse of Mexico's Hegemony over the Missionized Indians of California," *American Indian Quarterly* 15 (Fall 1989), 391–408; Edward Castillo, "The Assassination of Padre Andrés Quintana by the Indians of Mission Santa Cruz in 1812: The Narrative of Lorenzo Asisara," *California History* 68 (Fall 1989), 116–25, 150–52. In a curious debate published in *California History* 70 (Summer 1991), 206–15, 236–37, Doyce Nunis, a vocal advocate of the ongoing campaign to canonize Franciscan missionary Junipero Serra, attempted to discredit the Asisara account because it was an Indian account and presents a view that is in many ways unflattering to the Franciscans.

18. Castillo, "Indian Account," 398. Hugo Reed, who married a former mission Indian from San Gabriel Mission, records a similar form of punishment for sterile women at San Gabriel Mission. See Robert Heizer, *The Indians of Los Angeles County* (Los Angeles, 1968), 87.

19. Manuel Rojo, *Historical Notes on Lower California* (Los Angeles, 1972), 30–31.

20. On the mobility of the frontier population and the perceived problem of vagabondage, see Peter Stern and Robert H. Jackson, "Vagabondage and Settlement Patterns in Colonial Northern Sonora," *The Americas* 44 (1988), 461–81.

21. Michael Swann, *Migrants in the Mexican North: Mobility, Economy, and Society in a Colonial World* (Boulder, 1989), 159.

22. On population growth in Mexico in the eighteenth century, see, for example, William Taylor, *Drinking, Homicide, and Rebellion in Colonial Mexican Villages* (Stanford, 1979), 26.

23. Stern and Jackson, "Vagabondage and Settlement Patterns," 466–70.

24. Ibid., 472–73.

25. Max Moorhead, *The Presidio Bastion of the Spanish Borderlands* (Norman, 1975), 224–40.

26. For a useful summary of settlement patterns in Baja California, see George Deasy and Peter Gerhard, "Settlements in Baja California: 1768–1930," *Geographical Review* 34 (1944), 574–86.

27. Biennial Reports, Archivo General de la Nación, México, D.F.

28. On settlement in Baja California, see Robert H. Jackson, "Demographic and Social

Change in Northwestern New Spain: A Comparative Analysis of the Pimeria Alta and Baja California Missions" (master's thesis, University of Arizona, 1982).

29. Deasy and Gerhard, "Settlements in Baja California," 580.

30. See Robert H. Jackson, "Repeopling the Land: The Spanish Borderlands," *The Encyclopedia of North American Colonies* (New York, 1993); Robert H. Jackson, Edna Kimbro, and Maryellen Ryan, "Como la Sombra Huye la Hora: Restoration Research, Santa Cruz Mission Adobe, Santa Cruz Mission State Historic Park," unpublished manuscript.

31. The histories of Zephyrin Engelhardt, O.F.M., emphasize conflict between missionary and settler. Mission account books present a different view. Franciscans sold goods to local settlers and rented Indian laborers both to settlers and the military. Prominent colonists and soldiers worked for the Franciscans as overseers (*mayordomos*), who carried out the day-to-day management of the mission economies. The Franciscans supported the military through the supply of food, clothing, and Indian labor. See the sections on the Villa de Branciforte in Jackson et al., "Como la Sombra."

32. For a discussion of the failure of the development of the Villa de Branciforte, see ibid. For a general discussion of changes in Alta California following the secularization of the missions, see Jackson, "Post-Secularization Dispersion," 27–43.

33. Jackson et al., "Como la Sombra."

34. Leonard Pitt, *Decline of the Californios: A Social History of the Spanish-Speaking Californians, 1846–1890* (Berkeley and Los Angeles, 1968).

35. For a useful survey of Spanish and Mexican frontier policy in general and colonization policy specifically, see the two general histories of the Borderlands by David Weber: *The North Mexican Frontier, 1821–1846: The American Southwest under Mexico* (Albuquerque, 1982), esp. 79, 162, 180; and *The Spanish Frontier in North America* (New Haven, 1992), passim.

36. On the fate of California Indians following the conquest of the province by the United States, see Cook, *Conflict between the California Indian and White Civilization*, particularly the essay entitled "The American Invasion, 1848–1870"; Robert Heizer and Alan Almquist, *The Other Californians: Prejudice and Discrimination under Spain, Mexico, and the United States to 1920* (Berkeley and Los Angeles, 1971); James Rawls, *Indians of California: The Changing Image* (Norman, 1984); Albert Hurtado, *Indian Survival on the California Frontier* (New Haven, 1988).

37. Jackson, "Repeopling the Land"; Jackson et al., "Como la Sombra," 58–59.

38. Robert H. Jackson, "The Causes of Indian Population Decline in the Pimeria Alta Missions of Northern Sonora," *The Journal of Arizona History* 24:4 (1983), 420–24.

39. This tendency is particularly apparent in a series of detailed censuses prepared in 1796, 1800–1801, and 1813–1814 for individual Sonora parishes and missions. The censuses are preserved in the Archivo del Gobienro Eclesiastico de la Mitra de Sonora, Hermosillo, Sonora (hereafter cited as AGEMS).

40. The 1814 censuses are found in ibid.

41. Jackson et al, "Como la Sombra," 49–51.

42. Ms Santa Maria Soamca Mission Baptismal Register, Bancroft Library, University of California, Berkeley; Stern and Jackson, "Vagabondage and Settlement Patterns."

43. Stern and Jackson, "Vagabondage and Settlement Patterns."

44. Luis González R., *Etnología y misión en la Pimería Alta, 1715–1740* (México, D.F., 1977), 125–34.

45. Pedro Tueros, La Cieneguilla, Dec. 25, 1773, "Padrón general de los vecinos avitantes de esta Nueva población de el Real de sn. Yldefonso de La Cieneguilla," Archivo General de la Nación, México, D.F., Provincias Internas 247.

46. Jackson et al., "Como la sombra," 51–54.

47. James Hastings, "People of Reason and Others: The Colonization of Sonora to 1767," *Arizona and the West* 3 (1961), 321–40, provides a useful summary of the development of colonial Sonora.

48. Arbelaez, "Sonoran Missions and Indian Raids," 366–86; Cynthia Radding de Murrieta, "The Function of the Market in Changing Economic Structures in the Mission Communities of Pimería Alta, 1768–1821," *The Americas* 34 (1977), 155–69; Stern and Jackson, "Vagabondage and Settlement Patterns." The missionaries received stipends, but supplemented the stipends with the sale of livestock and particularly grain from the communal production that they managed. Moreover, the missionaries obtained most of the supplies they needed from local merchants from Sonora, and not from central Mexico. However, raids on mission herds by Apaches and other hostile indigenous groups cut into the profits of the missions, and were the source of numerous complaints by the missionaries. Despite the complaints over the loss of livestock, grain sales constituted the single largest source of revenue. For example, between 1720 and 1766 grain sales by the Jesuits stationed at San Pedro de Aconchi in central Sonora totaled 72,826 pesos as against 9,606 pesos for sales of livestock. Corn was the grain in greatest demand. Between 1749 and 1762, the Jesuits at Aconchi sold 42 percent of corn grown, but only 18 percent of wheat. Cynthia Radding, *Wandering Peoples: Colonialism, Ethnic Spaces, and Ecological Frontiers in Northwestern New Spain, 1700–1850* (Durham and London, 1997), esp. chap. 3.

49. For a discussion of the proposed closing of the Sonora missions and the Jesuit response drafted by Giuseppe Genovese, see González R., *Etnología y misión*, 125–87.

50. Robert H. Jackson, "Population and the Economic Dimension of Colonization in Alta California: Four Mission Communities," *Journal of the Southwest* 33 (1991), 387–439; Robert H. Jackson, "The Changing Economic Structure of the Alta California Missions—A Reinterpretation," *Pacific Historical Review* 61 (1992), 387–415.

51. Jackson et al., "Como la Sombra," 51–57.

Church of Nuestra Señora del Rosario, former Jesuit mission of Santa Cruz, in today's Valle del Rosario, Chihuahua. Photo by Susan Deeds

Coiffures de danse des habitans de la Californie.

habitants de Californie

Three males and two female neophytes from mission San Francisco. Notice details of female tattoos and coiffeur styles. The somber countenances reflect the culture shock and stress of the mission's program to rapidly transform the hunting and collecting peoples into a disciplined labor force. French artist Louis Choris made this disturbing observation that is amply reflected in this 1822 lithograph: "I have never seen one smile, I have never seen one look me in the eye." (Courtesy The Bancroft Library, University of California, Berkeley)

Facing page top: The elaborate flicker feather headdresses and feathered top-knots of mission San Francisco neophytes are highlighted in this lithographs done in 1822 by Louis Choris. As this and other illustrations demonstrate, some tolerance for ceremonial dancing was exhibited in some missions where the padres did not perceive any suspected paganism might be implied. (Courtesy The Bancroft Library, University of California, Berkeley)

Facing page bottom: A mixed group of mission San Francisco neophytes of Costanoan and Coast Miwok tribes as depicted in a Louis Choris lithograph in 1822. The woman with a garland in her hair is a member of the North Bay Coast Miwok Numpali. (Courtesy The Bancroft Library, University of California, Berkeley)

Ink and watercolor by Louis Choris in 1816 shows Costanoan and Bay Miwok neophytes playing a traditional gambling game. These Indians are wearing textile breechcloths and blankets given to neophytes at the time of their baptism. Note the sticks used to keep score and the shell bead money being wagered. These gambling games are accompanied by singing and are still being enjoyed today. Often decried as a vice by the padres, historical records indicate an uneven tolerance for these amusements existed from mission to mission. (Courtesy The Bancroft Library, University of California, Berkeley)

Facing page top: First site of La Purísima Mission. Photo by Robert H. Jackson.

Facing page bottom: Second site of La Purísima Mission. Photo by Robert H. Jackson.

Ruins of Rosario Mission. Photos by Robert H. Jackson.

"Saturiba Goes to War." Theodore de Bry's 1591 engraving (Plate 11) from the Brevis narratio *of Jacques le Moyne. (Published in Lorant,* The New World, *57).*

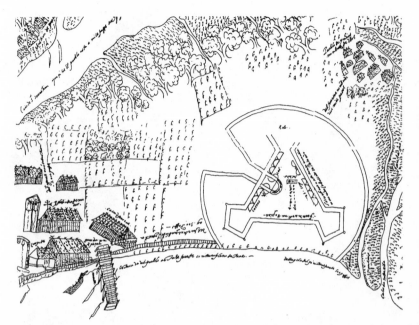

San Agustín. Plan of the City of San Agustín (lower left), its fort (lower right), and Nombre de Dios mission (upper right), 1593. (AGI 140-7-37. Published in Verne E. Chatelain, The Defenses of Spanish Florida, 1565–1763. *Washington, D.C.: Carnegie Institution, 1941).*

CHAPTER FOUR

SPANISH COLONIAL TEXAS

JESÚS F. DE LA TEJA

Until the early eighteenth century Texas was an almost completely neglected region, the very remoteness of which served as protection against foreign encroachment. The Gulf Coast and parts of the interior had been explored during the first half of the sixteenth century. Seaborne explorations in 1519 and 1558 vaguely outlined the coast. Alvar Núñez Cabeza de Vaca and the three other survivors of the Pánfilo de Narváez expedition to Florida, which wrecked on the Texas coast in 1528, traversed parts of Texas on their way to Mexico. A decade later, the De Soto-Moscoso expedition entered east Texas in a similar effort to reach Spanish-occupied territory. To the west at the same time, Francisco Vázquez de Coronado led his men in search of the mythical Gran Quivira.[1] Finding no great Indian kingdoms to conquer nor precious metals to exploit, the Spanish lost interest in these parts until the threat of foreign encroachment materialized a century and a half later.

THE FIRST TEXANS

These sixteenth-century Spanish intrusions into the geographic space of modern-day Texas resulted in contact with all the major native peoples that inhabited the region.[2] From the time he shipwrecked on one of Texas's barrier islands in 1528 until he entered Spanish-occupied northwestern Mexico in 1536, Cabeza de Vaca made the most observations. He met and lived among hunter-gatherer peoples, the Karankawa of the lower Galveston Bay area and various Coahuiltecan bands of southern Texas. If his claims of years as a trader and slave among these people are accepted, then he also had contact with the Caddoan-speaking people of eastern Texas, western Louisiana, and southwestern Arkansas. Finally, out beyond the Big Bend country of the Río Grande, he met and described the elusive semisedentary Jumanos, whom he called Cow People because of their buffalo-hunting practices. On the southern plains of eastern New Mexico and the Texas Panhandle, the Coronado expedition encountered the Querechos and Teyas, ancestors of the eastern Apaches, who apparently were part-time agriculturists before the introduction of the horse among them. In their abortive effort to reach New Spain overland from the Mississippi River following De Soto's death, Luis de Moscoso penetrated the Caddo country of east Texas, encountering numerous groups of well-organized, village-dwelling agriculturists. Unfortunately, the paucity and confusing nature of archival records has prevented scholars from venturing any guesses of population size at first contact.

Although acceptable population estimates have not been made, scholars have developed a clear picture of which Indian groups were present in Texas in the course of the next three centuries. Aside from the contact-period groups noted above, numerous Indian peoples made their way into Texas, at least in some degree owing to the impact of European expansion into the interior of North America. As Plains Indians acquired Spanish horses and French and English firearms and trade goods in the seventeenth century, a series of territorial adjustments took place that pushed the less-advantaged groups into contact with the northward-expanding Spanish. The eastern Apaches, specifically the Lipan, found themselves under increasing pressure from the more bellicose Comanches and by the 1720s had been pushed southward into the Texas hill country. The pressure, both from Comanches and Wichita-related groups, would continue, and by the early nineteenth century the Lipan Apaches were living southwest of San Antonio. The Comanches, who replaced the Lipan Apaches, established themselves as lords of the Southern Plains by the 1740s, when they are first mentioned in Spanish colonial records. Various Wichita groups, themselves under pressure from the Osages and Comanches by the late seventeenth century, settled in the Red River region at the beginning of the eighteenth. By the end of that century they had spread southward to the middle Brazos Valley.

At the turn of the nineteenth century, another period of Indian migration into Texas occurred following the transfer of Louisiana to the United States and the pursuit of Indian-removal policies in the U.S. South and Midwest. In part, this new settlement was possible because of the demographic collapse of east Texas Caddoan population. Members of the Five Civilized Tribes, Shawnees, Cherokees, and Creeks (Seminoles), as well as Delawares, Alabamas, Coushattas, and Kikapoos established themselves in Texas and sought protection from Spanish and, later, Mexican authorities, who found these predominantly sedentary peoples attractive residents. Their stay in the area after Texas independence was to be marked by increasing violence, so that by the Civil War only the Alabama-Coushatta (by now banding together for protection) survived in Texas at a small reservation in Polk County.

It is not necessary to have initial population figures for Texas Indian groups to note the devastating demographic collapse that followed Spanish occupation of the region. Only the Comanches and Wichita, with access to rich buffalo hunting grounds, European trade goods, and Spanish equine stock both in New Mexico and Texas seem to have escaped decline until after the passing of Mexican sovereignty. To the contrary, the Comanches reached their heyday during the Mexican period. The Lipan Apaches also managed to survive as independent agents until the end of Mexican rule, but in much reduced numbers. The Jumanos, who had prospered during the first three-quarters of the seventeenth century as traders between the Pueblo Indians of New Mexico and the Caddos, quickly declined following the Pueblo revolt of 1680 and encroachment of their hunting grounds by southward-moving Apaches. By the mid-eighteenth century the Jumanos incorporated themselves into the southward-moving Apache bands. These tribes remained beyond effective Spanish control, although individuals were incorporated into Spanish society and all adopted some Hispanic cultural practices.

It was among missionized Indians that the most severe demographic collapse occurred, in almost every case resulting in cultural extinction. Shortly after the first missions were established among Caddo groups in east Texas, in 1690–1691, an epidemic broke out that killed one missionary, approximately three hundred mission Indians and untold numbers of nearby villagers. Epidemic fever, which engulfed all of New Spain in the 1730s, reached Texas in 1739 and killed over one thousand Indians at the San Antonio missions. Between 1749 and 1757, the first decade of Spanish settlement along the lower Río Grande Valley, epidemics severely reduced local Coahuiltecan populations both within and outside missions. At the two missions established for the Lipan Apaches on the upper Nueces River in 1762, a smallpox epidemic in 1764 claimed the lives of seventy-four baptized natives and an unknown number of others. One of the most devastating epidemics occurred in 1777–1778, when large numbers of Caddos and Bidais succumbed to a disease that also affected the non-Indian populations of San Antonio, Bucareli, and nearby Natchitoches, Louisiana.[3]

In his *History of Texas,* written in part from personal observations made as a member of Commandant General Teodoro de Croix's inspection tour to the northern frontier in 1777–1778, Fray Agustín Morfí noted the impact of disease, missionary activity, and intertribal warfare on Texas Indians. After discussing the most important Indian groups, he concludes:

There are many other nations besides those already mentioned. Some of these were congregated in the missions; others do not deserve to be noted because of their idleness; still others disappeared or died out during the various epidemics; while some were absorbed by the nations described, such as the Nasones, Tatases, Quitseis, Yscanis, Yojuanes, Deadose, and Xanas [Xaraname].[4]

THE MISSION EXPERIENCE

The role of the missions in this disappearance or die-out of various Indian cultures is well documented, although it is as unquantifiable as the size of contact populations. Missionaries worked at not only training the Indians in the arts of agriculture and animal husbandry, but also at replacing their native cultural norms with Spanish colonial ones. Working with these goals in mind in mission fields in which the target groups were often small independent bands of people speaking distinct dialects or altogether different languages, Texas's Franciscan missionaries early gave up on learning the Indian languages and concentrated on using Spanish or, at the very least, using a standardized version of Coahuiltecan as a lingua franca.[5] The entire missionary program therefore contributed to the reduction in the number of native culture groups and their eventual disappearance altogether. After all, the product of a successful missionary endeavor *was* the transformation of natives into Spanish subjects.

A number of circumstances, some beyond the control of Spanish religious and secular authorities, combined to restrict and frustrate the missionary enterprise in Texas. Geographically, the province was so remote from the central parts of the viceroyalty that complete integration of the missions into the colonial economic system proved impossible. On the other hand, nearby French-influenced Louisiana offered many Texas Indians an attractive alternative to Spanish goods and services without the need to alter their lifeways. Not only the agricultural Caddos, but many of the hunter-gatherer cultures had easy access to the necessary subsistence resources, making mission life unattractive. The few colonials sent to Texas, both secular and religious, could not hope to control a territory of continental breadth, in which the natives effectively lost themselves when convenient. Too, European goods and horses, once introduced among the Indians who occupied North America between the Rockies and the Mississippi, set in motion a centuries-long rearrangement of the cultural landscape of Native Americans in which the Spanish were often only a marginal element. Many Indian groups quickly learned to set European rivals against each other, tell Spanish religious and secular authorities what they wanted to hear, and selectively submit to acculturation. Consequently, Texas Franciscans had only limited and spotty success.

In east Texas, missions for the Caddo were attempted in 1690–1693 and 1716–1773. Franciscan efforts among these sedentary agriculturists must be considered among the most sustained failures in Spanish colonial history. The 1690 epidemic that killed hundreds shortly after the first missionaries arrived was enough to convince the Caddos that baptism brought on death. When supplies failed to arrive in a timely manner and the villagers received no gifts, they lost interest in a continued relationship with the missionaries. By 1692 they were demanding that the Franciscans leave, which they did the following year. Returning in greater numbers a score years later to form a barrier against French penetration of Spanish territory, the Franciscans found a population indifferent to their ministry and still fearful of the deadly effect of baptism. Consequently, the ambitious field of six missions founded in 1716–1717 was reduced by half in 1730, and the remaining missions made only individual proselytes, most of them deathbed conversions when there was nothing to be lost. The failure of this mission field was acknowledged by the Franciscans themselves. Fray Morfí asserts in his history of Texas: "At the same time the useless missions of Nacogdoches, Aix, and others that had been maintained under the protection of the said presidios without Indians and *against the will of the missionaries in* charge of them, were to be abolished."[6] Although this statement does not square with the historical record entirely (apparently the missionaries did want to stay), the ineffectiveness of the east Texas missions is beyond dispute.[7]

The most graphic illustration of the deleterious effects of combined epidemic disease, missionary settlement, and intertribal conflict can be found in a decade-long struggle to operate a cluster of missions on the San Gabriel River. Between 1746 and 1751 three missions and a presidio were established to serve various central Texas tribes. During that time, the missions suffered attack from Lipan Apaches, a smallpox epidemic, and supply shortages that led to wholesale abandonment of the missions. The following four years saw more of the same: smallpox and measles epidemics, drought, summer outbreaks of typhoid, and Indian desertions to pursue foraging, self-defense, and campaigns against the Apaches. By the summer of 1755 the Spanish gave up on the mission-presidio complex that had been permanently abandoned by most of the Indians for whom it had been intended.[8] The missionaries and soldiers were then assigned to a mission for the Apaches, but that effort proved even more disastrous. The first mission, on the San Saba River near present-day Menard, was destroyed in 1758, within months of its founding, by a large force of Plains and Caddo Indians hostile to the Lipans. A subsequent effort, an Apache mission on the upper Nueces that lasted from 1762 to 1769, proved equally ineffective, although the Lipans found it a useful haven from their enemies and some individual conversions were made.[9]

The most successful missions, judged by physical infrastructure and peak agricultural output, turned out to be those located along the San Antonio River Valley from San Antonio down to present-day Goliad. In the vicinity of the presidio founded at the headwaters of the river in 1718, five missions were active by 1731. Near the coast, Mission Espíritu Santo followed Presidio La Bahía as it was moved from Matagorda Bay (hence the name) to the Guadalupe River, and in 1749 to its present location. There, the missionaries established a sister mission, Rosario, for Karankawan bands in 1754.

Activity at these missions concentrated on the seemingly most pliable and defenseless hunter-gatherers, the Coahuiltecans and some Karankawan bands. Pulled to the missions by trinkets and food offerings from the Franciscans and pushed there by pressure from aggressive Apaches, the Coahuiltecan and Karankawans nevertheless accepted acculturation on their own terms. Witnesses called to attest to the progress of the San Antonio missions in 1745 declared that "the tribes that are unconverted have been gradually brought under the influence of the missionaries, replacing from these [Indians] many of those who have died in the mission." They went on to state that

> although these missions have reached the flourishing state of develop-
> ment which is known to everyone, they do not believe they are ready to be
> turned over to the secular [priest] because new converts are brought daily,
> and even among those who have been in the missions a long time, there
> are many who frequently run away, making it necessary for the mission-
> aries to go after them and start their labors anew to bring them back to the
> bosom of our Holy Mother the Church.[10]

The above statement is only one piece of evidence indicating the inherent instability of mission populations. Evidence from the sacramental records indicates that the initial mission populations were unviable over the long term, as death rates consistently exceeded birthrates. This conclusion is further supported by the steady decline in mission populations as the sources for new recruits disappeared. Additional instability arose from the behavioral patterns of the would-be converts. The refusal of many Indians to accept the regimentation of the sedentary-agricultural life the missionaries preached along with the Gospel led to periodic and prolonged absenteeism. Indians also abandoned missions upon the outbreak of epidemics, which were sometimes occasioned by poor sanitary and living conditions and inadequate diets. The approach of Indian enemies likewise provoked flight. Among the Karankawa, and likely too among the Coahuiltecans, the missions represented little more than one stop among the various ones that made up their seasonal migrations. Consequently, the missions were often occupied only by the infirm, the elderly, some of the very young who were under the direct supervision of the missionaries, and small core groups of converts that had accepted the new way of life.[11]

That Spanish secular and religious authorities did not learn important lessons from their seventy-five years of work with south Texas hunter-gatherers is best illustrated in the experience of Mission Nuestra Señora del Refugio, the last mission founded in Spanish Texas. Established in 1793 for the Karankawa proper, one of whose chiefs had solicited a mission the previous year, the authorities considered this the best opportunity yet to civilize one of the most recalcitrant tribes in the province. The Karankawa had their own agenda, however, and the relationship soon soured as the supplies of cattle and other victuals did not turn out as bountiful as the Indians expected, and sickness spread among those residing in the mission. Chief Frezada Pinta and his followers, who had asked for the mission, refused to enter it, and a group of Indians vandalized the mission compound and its ranch. By the middle of June 1794 most of the Karankawa had abandoned Mission Refugio. The friar in charge then moved the mission to the present-day location of Refugio, where, employing paid labor from the province's settler population, permanent buildings and a farm were established. There, the mission attracted Karankawa from the older Mission Rosario, probably because it placed them closer to their coastal home range. From 43 Indians at this time, the mission grew to 224 in December 1804, and then down to 21 when the mission was secularized in 1830.[12]

By the time the various missions were secularized, the transfer of chattels and real property was most often made to settlers, some of whom had always been present at the missions. Although the Franciscans feared the corrupting influences of mixed-blood settlers, they required the presence of Hispanics in order to properly train the neophytes in the crafts and skills of Spanish colonial life. The small "Spanish" population that always resided at the missions, whether military or civilian, was augmented in 1770s and 1780s by increasing numbers of civilians, on whom the missionaries came to rely as a dependable workforce. Some intermarriage necessarily took place between mission Indians and settlers, contributing to the small stable population at the missions.[13]

THE HISPANIC TEXANS

Throughout the Spanish colonial period Texas never generated a successful economy. This important handicap, when combined with the chronic state of Indian depredations created a considerable disincentive for settlement. A letter from Texas governor Domingo Cabello to Louisiana governor Bernardo de Gálvez in July 1779 puts Texas's problems in perspective more than sixty years after the province had been occupied. In it, Cabello asks that the Louisiana official use the proceeds from the sale of two hundred head of cattle he is sending to Louisiana to purchase a male slave cook or female slave cook who can also sew, wash, and iron,

> because here all that is lacking, and particularly a cook, for a very good one that I employed in Cádiz in 1763, when I went to serve in the government of Nicaragua, was told so many things about this place as soon as we arrived in Mexico City last year, that he came to believe that the Indians would eat him, for which reason he resigned from my service. And the same thing happened with my manservant and a secretary, so that I am reduced to the most deplorable state. Although I recognize that they did right, because this [place] is worse than Siberia and Lapland.[14]

Throughout the eighteenth century the Spanish population remained small and heavily dependent on military settlers. The initial expeditions that served to occupy the province, those of Domingo Rámon in 1716 and Martín de Alarcón in 1718, brought the first two hundred or so settlers. In 1721–22 the Marqués de San Miguel de Aguayo reinforced the existing presidios and established two additional ones, leaving another two hundred soldiers in the province, many of them with families. In 1731 the population of San Antonio was augmented by the arrival of fifty-five Canary Island colonists sent to Texas at royal expense. Twenty years later a number of recruits, perhaps twenty, and their families were brought to Texas as part of the new presidio at San Xavier, where they were joined by another twenty-or-so families of volunteers from San Antonio. In 1756, when the garrison was transferred to the San Saba River, it was augmented to one hundred men, mostly by reducing San Antonio's garrison and recruiting among the civilian population.[15]

Despite the unattractiveness of frontier Texas, there was a small but steady stream of incoming settlers who contributed significantly to what little demographic growth the province experienced in the last fifty years of Spanish rule. Lax control of the border with Louisiana and the dire need for set-

tlers meant that official regulations against frontier settlement by foreigners was ignored. At Nacogdoches in 1793, among a total population of about
460 there lived 24 foreigners, including 5 European Frenchmen, 8 Louisi-
anians, 5 French Canadians, 2 Englishmen, 2 Irishmen, 1 Italian, and 1 Guin-
ean black.[16] Most of the late-colonial immigrants to Texas came from other
parts of northern New Spain, however. Coahuila, Nuevo León, and Nuevo
Santander were the provinces of origin for most of them, with the one supplying the largest number being Saltillo, the oldest population center in the
northeastern corner of the viceroyalty. The 1793 census of San Antonio, for
instance, indicates that over 12 percent of the town's residents were from other
parts of New Spain, and that 130 of these 164 Mexicans came from the three
above-named provinces.[17]

If this remote province's population had disparate national origins, it also
had a very mixed racial background. As early as 1718 the missionaries with the
Alarcón expedition complained that the colonists the governor had recruited
belonged to the baser castes—mestizos and mulattos. Other outside observers
throughout the colonial period, from governors to visitors, also commented on
the mixed racial characteristics, and the parish registers and census reports
support their conclusion of widespread miscegenation.[18] The fluidity of racial
boundaries on the frontier, and especially in isolated Texas, was helped by royal
requirements that soldiers in the service of His Catholic Majesty be Spaniards.
Hence, no matter what their baptismal records indicated or the way they were
described in their enlistment papers, company commanders routinely listed
their men as "Spaniards." Also contributing to racial mixing was the limited
availability of marriage partners for the predominantly male immigrants. The
evidence is clear that whatever their true racial composition, about half of
Texas and Laredo settlers considered themselves "Spanish," with mestizo and
other mixed-blood groups making up most of the rest, and Indians within the
civil settlements accounting for between 10 and 15 percent of the population.[19]

Following the transfer of Louisiana to the United States in 1803, the crown
stationed in Texas hundreds of additional troops from the militias of neighboring provinces, reaching a high of 1,368 in 1806.[20] This population boom proved
transitory, however, as the disruptions of the Mexican War of Independence
led to the transfer of troops, the rebellions in the province, the death of
hundreds of Tejano insurgents, and the flight of hundreds of others to Louisiana. Although the numbers available are very problematical, it is certain that
Texas had a smaller Hispanic population on the eve of Mexican independence
—fewer than twenty-five hundred men, women, and children—than it did at
the turn of the century.

SETTLEMENT PATTERNS ON THE TEXAS FRONTIER

Throughout the colonial period Texas's small population was concentrated at three geographic centers. The most stable center of settlement was located in the upper San Antonio River Valley, at present-day San Antonio, where Spanish occupation began in 1718 with a presidio and Mission San Antonio de Valero (the Alamo). In 1720 a second Franciscan mission, San José y San Miguel de Aguayo, opened its doors some miles downstream. In 1731 three other missions, Nuestra Señora de la Concepción, San Juan Capistrano, and San Francisco de la Espada, which had failed to take root in east Texas, relocated along alternating sides of the river below the older settlements. That same year, the fifty-five Canary Islander immigrants founded the only chartered civil settlement in the province, San Fernando de Béxar. Located adjacent to the presidio for protection, the two entities merged so thoroughly that by the late colonial period the entire settlement was commonly referred to as Béxar. Because of its location on the road from the interior of New Spain to the other Texas settlement, Béxar quickly grew into the largest and most diversified settlement. In recognition of its strategic importance, in 1771 Béxar became the provincial capital.

East of San Antonio, in the coastal region near Matagorda Bay, was located the second population center of the province, the presidio-mission complex known as La Bahía. Originally established at the site of La Salle's Fort St. Louis by the Marqués de San Miguel de Aguayo in 1722, the presidio and mission were removed some thirty miles inland to a more healthful location in 1726. In an effort to give José de Escandón's plans for settling the coastal region between the Río Grande and the Texas border a northern anchor, the complex was moved once again in 1749 to its present location on the San Antonio River at Goliad. Here the original mission, Espíritu Santo de Zúñiga, was joined by Nuestra Señora del Rosario in 1754. At the end of the century, just when the other missions were moribund and about to begin the secularization process, the last Texas mission, Nuestra Señora del Refugio, was established about twenty miles south of La Bahía for nearby Karankawan bands. Although a sizable civilian settlement grew around the presidio from an early date, La Bahía remained under the administrative jurisdiction of the military commander until 1820, when the settlement was raised to the status of villa and established a town council.

The third area of permanent settlement in the province was in eastern Texas. In 1716 the Domingo Rámon expedition established a short-lived presidio and four missions on the Neches and Angelina rivers near present-day Nacogdoches. The following year two more missions were founded, including San Miguel de los Adaes, which was located near the French settlement at Natchitoches. In his effort to reinforce the frontier against French encroachments, the Marqués de San Miguel de Aguayo established another presidio, Nuestra Señora del Pilar de los Adaes, between Mission San Miguel and Natchitoches. The presence of this border military post and the moribund status of most of the missions of the Neches-Angelina area brought about the closure of the presidio protecting them in 1729 and the transfer of three of the missions to central Texas in 1730. Between that year and 1773, when the area was abandoned on the recommendation of the Marqués de Rubí, Spanish east Texas consisted of the Presidio de los Adaes, its companion mission of San Miguel, and missions Nuestra Señora de los Dolores de los Ais and Nuestra Señora de Guadalupe de los Nacogdoches.

As in the case of La Bahía, the east Texas presidio became the hub of a considerable civil settlement with substantial ties to the neighboring French colony. Not surprisingly, many of the residents resented being moved to the San Antonio area when Los Adaes was disbanded as no longer necessary in light of Louisiana's transfer to Spain following the Seven Years War. A large group of Adaesanos successfully petitioned for permission to return to east Texas and in 1774 founded the short-lived pueblo of Bucareli on the Trinity River crossing of the Camino Real. Indian depredations and floods led to the abandonment of this site in 1779 for the vicinity of the abandoned mission of Nacogdoches, where the settlers established a town by that name. Although it had its roots in the military settlement of Los Adaes, Nacogdoches was a civil settlement governed by a lieutenant governor appointed by the governor. Following United States acquisition of Louisiana, Nacogdoches was garrisoned by royal troops beginning in 1795, and during the Mexican War of Independence became the target of filibustering expeditions, which left it almost totally abandoned until 1821.[21]

Aside from the above-described settlement areas, Spanish officials undertook a number of abortive efforts to expand the province's area of settlement. The failed effort to establish the San Xavier Mission-Presidio complex in central Texas in the early 1750s gave way to the disastrous Apache mission experiment at San Sabá. Although the accompanying presidio remained in that location for more than a decade, and two new Apache missions were opened on the upper reaches of the Nueces River, by 1772 the crown recognized the uselessness of such a remote post and ordered the area's abandonment. As San Sabá was failing to the west, the presidio-mission complex known as Orcoquisac was meeting a similar fate to the east. It was established in 1755 at the northern end of Galveston Bay for the Christianization of the Akokisa Indians and the defense of Spanish territory against French and English intruders. The location proved unhealthful, however, the Indians uncooperative, and the garrison querulous. Unable to attract settlers, and its garrison in greater demand at Béxar and La Bahía, the post was often undermanned. It too was closed at the time Los Adaes was abandoned, although the garrison had been removed sometime before.[22]

With the exception of the Adaesanos' efforts to relocate themselves at Bucareli and, finally, at Nacogdoches, no other settlement efforts were made until after the turn of the century. The Louisiana Purchase by the United States drew that expansion-minded country much closer to the rich mining regions of northern New Spain than Spanish officials felt comfortable with. The debate between those officials who wanted to accept French- and Anglo-American émigrés as settlers in Texas and those who did not want any foreigners so close to the border was won by the former. The commandant general gave permission for settlements on the Trinity, Brazos, Colorado, San Marcos, and Guadalupe rivers. But only two of these were actually realized, Santísima Trinidad de Salcedo (1806) and San Marcos de Neve (1807). Salcedo, as the former was known, was settled with a few families from Béxar and a larger number of émigrés from Louisiana. San Marcos, on the other hand, was founded by a group of colonists from Nuevo Santander. Both succumbed to the disruptions of the Mexican War of Independence. In 1810 Governor Cordero, using his authority as governor of Coahuila, established one last settlement in the territory of present-day Texas. The town of Palafox, located on the east bank of the Río Grande halfway between Laredo and San Juan Bautista, went untouched by the insurrections in Texas, but fell prey to repeated Indian assaults, which brought about its abandonment by the mid-1820s.[23]

Another town with civilian origins was Laredo, which, although part of present-day Texas, was until the Treaty of Guadalupe Hidalgo part of Tamaulipas. Laredo was the last northwesternmost of the Río Grande settlements founded by José de Escandón, the colonizer of Nuevo Santander (renamed Tamaulipas after Mexican independence); it was also the only one on the east bank of the river. Founded in 1755 with a handful of ranching families from the downstream Hacienda de Dolores, the settlement was quickly augmented by families from another Río Grande settlement, Revilla, and in 1767 Laredo received a royal charter as a villa and was granted a local government. Indian depredations in these years proved too much for the local militia, and in 1775 the governor stationed a small garrison there, although from the available evidence it is clear that it did not play an important role in community development.[24]

TEXAS COLONIAL SOCIETY

The social structure of colonial Texas was a simpler and more fluid version of broader Mexican colonial norms. Outside the governor and presidio commanders, there were no governmental representatives of the crown. The only members of the ecclesiastical hierarchy present were the missionaries, who also served the needs of the Hispanic residents at La Bahía and Los Adaes/Nacogdoches, and the lone diocesan priest in the province, who served at Béxar. Because the province had no mines or well-developed estates, there were no rich residents.[25] A limited number of the most successful rancher-farmers (many of them one-time soldiers) and merchants constituted the local elites of the various settlements, although even these would have been recognized as little more than poverty-stricken yokels in the central parts of the empire.

Within the confines of the limited economic and social world that Tejanos constructed for themselves, there was room for mobility, however. The reality of miscegenation, combined with the demands of a hierarchical social system that emphasized the primacy of Spaniards, produced widespread "passing." Mulattos and Indians tried to pass as mestizos and mestizos tried to pass as Spaniards. As mentioned above, military service, which tended to "whiten" individuals socially, provided an additional avenue of mobility through promotion. Because the frontier presidio system was separate from the regular Spanish army and relied on men with knowledge of Indian warfare, competent frontiersmen could and did rise to command.[26]

In the case of San Antonio there was an important additional element that contributed to social status, descent from the Canary Island settlers who arrived in 1731. Because the king had granted privileges as original settlers (*primeros pobladores*), the original Isleño group and its descendants took pains to point out their social rank, although it did not necessarily correspond to economic or political status. In the course of time the Canary Islanders had to seek spouses among the much larger Mexican population, so that by the latter part of the eighteenth century most second- and third-generation Bexareños could claim Isleño status.[27]

As a military-agricultural society, property ownership was the most important measure of social status. Limited access to farmland—irrigated fields were only available at Béxar—and the financial requirements for obtaining ranch land divided society into the few haves and the many have-nots. Although anyone showing a little industry and the intent of establishing and maintaining a family could gain access to a town lot and, therefore, the status of *vecino,* participation in local affairs was limited to individuals of substance. The few merchants and craftsmen who braved the frontier did not, by their mere presence, gain status within their communities. They too had to acquire landed property and, if possible, marry into an established family in order to climb the local social ladder.[28]

As in the greater colonial society, the trappings of social status were many and readily evident in colonial Texas. Length of family residence in the community, for example, claim to Isleño descent; location of one's residence in proximity to the town's plaza; participation in local government; undertaking some form of conspicuous consumption, like sending a son to train for the priesthood or assuming the expenses of religious celebrations; and having one's name prefaced by the honorific *don* or *doña* were all symbols of rank within one's community. Because of the limited financial means of all members of local society, manual labor consisting of farming and ranching did not reduce one's status. In colonial Texas everyone had to work.[29]

COLONIAL TEXAS: AN ECONOMIC BACKWATER

Unlike other parts of the frontier, where mining or large-scale sheep and cattle operations extended the zones of Spanish control, in Texas the military served that function. It is not surprising that at the end of the colonial period the surviving pre-independence settlements (including the almost abandoned Nacogdoches) had military origins. What little market economy existed in colonial Texas relied heavily on meeting presidial needs. Not only did the presidios serve as markets for foodstuffs produced both by the missions and civilian settlers, they also supported tailors, blacksmiths, carpenters, shoemakers, and other artisans. After economic control over the garrisons was wrested away from governors and presidio commanders in the latter part of the eighteenth century, a handful of petty merchants made a meager livelihood supplying soldiers and their families with second-grade goods from central Mexico and a few imported luxuries. The military payrolls proved to be the only consistent, if inadequate, source of money supply in the province. Of the colonial settlements within present-day Texas, only Laredo had a history of independence from this military economy.

Outside of military service, economic opportunity was by and large limited to farming and ranching. Most farming took place near the towns and, of course, at the missions. Farming at La Bahía and in east Texas seems to have been a strictly subsistence practice, which at the former often did not meet local needs. In San Antonio, where the terrain lent itself to irrigation, Mission San Antonio de Valero and the presidio both opened acequias in 1718. It was the presidio's acequia and farm that the Canary Islanders appropriated when they arrived in 1731. Another farm for the town opened in 1778, with the construction of a second public acequia spanning the San Antonio River and San Pedro Creek. By the 1750s all five Béxar missions had sophisticated irrigation works that, in the case of San Francisco de la Espada, included an aqueduct that has remained in service to this day. The productivity of the San Antonio farms was such that they regularly supplied other Texas communities with agricultural products, mostly maize, and sometimes sold crops as far away as the Río Grande and Coahuila. But the limited range of Texas agriculture is evinced in the absence of gristmills until the beginning of the nineteenth century at all establishments except Mission San José.[30]

Not surprisingly, the limited markets available to Béxar farmers contributed to periodic disputes between settlers and missionaries. Soon after the Canary Islanders arrived, they complained to the viceroy that the presidio commanders and missionaries were conspiring to prevent the sale of Isleño corn to the garrisons. Throughout the rest of the colonial period, the town's civilian farmers used the viceregal order that resulted from the complaint to force the presidios to purchase their crops in preference to that of the missions. The townspeople did not get everything they wanted, however, for the missionaries were successful in preventing the settlers from gaining access to neophyte labor.[31]

Disputes between missions and civilians extended to ranching as well. The ranching practiced by Tejanos also remained at a rudimentary level. Because of chronic Indian hostilities, operations during the colonial period remained limited in size and in ranching methods. Prior to their decline in the 1780s, the missions developed the earliest ranches and owned the largest herds. Overall, there were few standing herds, however, most branded animals being allowed to roam at will until roundup time. Until the late 1780s missionaries protested that settlers raided mission pastures, indiscriminately slaughtering cattle that clearly belonged to the Indians. Civilian ranchers, for their part, complained that the missions had not only appropriated excessive amounts of land in order to prevent settlers from establishing viable ranches, but that they claimed the descendants of animals originally brought to the province by the colonists.[32]

Notwithstanding the continual disputes, ranching proved, overall, the most lucrative economic pursuit available from the Río Grande to the Louisiana border. In the first decades following Spanish settlement, animals were slaughtered at temporary work sites, where vaqueros dried the meat and extracted useful by-products. Hides, tallow, and dried beef made their way out of the province in mule trains organized both by local settler and mission ranchers and by outsiders who had brought in merchandise. For a quarter-century beginning in 1770, economic conditions in New Spain and Louisiana combined with impressive growth in the wild cattle population to create a market for live-cattle exports. Tejanos made cattle drives to New Orleans in the east and Coahuila, Nuevo León, and Nuevo Santander to the south. One favorite destination was the annual trade fair at Saltillo, where ranchers could exchange cattle for goods that they brought back to Texas for sale. As the wild cattle population succumbed to unbridled exploitation, Tejanos turned to horse and mule trading at the end of the eighteenth century.[33]

Trade in colonial Texas was limited not only by the geographic isolation of the region, but also by imperial regulations aimed at preventing foreign access to colonial markets. Commerce with Natchitoches was officially proscribed, even during the decades when it was a Spanish possession. Bernardo de Gálvez's efforts to acquire Texas cattle for Spanish military efforts against the British during the United States War of Independence required special dispensation from the viceregal officials. Contraband, nonetheless, was widespread, particularly in east Texas, but its overall economic importance remains the subject of debate.[34]

The possibilities for trade with the Indians were likewise limited by official Spanish policy. Until late in the eighteenth century it was illegal for Spanish subjects to trade in firearms with the Indians. Even after it became permissible, many limitations were placed on it, as at Béxar, where the governor refused the settlers permission to trade in firearms with the Lipan Apaches. European trade goods, also in demand by the Indians, were expensive for would-be Spanish traders because of the costs of bringing them overland from Veracruz. Another obstacle to trade was that the Spanish never acquired the interest in pelts and furs that other Europeans did. Consequently, French, English, and (after the turn of the nineteenth century) American traders held the upper hand in dealing with the Indians. Nevertheless, some commerce between Indians and settlers did take place, especially in locally produced agricultural goods and services (for example, in smithing) in return for buffalo hides, deerskins, horses (often taken from other Spanish settlements), and, on occasion, human captives. In the absence of any account books documenting such transactions, any estimate of the scope of this activity is impossible.[35]

The economic development of Texas during the colonial period was largely limited to these incipient, rudimentary activities. Outside the mission textile shops, with their looms and spinning wheels, Texas contained no intensively organized economic enterprises. Activities such as soap and candle-making made up small cottage industries that sometimes produced enough surplus to provide export quantities, but most often only served local needs. *Piloncillo* (brown-sugar cones) and *chinguirito* (a crude rum) were also manufactured for local consumption, although production of the latter was illegal until the mid-1790s.[36]

There are indications that conditions improved in the first decade of the nineteenth century. The arrival of additional troops to defend the new border with the United States, efforts on the part of the governor and other royal officials to foster the province's development by establishing new settlements, and a lull in Indian depredations all contributed expanding economic opportunities. But this period was short-lived. The outbreak of the Mexican War of Independence brought an end to government subsidies for Indian gifts, and the disgruntled tribes increased their raids on Spanish settlements and ranches. Rebellion and filibustering threw provincial government into disorder, led to the abandonment of Nacogdoches and the new settlements, and resulted in the flight of hundreds of settlers.[37] Governor Martínez, the last Spanish colonial governor of Texas, documented the deplorable state of the province on the eve of Mexican independence. About Béxar he had the following to say:

This citizenry has no other occupation than farming, and he who cannot practice it employs himself in hunting bear and deer. The crops that they work are reduced to maize, wheat, and sugarcane. There is no manufacturing at all nor any freighting, nor are there any miners.

The number of livestock upon which this citizenry can count at this time is small, and cannot be detailed because it has fled from its respective pastures; there being no wool-bearing livestock left now, with the exception of some sixty head of sheep and about thirty goats. There are also no breeding mares and the number of tame horses reaches sixty.[38]

SOCIAL MOBILITY ON THE FRONTIER: A FAMILY CASE STUDY

The various characteristics of social and economic development in colonial Texas can be seen at work in numerous families whose Texas roots stretch from the earliest days of settlement to the present. One such family is the Seguíns, among whose colonial ancestors can be counted soldiers, artisans, town councilmen, farmers, ranchers, and legislators.[39]

The first Seguín in Texas was linked to the early military history of the province. Santiago Seguín was in San Antonio by 1722, as a member of the presidio company, most probably having been recruited for the Marqués de San Miguel de Aguayo's expedition to drive the French out of east Texas. His son, José Miguel, had the distinction of being one of three Bexareños who, in 1756, accompanied Bernardo de Miranda y Flores on his search for the fabled silver mines of Los Almagres.[40]

In the 1740s Santiago was joined by Bartolomé, who was probably his nephew. Bartolomé did not enter military service, for he was a carpenter. He did marry the daughter of a Béxar alderman, who himself had been a local soldier in the 1720s. Also unlike his kinsman, Bartolomé prospered in Béxar. Aside from his extensive carpentry work, which included providing estate appraisals and led to a grant of land on which to build a shop, he did some farming. In 1776 he received a grant for an irrigated field in the town's new farm. Other signs of his rise in local society included his purchase of an expensive plot of land near the military plaza, his service as an officer for one of the town's religious feasts, and his three-time election to the town council. Bartolomé died in 1791 at about age seventy, leaving behind children and grandchildren by his first two wives, and having buried his third wife some time before.

The vagaries of achieving and maintaining social status on the frontier are illustrated in the fortunes of two of Bartolomé's sons. His only child by his first wife, Santiago, inherited his maternal grandfather's farming and ranching interests and parlayed them into enough wealth to join the ranks of San Antonio's prosperous. In contrast, Bartolomé's second son by his second wife, Esmeregildo, remained a landless farmhand throughout his later life after a brief military career in the 1780s. Béxar's census of 1793 makes the distinctions between the two clear.[41] Santiago is listed as a *labrador* (farmer) and bears the title of *don*. Esmeregildo, meanwhile, appears simply as a *jornalero* (farmhand) with no honorific preceding his name.

As was the case with most other successful colonial Texans, Santiago had his hand in a number of different economic activities. He farmed, hauled stone, and perhaps even served as a mule skinner. It was in ranching that Santiago found the most success, however. From the late 1770s onward, he was one of the town's most prominent cattle ranchers, driving a number of herds to Coahuila during the period. Although his herds consistently numbered in the hundreds, he, like a number of other ranchers, did not own his own ranch land, instead keeping his cattle with those of relatives. Santiago's prospects were good enough that in 1778 he married María Guadalupe Fuentes, sister of the parish priest. In 1784, at age thirty, he was already serving as a member of the town council.

As he grew older, Santiago also grew more unsettled, however. Trouble with the authorities over compensation for construction work, beginning in 1790, at least in part contributed to Governor Manuel Muñoz rejecting his selection to the town council in 1795. The following year, he was found guilty of assaulting one of the town's aldermen. By the end of the century Santiago had moved his family to Saltillo, although in 1803 his brother-in-law, Father Pedro Fuentes, asked the governor to order his return to *Saltillo*.

At least two of Santiago's sons decided to make Texas their home after Santiago's family moved away. Juan made his way to Nacogdoches, where he got into trouble with the authorities in 1805 for displaying an anticlerical poster. Despite the disruptions of the Mexican War of Independence, Juan remained attached to the Nacogdoches area, and served as *alcalde* during the mid-1820s. He died there in August 1836.[42]

Juan's older brother Erasmo led a longer and more influential life as one of San Antonio's leading citizens during the first four decades of the nineteenth century. In 1807 the twenty-five year old Erasmo, already described as a merchant, became Béxar's postmaster. The post proved profitable enough that, despite two or three interruptions, he occupied it for almost thirty years. Of course he also worked the fields he had inherited from his father's family, and by 1810 managed to acquire a considerable amount of ranch land that had belonged to the now secularized Mission San Antonio de Valero. The invasion of Texas by the Gutiérrez-Magee expedition of 1812–1813 brought a sharp but temporary decline in Erasmo's fortunes. Accused of treason, his property was confiscated. He refused to participate in a general amnesty, however, and sought to prove his innocence. Although he was cleared of the charges by 1818 and his house and ranch were restored to him, Erasmo never recovered approximately eight-thousand-dollars worth of other property that he claimed.

A man of considerable talents, Erasmo quickly rebuilt his position in the community. In 1820 he served as alcalde of San Antonio—the first of a number of municipal posts he was to hold throughout the next decade. The following year he was selected by Governor Antonio Martínez as his emissary to Moses Austin, to carry word that the Anglo-American's colonization plan had been approved. And his protestations of loyalty to the crown did not prevent his early emergence as one of the town's post-independence political leaders. In 1822 he recovered the postmastership, and in 1825 added that of quartermaster. Having been selected as backup representative to Mexico's first constitutional congress, he was elected as the Texas delegate to the second, and helped draft the Federal Constitution of 1824. A strong proponent of Anglo-American settlement, he would eventually side with the Texans in the Texas War of Independence. His son, Juan Nepomuceno, not only served as an officer in the Texas army, but went on to have a colorful political-military career in the border region.

CONCLUSION

Under such circumstances, it should not surprise us that Tejanos supported liberal immigration and economic policies throughout the Mexican period. A few Tejanos even managed to prosper through their dealings with the new Anglo-American settlers, but most of the Mexican population did not benefit from the growing population. Anglo-Americans directed their commercial and productive activities toward markets in the United States, New Orleans in particular. Most were yeomen farmers who produced the very types of goods Tejanos would have been in a position to sell them—agricultural products. Those Anglo-American immigrants who came as cotton farmers tended to bring their own labor with them—slaves—and, therefore, had little need of Mexican agricultural workers. Consequently, by the end of the Mexican period, Texas was well on the way to the kind of economic development that had eluded the region during the colonial period. But the beneficiaries of that development were by and large the new arrivals. Having attained economic and demographic predominance within fifteen years of their initial legal arrival in 1821, Anglo-Americans were ready by 1835 to wrest political control from Mexico and from a Tejano population that had come to be looked upon as alien to Texas.

TABLE 4.1

Estimated Population of Texas Settlements and Laredo

	1740	1747	1754	1757	1789	1790	1793	1794	1830
Bexar Presidio & Civilian	400					1,383			
Mission Valero	238					48			
Mission San José	249					144			
Mission Concepción	210					47			
Mission Capistrano	169					21			
Mission Espada	121					93			
La Bahía Presidio & Civilian	200					633			
Mission Espíritu Santo		400						125	
Mission Rosario			500			67			
Mission Refugio							138		21
East Texas	300					524			
Laredo				85	708				

SOURCES: Peter Gerhard, *The North Frontier of New Spain* (rev. ed., Norman: University of Oklahoma Press, 1993), 341; Gilberto M. Hinojosa, *A Borderlands Town in Transition: Laredo, 1755–1870* (College Station: Texas A&M University Press, 1983), 9–19; Robert H. Jackson, "Congregation and Population Change in the Mission Communities of Northern New Spain: Cases from California and Texas," *New Mexico Historical Review* 69, 2 (1994): 174, 176; Alicia V. Tjarks, "Comparative Demographic Analysis of Texas, 1777–1793," *Southwestern Historical Quarterly* 77, 3 (1974): 303.

NOTES

1. For the Pineda and Lavazares expeditions, see Robert S. Weddle, *Spanish Sea: The Gulf of Mexico in North American Discovery, 1500–1685* (College Station, 1985), 99–101, 257–58. Narratives of the Cabeza de Vaca and De Soto journeys are collected in Frederick W. Hodge and Theodore H. Lewis, eds., *Spanish Explorers in the Southern United States, 1528–1543* (repr., 1907; Austin, 1984). The best monograph on the Coronado expedition is Herbert E. Bolton, *Coronado: Knight of the Pueblos and Plains* (repr., 1949; Albuquerque, 1964).

2. The following discussion of the region's Indian cultural landscape is based on W. W. Newcomb, Jr., *The Indians of Texas: From Prehistoric to Modern Times* (Austin, 1961). An excellent brief account can be found in Donald E. Chipman, *Spanish Texas, 1519–1821* (Austin, 1992).

3. Peter Gerhard, The North Frontier of New Spain, rev. ed. (Norman, 1993), 340; Elizabeth A. H. John, *Storms Brewed in Other Men's Worlds: The Confrontation of Indians, Spanish, and French in the Southwest, 1540–1795* (Lincoln, 1981), 189, 369, 498–99; Martín Salinas, *Indians of the Rio Grande Delta: Their Role in the History of Southern Texas and Northeastern Mexico* (Austin, 1990), 140.

4. Agustín Morfí, *The History of Texas*, 2 vols. (Albuquerque, 1935), 1:92.

5. Gilberto M. Hinojosa, "The Religious-Indian Communities: The Goals of the Friars," in Gerald E. Poyo and Gilberto M. Hinojosa, eds., *Tejano Origins in Eighteenth-Century San Antonio* (Austin, 1991), 71.

6. Morfí, *History of Texas*, 2:421; italics in original. The other missions to which Morfí refers include Nuestra Señora del Pilar de los Adaes, near the Red River and the Louisiana settlement of Natchitoches, and Nuestra Señora de la Luz del Orcoquisac, on the Trinity River just above Galveston Bay.

7. Carlos E. Castañeda, *Our Catholic Heritage in Texas, 1519–1936*, repr. ed. (New York: Arno Press, 1976), 2:225–26, 237–38, 4:33; Hinojosa, "Religious-Indian Communities," 74.

8. Bolton, Coronado, 137–278; John, Storms Brewed in Other Men's Worlds, 279–92.

9. The most detailed account of the San Sabá Mission is Robert S. Weddle, *The San Sabá Mission: Spanish Pivot in Texas* (Austin, 1964).

10. Castañeda, Our Catholic Heritage in Texas, 3:121.

11. Robert H. Jackson, "Congregacíon and Population Change in the Mission Communities of Northern New Spain: Cases from the Californias and Texas," *New Mexico Historical Review* 69:2 (1994), 171–75; Hinojosa, "Religious-Indian Communities," 74–78.

12. Castañeda, *Our Catholic Heritage in Texas*, 5:67–109, 6:126, 324–26; Jackson, "Congregation and Population Change," table 6, p. 177.

13. Hinojosa, "Religious-Indian Communities," 79–80; Castañeda, *Our Catholic Heritage*, 5:96–108.

14. Domingo Cabello to Bernardo de Gálvez, July 25, 1779, Papeles de Cuba, leg. 70, Archivo General de Indias, transcripts at the Texas State Archives, Austin.

15. Oakah L. Jones, *Los Paisanos: Spanish Settlers on the Northern Frontier of New Spain* (Norman, 1979) 46–47; Herbert E. Bolton, Texas in the Middle Eighteenth Century: Studies in Spanish Colonial History and Administration, repr. ed. (Austin, 1970), 84–85, 246–47.

16. Alicia V. Tjarks, "Comparative Demographic Analysis of Texas, 1777–1793," *Southwestern Historical Quarterly* 77 (Jan. 1974), table 23, note a.

17. Tjarks, "Comparative Demographic Analysis," table 21.

18. Castañeda, *Our Catholic Heritage,* 2:87; Jesús F. de la Teja, "Indians, Soldiers, and Canary Islanders: The Making of a Texas Frontier Community," *Locus* 3 (Fall 1990), 88.

19. Tjarks, "Comparative Demographic Analysis," 322–28; Gilberto M. Hinojosa, *A Borderlands Town in Transition: Laredo, 1755–1870* (College Station, 1983), 17.

20. Odie B. Faulk, *The Last Years of Spanish Texas, 1778–1821* (The Hague, 1964), 124; Mattie Austin Hatcher, *The Opening of Texas to Foreign Settlement, 1801–1821,* repr. ed. (Philadelphia, 1976), 61–62, 70–71.

21. Bolton, *Texas in the Middle Eighteenth Century,* 377–446; Chipman, *Spanish Texas* 240–41; James M. McReynolds, "Family Life in a Borderland Community: Nacogdoches, Texas, 1779–1861" (Ph.D. diss., Texas Tech University, 1978), 7–25.

22. Chipman, *Spanish Texas,* 147–66; Weddle, *San Sabá Mission,* 156–83.

23. Hatcher, *Opening of Texas,* 94–105, 124–26, 202, 224–25, 230.

24. Hinojosa, *Borderlands Town,* 5–16.

25. A good contemporary description of the little progress Texas had made by the beginning of the nineteenth century is a report by Juan Bautista Elguezabal, governor of Texas, to the commandant general of the Interior Provinces in 1803. See Hatcher, *Opening of Texas,* appendix 5.

26. Tjarks, "Comparative Demographic Analysis," 322–30.

27. De la Teja, "Indians, Soldiers, and Canary Islanders," 93–94.

28. McReynolds, "Family Life in a Borderland Community," 243–47; de la Teja, "Indians, Soldiers, and Canary Islanders," 86–87, 92.

29. Jesús F. de la Teja, "The Structure of Society: The Spanish Borderlands," in *Encyclopedia of the North American Colonies,* Jacob Cooke, ed. (New York, 1993), 379–80.

30. Jesús F. de la Teja, *San Antonio de Béxar: A Community on New Spain's Northern Frontier* (Albuquerque, 1995), chap. 4; McReynolds, "Family Life in a Borderland Community," 243–45. Scattered throughout vols. 2–6 of Castañeda's *Our Catholic Heritage in Texas* are descriptions of the economic activities of all the Texas missions; see, for example, 4:22– 39. A good compact survey of the San Antonio missions that gives considerable attention to material development is Marion A. Habig, *The Alamo Chain of Missions: A History of San Antonio's Five Old Missions,* rev. ed. (Chicago, 1968).

31. Castañeda, *Our Catholic Heritage in Texas,* 3:103–4; Jesús de la Teja, *San Antonio de Béxar: A Community on New Spain's Northern Frontier* (Albuquerque, 1995), chap. 4.

32. De la Teja, *San Antonio de Béxar,* chap. 5; Jack Jackson, *Los Mesteños: Spanish Ranching in Texas, 1721–1821* (College Station, 1986), 33–41, 53–54.

33. De la Teja, *San Antonio de Béxar,* chap. 5; Jackson, *Los Mesteños,* 503–4.

34. Jackson, *Los Mesteños,* 250–51, 508–10; McReynolds, "Family Life in a Borderland Community," 14; Robert S. Weddle and Robert H. Thonhoff, *Drama and Conflict: The Texas Saga of 1776* (Austin, 1976), 170–71.

35. Ordinances of Governor Muñoz, Oct. 24, 1793, Béxar Archives (hereafter cited as BA); McReynolds, "Family Life in a Borderland Community," 19–21.

36. Nava to Muñoz, Dec. 27, 1796, BA.

37. Castañeda, *Our Catholic Heritage in Texas*, 6:56, 118, 121–26; Chipman, *Spanish Texas*, 238; McReynolds, "Family Life in a Borderland Community," 15, 23.

38. Ciudad de Béxar, Jurisdicción de la Provincia de los Texas, Jan. 1, 1820, BA.

39. Unless otherwise stated, the following paragraphs are based on Jesús F. de la Teja, ed., *A Revolution Remembered: The Memoirs and Selected Correspondence of Juan N. Seguín* (Austin, 1991), 1–56; and Frederick C. Chabot, *With the Makers of San Antonio* (San Antonio, 1937), 118–29.

40. Roderick B. Patten, trans. and ed., "Miranda's Inspection of Los Almagres: His Journal, Report, and Petition," *Southwestern Historical Quarterly* 74:2 (1970), 229.

41. Padrón de las almas que hay en esta villa de San Fernando de Austria [*sic*], Dec. 31, 1793, BA.

42. Nettie Lee Benson, "Bishop Marín de Porras and Texas," *Southwestern Historical Quarterly* 51:1 (1947), 23–24; Anthony R. Clarke to Austin, May 22, 1824, Eugene C. Barker, ed., *The Austin Papers*, vol. 2, part 1 of the *Annual Report of the American Historical Association for the Year 1919* (Washington, D.C., 1924), 797; Columbia *Telegraph and Texas Register*, Sept. 21, 1836.

CHAPTER FIVE

THE FORMATION OF FRONTIER INDIGENOUS COMMUNITIES
Missions in California and Texas

ROBERT H. JACKSON

Two previous chapters in this book have outlined patterns of development in the northern frontier provinces of colonial Mexico. This essay examines, in a comparative fashion, the evolution of missions in California and Texas. The mission was an important colonial institution on the frontier. While it is generally viewed as a religious rather than a government institution, in this essay I argue that the development of missions should be viewed as an effort to create sedentary indigenous communities on the frontier. Such efforts to concentrate natives were based upon the model of indirect Spanish rule in central Mexico. However, as shown by the analysis of Texas and California missions, plans to create stable sedentary communities met with varying degrees of success, from the perspective of government policy.

This essay provides a case study of the development of La Purísima Mission, established in 1788 among the Chumash. La Purísima provides an example of a relatively successful evangelization and acculturation program, from the perspective of the missionaries and Spanish officials. The Franciscan missionaries congregated hundreds of Chumash, developed extensive functional building complexes, and organized thriving farming and ranching operations that produced large surpluses used to feed the Indian populations as well as to supply the local military. Life in La Purísima Mission, however, had a downside. Health conditions were poor, and mortality rates among the Chumash consistently ran higher than birthrates. In the long run, the Chumash population in the mission declined. In contrast to the success of the California missions (at least from the official point of view), the missions in Texas achieved mixed results. I examine here mission programs that did not lead to the creation of

Indian communities: two missions established among the Karankawas who lived along the Texas Gulf Coast (Rosario, 1754, Refugio, 1795); and two missions established in 1762 for Lipan Apaches (San Lorenzo, Candelaria). This is not to say that all missions in Texas failed from the perspective of policymakers, but an examination of the Karakawan and Apache missions highlights factors that limited the effectiveness of frontier-mission programs, and particularly how the responses of indigenous peoples could limit Spanish policy objectives. Taken together, these case studies provide a useful overview to the limits of Spanish frontier Indian community policy.

LA PURÍSIMA MISSION: BACKGROUND

In mid-March of 1788, Ensign Pablo Cota and a group of soldiers from Santa Bárbara Presidio went to a site known by the local Chumash as Alsacupi, near the village called Lompoc. The troops began the construction of crude buildings that would serve as a temporary chapel and residence for the two Franciscans assigned to the new mission. Although December 8, 1787, is given as the traditional date for the establishment of La Purísima Mission, the occupation of the site by the soldiers in March and the arrival of the Franciscans on April 1, 1788, initiated the development of the mission community.[1]

La Purísima was the fourth of five missions established among the Chumash between 1772 and 1804. The other four were San Luis Obispo (1772), San Buenaventura (1782), Santa Bárbara (1786), and Santa Ynez (1804). The Chumash were among the most socially and politically sophisticated indigenous groups in coastal California. The Chumash were hunter-gatherers, but the richness of the environment supported relatively dense populations. Villages were permanent. The acorn was the staple, but other food sources included grass seeds, fish and other marine life, and animals. The Chumash classified as Purísimeño lived on an exposed coast, and did not develop the same type of seagoing canoes as did the Chumash living along the more protected Santa Bárbara Channel. The Chumash also traded with neighboring groups.

Nine historical Purísimeño villages ranged in size from twenty to three hundred people, and the estimated population was around sixteen hundred. The nine villages provided a large enough base population for Spanish officials to authorize the expense of building a mission. The villages were patrilineal-descent groups, but were not closed communities. Many men selected wives from other villages. Chiefs were hereditary patrilineally, and the record shows that four of the nine Purísimeño Chumash villages had resident chiefs. The chief did not, however, have to be a man. The sisters or daughters of a chief could become the chief. Chumash society was, to a certain extent, stratified, with inequality of wealth. There were also specialists: healers and religious leaders who interpreted the complex Chumash religion and conducted the different ceremonies that marked each stage of life.[2]

THE IDEA OF THE MISSIONS[3]

The mission programs that operated in Texas after 1716 and in California after 1769 represented several centuries of development of Spanish colonial Indian policy. The Spanish objective was to recast California and Texas indigenous societies as sedentary agriculturists, much like the peasants that were the largest group in Spanish society and the sedentary Nahuatl agriculturists of central Mexico. The colonial system in central Mexico served as the model for California, although the California missions did not completely transform Indian society. The Indians of central Mexico provided labor to individual Spanish entrepreneurs and the colonial government through a labor draft regulated by Spanish officials. Indians also paid a special tax called tribute. Finally, the government promoted the evangelization and conversion of the Indian populations to Catholicism, the official state religion, and attempted to wipe out the indigenous religion. The Spanish created a system of indirect rule that relied on local Indian leaders, who became responsible for organizing the labor drafts, delivering tribute payments, and ensuring that Indians attended mass and other church ceremonies and functions.

In the century following the Spanish conquest of central Mexico (1519–1521), lethal epidemics of diseases introduced from the Old World, exploitation, and ecological degradation combined to cause drastic declines in the size of the Indian population. At the end of the sixteenth century civil and ecclesiastical officials relocated the populations of communities with small numbers of people to form larger communities. The creation of communities with larger populations facilitated the collection of tribute, the organization of labor drafts, and the continued conversion of the indigenous population. The resettlement policy known as *congregación* served as the basis for the frontier-mission system, since the missionaries resettled Indian populations from a number of villages to a single mission community.

The frontier missions were both government and ecclesiastical institutions. Through a series of papal concessions known as the royal patronage (*real patronato*), the Spanish government gained control over the Catholic Church in the New World. For example, royal officials approved the establishment of new parishes and missions, as well as the naming of priests to specific posts. Moreover, the Spanish government collected tithes, a special tax that supported the Catholic Church, and paid the salaries or stipends of priests. Church officials retained control over doctrine and maintained some autonomy from the government, but the lines separating civil and ecclesiastical authority blurred. Although staffed by members of missionary orders such as the Franciscans, the missions were primarily government institutions organized to further the goal of frontier settlement and pacification and incorporation of the Indian populations into colonial society. The government gave representatives of the missionary orders direct responsibility for the management of the missions. In the case of the California missions, the Franciscan Apostolic College of San Fernando in Mexico City not only provided the missionaries to staff the missions, but also managed the entire mission province.

The government, in most instances, gave the missionaries considerable control over the day-to-day management of the missions, including the right to discipline the Indians. Indians, legally defined as minors and under the care of the government and the missionaries who acted as agents for the government, provided the labor to construct the buildings at the missions, to grow crops, tend the livestock, and produce leather goods, clothing, and other items needed for the missions. In most frontier regions where the government established missions, the economic objective was to attain basic self-sufficiency. In some areas, such as northern Sonora, the missionaries sold small surpluses to local settlers and the military garrisons. As in central Mexico, the government set aside certain lands as the collective property of the Indians living in the missions, to be administered by the missionaries in a form of trust, and considered many buildings, livestock, crops, and tools and other equipment to be communal property as well.

The management of the California missions differed from other missions in the larger region, such as the Baja California and Texas establishments. In 1773, Fr. Junipero Serra, O.F.M., the president of the newly established California missions, signed a formal agreement with the government to supply food, clothing, and leather goods to the military garrisons, at prices set by a price guide drafted by the governor. The 1773 agreement changed the development of the California missions. The Franciscans developed agriculture and ranching, with the goal of producing large surpluses above what they defined as the basic needs of the Indians living in the missions. This, in turn, made it even more imperative from the perspective of the Franciscans to convert the Indians into a disciplined labor force, and to employ corporal and other forms of punishment to ensure discipline and social control based on puritanical notions of morality. Missionaries stationed in missions throughout the northern frontier of Mexico introduced new rules to regulate the lives of the Indians and punished transgressions of the rules, but the Franciscans in California developed measures of social control to a greater extent than in neighboring regions such as Baja California and Sonora.

The Franciscans based the organization of labor in the missions on Spanish notions of the roles of men and women in the household economy. The Spanish division of labor differed from the division of labor among California Indian groups. For example, Indian women generally collected and processed plant foods. In the missions, on the other hand, the Franciscans put Indian men to work in the fields producing crops, which was an activity that most closely resembled the collection and processing of plant foods. The Franciscans instituted a labor regime that required sustained work in a fashion alien to California Indians, and was just one aspect of a general program of social and cultural change that sought to radically transform Indian society and culture and, in a generally intolerant fashion, completely eliminate all activities that the Franciscans associated with traditional religious practices.

The tenure of the missionaries was legally limited by laws first passed in the 1570s, in response to conditions in central Mexico, that envisioned missionaries converting the Indians and then moving on within ten years and leaving the administration of the former missions to secular clergy who answered to bishops. However, missionaries in northern Mexico frequently postponed indefinitely secularization, the transfer of authority from the missionaries to the secular clergy and the division of mission property among the Indians, by arguing that they still were actively involved in the conversion of Indians only recently brought to the missions. Letters written between Franciscans stationed in California indicate that the missionaries developed a strategy to counter government pressures to secularize the missions by emphasizing that the California missions were still actively converting Indians. Nevertheless, in the 1820s and 1830s politicians influenced by liberal ideas first ordered the legal emancipation of acculturated Indians, and in 1833 the secularization of the missions. One rationale given by liberal Mexican politicians for secularization was to remove the Indians from the paternalistic authority of the Franciscans and to fully incorporate the Indians into Mexican society. Writing in the first decade of this century, the Franciscan historian Zephyrin Engelhardt, O.F.M., decried mission secularization in the 1830s. However, within the context of colonial policy and law, mission secularization was inevitable, and it was within the powers of the government to order secularization. The Spanish government initiated the secularization of the Texas missions in the mid-1790s.

THE BUILDING OF LA PURÍSIMA MISSION[4]

La Purísima Mission occupied two different sites for twenty-five and twenty-one years, respectively, and the Franciscans directed the construction of extensive building complexes at both sites. The devastating 1812 earthquake forced the abandonment of the site chosen for the mission in 1787, and relocation to a new site several miles away. There are several examples of the relocation of missions to new sites, but the shifts came within several years of establishment. For example, the Franciscans relocated San Diego, San Juan Capistrano, San Gabriel, and Santa Clara. Santa Clara offers the only other case of one of the California missions being relocated after the development of an extensive building complex, but the change was only a short distance.

Annual reports prepared by the Franciscans at the end of each year contain summaries of any building construction projects, including in some instances the dimensions as well as the building use. The reports describe the development of extensive and functional building complexes designed to form the core for self-sufficient towns. Churches stood as the largest and dominant structures, built on a scale to impress upon the Indians the grandeur of the new religion. The Franciscans had three churches built at the first mission site. The first was a temporary structure of palisade, with a packed-earth roof on beams erected in 1788. The temporary church was replaced in the following year with an adobe structure, also with a packed-earth roof. During the 1790s the number of Indians living at the mission increased, and the 1789 church was not large enough. In 1792, the Franciscans had the adobe church enlarged and added a tile roof. In 1798, the cornerstone was laid for a new and larger adobe church completed in 1802 or 1803. This was the church destroyed in the 1812 earthquake. The Franciscans directed the construction of a variety of other buildings at the first site. Residences for the missionaries had a top priority in building projects, and the record shows the construction of apartments for the Franciscans in 1788, 1793, and 1797. Granaries to store mission crops were an important part of the building complexes, and granaries appear in the record in 1788, 1791, and 1795. Additionally, the Franciscans had buildings erected at farms located at different spots within the mission territory. In 1810, a granary and residence were built at Rancho San Antonio, to the north of the mission.

Other structures served to enhance social control at the mission. A permanent detachment of soldiers resided at the mission to protect the Franciscans and control the Indian populations. Indian laborers built barracks for the mission guard in 1794, and a new and larger barracks in 1804. The Franciscans ordered the incarceration at night of single women and older girls in dormitories, and a dormitory had been built at La Purísima by 1802. The Franciscans ordered the construction of dormitories from the beginning of the development of the missions. Ecclesiastical authorities later directed the construction of dormitories in Baja California and perhaps in other frontier missions. The missionaries also had European-style housing for Indian families. The report on the damage to mission buildings caused by the 1812 earthquake included one hundred small apartments for Indian families. The configuration of the Indian housing at the first site of La Purísima is not known, but evidence from several other missions including Santa Bárbara shows that in some instances walls enclosed Indian housing.

The 1812 annual report, dated December 31, contained a description of the damage caused by the severe earthquake on December 21, 1812.

> Some of the work shops went down. but some more strongly built may serve as habitations if not for minor uses which require no such security. One hundred houses of neophyte Indians and the *pozolera* [community kitchen], the walls of which were an adobe and a half thick and roofed with tiles, have become unserviceable. The garden walls of adobe, covered with tiles, have either collapsed or threaten to fall.[5]

Three months later, in March of 1813, Fr. Mariano Payeras, O.F.M., wrote to propose relocating the mission several miles north to a site known as Los Berros. Payeras also provided further details on the damage to the mission buildings at the first site.

> In view of what this promises we have examined the interior of the granaries, and we have observed with sorrow that all these structures are ruined from the foundations to the roof: that the church is demolished from the foundations up: and that neither Fathers, nor soldiers, nor neophytes will or can, without terror or risk, live in their habitations, which have partially fallen, are partly out of plomb, and all in many parts [are] seriously cracked.[6]

The Franciscans moved the mission to Los Berros in April of the same year, and directed the construction of temporary buildings built of palisades with an adobe veneer. Over the next decade, Payeras had a new complex of buildings constructed in an unusual configuration. Instead of a quadrangle, as had been built at the first mission site and at most of the other missions, the new buildings were laid out along a line at the base of one of the hills that borders the Los Berros Valley. In 1815, the church erected in 1813 was repaired and replastered, and a building with twenty-one rooms, including a residence for the missionaries and a small private chapel for the use of the Franciscans, was built. In the following year, another long building containing quarters for the mission guard and *mayordomo* (overseer) and workshops was built.

In 1817, foundations were laid for a new permanent church that, however, was never completed. In 1818, the temporary church built in 1813 collapsed, and was replaced by another adobe structure that remained in use until the early 1830s. After abandoning plans to complete the church started in 1817, the Franciscans had a cemetery and bell tower added in 1821 to the church built in 1818. One wall of the 1818 church rested on a small spring that so damaged the structure that it had to be abandoned around 1835. The small chapel in the long building erected in 1815 was remodeled to serve as a temporary chapel, and was large enough for the Indian population already reduced in size to about four hundred.

Details on the construction of housing for the Indian population are incomplete. In 1816, a hospital was built for the Indian population, and older buildings were remodeled to provide additional hospital space. The 1817 report mentioned the Indian *rancheria* (village), but provided few details. The 1823 annual report mentioned the construction of ten residences for as many Indian families. In the late 1950s and early 1960s archaeological excavations identified two adjoining structures that consisted of small apartments for Indian families. The two structures measured 335 feet and 200 feet in length, respectively.

THE MISSION ECONOMY

The economy of La Purísima Mission was based on agriculture, ranching, and craft industries such as textile production. The Franciscans controlled two important resources: abundant land and Indian labor. The mission domain granted to La Purísima covered some 84 square leagues, or about 149,000 hectares of land. Within this territory, the Franciscans developed farming and ranching at different sites.[7] In the 1830s, the mission included seven ranchos dedicated to agriculture and ranching.[8] The 1773 agreement between the Franciscans and the colonial government stipulated that the missions would supply the military with food, textiles, and leather goods. Therefore, the missionaries organized the economy of La Purísima to produce large surpluses. The Franciscans also hired out Indian labor to both the military and local settlers. In 1807, for example, one Antonio Reyes hired skilled and unskilled Indian workers from La Purísima.[9]

The Franciscans supplied food and other goods directly to the presidios and the military guard stationed at each mission. The common practice was to hire mayordomos to be directly responsible for the day-to-day management of the different economic activities at the missions. The Franciscans recruited overseers from either the local settler population or from the soldiers. Members of the mission guard often doubled as overseers. Overseers earned a salary in addition to food rations. In 1814 and 1815, for example, Ignacio Yguera earned twelve pesos a month and a ration for services as overseer.[10]

Wheat, corn, and barley were the most important crops grown at La Purísima (see Table 5.1). Cultural factors played an important role in the decision on the choice of crops grown. Spaniards and settlers in northern Mexico perceived corn to be an inferior "Indian" grain, and preferred wheat. Even today, the population of northern Mexico consumes wheat tortillas, whereas the more indigenous population of central Mexico eats corn tortillas. However, corn produced more grain per unit planted than wheat. At La Purísima, the ratio of wheat harvested to planted ranged between 2 to 24 *fanegas* (2.6 bushels), but ranged from a low of 1 to 333 *fanegas* for corn, and was consistently higher than wheat. Production levels fluctuated from year to year, but the largest wheat harvest was 4,000 *fanegas* in 1821 and for corn 2,000 *fanegas* in 1813 and 1814.

In most years La Purísima produced more wheat than corn and barley combined. The Franciscans emphasized wheat over corn, despite the greater productivity of corn and the large Indian population at the mission who primarily ate corn. The obligation to supply the military prompted the decision to grow more wheat than corn. Moreover, the Franciscans supplied the needs of the military without regard to actual production levels. In other words, the missionaries provided less food to the Indians following poor harvests, in order to supply the military.

The mission also owned large herds of cattle, sheep, and horses (see Table 5.2). Slaughtered livestock provided protein for the diet of the Indians, and also leather and wool for producing clothing, shoes, and other items consumed by the Indians, soldiers, and settlers. After about 1800 an increasing number of foreign ships visited the California coast, and in particular Americans who developed trade with the missions and to a lesser extent settlers. After 1820 the scale of trade grew, and the Franciscans sold large numbers of cattle hides and tallow (rendered fat). The annual reports indicate the overculling of cattle herds to produce hides and tallow for export at some missions after 1800. There is some evidence of overculling at La Purísima. In 1809, the missionaries reported ten thousand cattle, but this number rapidly dropped over the next several years to a low of four thousand in 1812. The numbers slowly grew and reached eleven thousand in 1821. However, there were several significant one-year drops in the 1820s. For example, from 1824 to 1825 the number of cattle reported declined from 10,500 to 6,000. This may represent a weakness in the count of the number of animals, perhaps related to the 1824 Chumash uprising.

THE DEMOGRAPHIC DECLINE OF THE CHUMASH POPULATION

The congregation of Chumash into La Purísima Mission led to increased mortality rates and, over the long run, declining birthrates. The mission population was unstable and did not reproduce through natural reproduction. The numbers of Indians living at La Purísima Mission only increased during periods of recruitment and resettlement of new converts to the mission community. The Franciscans stationed at La Purísima baptized large numbers of Chumash converts from 1788 until about 1804, which was the last major surge of resettlement. The reasons why the Chumash and other California Indians entered the missions has been debated. One recent analysis argues that subsistence variability, recurring droughts in southern California that reduced available plant foods, was a very important factor in the 1780s and 1790s.[11] Once large numbers of Indians moved to the missions, the support and trade networks that had existed in pre-contact Chumash society collapsed. In these years, the mission population grew to a recorded maximum of 1,520, in 1804. After that year the number of new recruits dropped, and the population declined. In 1834, on the eve of secularization, only 407 Chumash remained at La Purísima (see Table 5.3).

A complex series of factors contributed to the demographic decline of the population of La Purísima Mission. Birthrates, although moderate to high by contemporary standards, lagged behind death rates. In the years 1813 to 1832, crude birthrates per thousand population averaged 30, whereas crude death rates during the same period averaged 87 per thousand population. Put into simple terms, on average out of 1,000 people 943 would be alive at the end of the year, with a net decline of 57 per thousand population. Over the long run the mission population would have gradually disappeared, unless replenished with new recruits brought from outside the mission community.[12]

What caused the high death rates at the mission? Epidemics of highly contagious crowd diseases, which rapidly spread among large populations living close together, were one factor. After 1800, five lethal epidemics struck La Purísima and raised death rates significantly. Chronic ailments such as respiratory illness and syphilis also debilitated the Indian population. Unhealthy living conditions at the mission also contributed, particularly the practice of locking single women and older girls at night in unhealthy and crowded dormitories. In a general report on the California missions written in 1797,

California governor Diego de Borica reported how he had entered a dormitory at one of the missions, and was overcome by the stench of human feces and had to leave the building.

Two groups within the Indian population experienced particularly high death rates: women and girls and young children. Census data for La Purísima Mission shows a widening gender imbalance in the years after about 1810, as recruitment of new converts declined. In 1832, there was only 0.62 females for every male at La Purísima. This translates to a male:female ratio of almost 2:1, and a rapidly declining number of women of child-bearing age. Infant and child death rates were also high, and life expectancy low. In 1832, children under age nine, the age group classified by Spaniards as children and hence not liable for adult labor, made up only 9 percent of the population of La Purísima Mission. Between 1813 and 1832, the mean life expectancy at birth for children born at the mission was only 3.5 years. By the 1830s the Indian population of La Purísima Mission had a gender and age imbalance, and adult males increasingly made up a large part of the population. This ensured a relatively large labor force at the command of the missionaries, but also doomed the Chumash living at the mission to gradual but steady decline.[13]

In 1834, 407 Indians remained at the mission, and the population dropped rapidly following the secularization of the mission. In 1838, there were 242 still at the mission, and 170 in 1840. A smallpox epidemic in 1838 caused excess mortality. But much of the decline resulted from the dispersion of the Chumash after 1834. In 1856, fifty-five Indians remained at the mission.

RESISTANCE AND SOCIAL CONTROL[14]

The Franciscan missionaries systematically attempted to wipe out all social and religious practices, and imposed different forms of social control, including corporal punishment such as flogging, incarceration, stocks, and a weighted wooden shoe. Some Chumash chose to come to live at the missions as the Franciscans brought more and more people into the Spanish orbit, and traditional networks of trade and support disappeared. Not all who accepted baptism passively adhered to the rules imposed by the missionaries, and resisted in a variety of ways. Some fled the missions, and sought refuge as far away as the Central Valley. Sherburne Cook estimated that up to 1817 some fifty-two Indians fled from La Purísima Mission. Others faced retaliation for behavior defined by the Franciscans as unacceptable. In 1811, five Indians received hard labor reportedly because of their bad behavior.[15]

California Indians also resisted the Spanish presence violently, and the most serious Indian uprising against the new colonial order involved the Chumash at Santa Inés and La Purísima. The Chumash uprising began at Santa Inés Mission on February 21, 1824, when a member of the mission guard flogged an Indian. News of the rebellion soon spread to La Purísima, and the Indians there seized control over most of the mission, except for the soldier's barracks that was defended by the mission guard. However, on the following day, Sunday, February 22, the soldiers surrendered and were allowed to go to Santa Bárbara unharmed.

The Indians remained in control of the mission for about three weeks, until a force of 109 soldiers returned to crush the uprising. The soldiers attacked on March 16, 1824, and rapidly subdued the rebel Chumash. One Indian died during the attack. In the aftermath of the uprising, retribution was swift and harsh. The military executed seven Indians from La Purísima, and sentenced another eight to different terms of imprisonment. More than four hundred Chumash, most from Santa Bárbara Mission, fled en masse to the Central Valley after the suppression of the uprising, and established a community that blended traditional Chumash and Spanish/Mexican culture.

What caused the Chumash uprising of 1824? An older interpretation maintained that the Chumash rebelled against the excessive demands for supplies and abuses of Indians by the soldiers. However, a dynamic symbiosis existed between the Franciscan missionaries and the military in California, cemented by the 1773 agreement signed by Fr. Junipero Serra, O.F.M. A more recent interpretation suggests that Franciscan probing for certain social and sexual practices was a key factor. The uprising occurred soon before Easter, when Indians were expected to confess. Upcoming confessions, coupled with the preparation by at least one Franciscan of a confessional aid to probe for prohibited social and sexual practices, may have prompted the uprising more than the flogging of the Indian at Santa Inés. Moreover, several of the Franciscans stationed in the Chumash missions had spent some time at the missions already, and learned the language and the intricacies of Chumash culture and social practices. The uprising most likely was a last attempt to defend traditional Chumash culture against the Franciscans.

THE SECULARIZATION OF LA PURÍSIMA MISSION[16]

The Franciscan most responsible for the later development of La Purísima Mission was the Mallorcan Mariano Payeras, stationed there for nearly twenty years between 1804 until his death in April of 1823. Payeras died one year before the Chumash revolt, and several years before government frontier Indian policy began to shift. In 1813, the liberal Spanish Cortes (parliament) legislated the secularization of missions in Mexico, a law suspended with the return to power of the absolutist king Ferdinand VII. Nevertheless, the 1813 law provided a legal precedent for later secularization laws.

The newly created republican Mexican government, installed in 1824, challenged colonial-era Indian policy viewed as being too paternalistic. As the liberal ideologue José María Luis Mora put it, the extreme paternalism of the frontier missions prevented the Indian populations from being fully integrated into Mexican society. Liberals, particularly the radicals, were also anticlerical, and challenged the fundamental role of the Catholic Church in all aspects of Mexican life. Church wealth especially attracted the attention of liberal reformers because of the perception that the wealth of the church retarded Mexican economic development.

The California missions received attention from liberal reformers because the missions were seen as preventing the full integration of Indians into Mexican society, because of the wealth of the missions including the endowment known as the Pious Fund, and also because many of the Franciscans still stationed in California were Spanish born. In the late 1820s the Mexican government expelled many Spaniards, but exempted the California Franciscans because replacements were not available until 1833. The letters of several of the Spanish Franciscans indicate that their loyalty to the new regime was lukewarm at best, and that they resented the interference of the Mexican government in the missions.

The new mission policy developed in several stages. In 1826, the governor of California issued an emancipation decree that freed the more acculturated Indians in the southern and central California missions from the legal control of the missionaries. Several missionaries complained about the emancipation decree, and particularly the loss of labor and control over the Indians. Some neophytes left the missions and went to work on local ranches and in towns such as Los Angeles and Monterey. Seven years later, in 1833, the governor issued a second emancipation decree, and attempted to establish an experimental "Pueblo de Indios" at San Juan Capistrano that was designed to be an autonomous self-governing community along the lines of the corporate indigenous communities of central Mexico. During an inspection of the former missions on behalf of the government, William Hartnell documented the presence of forty-seven emancipated Indians living at Los Alamos, one of the ranchos of La Purísima Mission.

In the same year, 1833, a radical liberal group headed by Valentín Gómez Farias dominated the Mexican Congress for almost a year, and passed a large volume of reform legislation, including a law for the secularization of the missions in Baja and Alta California. The secularization law was separate from the emancipation decrees, and placed control over the mission temporalities, buildings and economic activities in the hands of civil administrators. The Franciscans remained as parish priests, but no longer controlled the lives of the Indians. However, secularization did not immediately lead to the emancipation of the remaining Indians, who were still legally defined as wards of the government. Final emancipation did not occur until 1840.

One consequence of emancipation was the dispersal of the Indians living at many of the missions, particularly at those missions that had large numbers of recent converts brought from some distance from the missions, such as the Central Valley. Between 1834 and 1839, the average rate of out-migration from the missions was 8.6 percent per year, and 5.6 percent from 1839 to 1842. Many of the missionaries complained about the out-migration. The more homogeneous population of La Purísima, made up primarily of local Chumash, did not experience the large losses from out-migration until the mid-1840s and the alienation of much of the former mission lands as private ranches.

The civil administrators responsible for running the missions, which included providing clothing for the Indians, used mission resources to pay for day-to-day expenses as well as covering their own salaries set by law. Among other things, the administrators slaughtered cattle to sell hides and tallow. Politically connected settlers also used the mission herds to stock their own newly granted ranches, borrowing livestock with a later obligation to return the borrowed animals. Under civil administration, the value of the La Purísima Mission estate declined from 61,976 pesos in 1834 to 25,845 in 1845. The loss of livestock and mission lands granted as private ranches accounts for most of the decline. The depletion of mission herds can be seen in a comparison of figures from 1834 and 1839. In the former year, La Purísima herds totaled 6,200 cattle, 6,458 sheep, and 1,200 horses. In 1839, 3,824 cattle and 1,300 sheep remained, but the number of horses had actually grown to 1,532.

When Mexico became independent in 1821, the new regime faced the challenge of an underpopulated frontier bordered on the east by the aggressively expansionist United States. Colonization laws passed in 1822 and reissued in 1824 attempted to promote colonization of the frontier by authorizing local governors to issue land grants. Offers of land, then, provided the major incentive to attract settlers to the frontier. In the 1830s and 1840s, up to 1846, California governors issued more than eight hundred land grants, many coming from mission lands. The most valuable grants were often centered on farms and ranches developed by mission-Indian labor, such as Los Alamos, which was one of the ranchos of La Purísima Mission that had a population of forty-seven emancipated Indians in 1839. Some former mission Indians received lands and sections of mission buildings, but the bulk of the mission estates went to prominent local settlers. Most Indians either returned to a modified aboriginal life along the coast or in the Central Valley, or else became workers on ranches and in the towns. With the passage of time, non-Indians bought out the interests of Indian property owners. The majority became laborers at the bottom of California society. However, this outcome was also consistent with Spanish and, later, Mexican social policy and racial attitudes among Mexico's elite.

Under the Spanish colonial caste system, Indians were legally a separate group and theoretically isolated from the rest of society under the special protection of the government. Indians were also legally and socially inferior. Although Mexican liberals wanted to integrate Indians into Mexican society, integration did not imply social equality, only legal equality under a single rule of law that applied equally to all citizens. Members of Mexico's elite of all political orientations generally viewed Indians as being backward and an impediment to development, but the more progressive also believed that the paternalism of the colonial era, as typified by the frontier missions, contributed to this backwardness. When fully integrated into Mexican society, Indians would be at the bottom. In the colonial era this also meant that the Indian populations could be exploited through labor drafts and the collection of special taxes for the benefit of both the government and prominent colonists. The Mexican government abolished the most overt forms of exploitation of Indians, and mission secularization was viewed within this context by some politicians, but the underlying social prejudices remained. The very word *indio* was and even today is a derogatory term.

At the end of 1845, Governor Pío Pico sold the building complexes at a number of mission sites. Pico included La Purísima in the sales. On December 4, 1845, John Temple paid eleven hundred pesos for the second mission site. The United States government returned title to the second mission site to the Catholic Church in 1855.[17]

MISSIONS FOR THE KARANKAWAS OF THE TEXAS GULF COAST

The Karankawas were hunter-gatherers who occupied seasonal camps on the coast and along streams and rivers in the coastal prairie environment. The availability of different food resources defined seasonal migration within a clearly defined territory. During the fall and winter Karankawan bands occupied large camps on the coast to exploit estuarine foods, particularly redfish and black drum. During the spring and summer Karankawas occupied smaller camps in the coastal prairie and hunted bison, deer, and other animals and collected plant foods. Large deposits of artifacts and food remains, particularly at the coastal sites, indicates long-term occupation of camps.[18] Seasonal migration figured into decisions by bands to enter the missions established for the Karankawas. The Franciscans located both Rosario and Refugio missions in the coastal prairie environment, at locations that best suited plans for the development of agriculture and ranching. Most documented instances of Karankawan bands moving to the two missions occurred during the spring, which coincided with the traditional occupation of camps in the coastal prairie.[19]

The Franciscan missionaries never broke the pattern of seasonal migration between the coast and coastal prairie, and they frequently complained about how the Karankawas abandoned the missions to return to the coast, and in fact abandoned Rosario en masse in 1779, forcing the abandonment of the mission for a decade. This was particularly a problem at Rosario Mission, located well outside the traditional territory of the Karankawas, on the lower San Antonio River (near modern Goliad), whereas Karankawan band leaders told the Franciscans that they would be more willing to settle at Refugio Mission, which was located within their territory.[20] One important factor in the continued independence of the Karankawas was the inability of Spanish troops to follow runaways from the missions in an estuarine environment they were not familiar with. Moreover, the soldiers did not have boats to follow the Karankawas to offshore Islands.[21]

Censuses show considerable short-term fluctuations in the populations of both Rosario and Refugio missions (see Table 5.4). Moreover, a number of the fluctuations can be directly tied to the traditional pattern of seasonal migration. For example, in June of 1797, 254 Indians reportedly lived at Rosario, which coincided with the period when the Karankawas returned to the coastal prairie. In December of 1798, however, the number was down to 70, which was the period when the Karankawas returned to the coast. The gender and age structure of the mission populations provides additional evidence of the patterns of migration from the missions. A 1794 census of Rosario Mission recorded a total of eighteen men as against twenty-five women, and twenty-nine boys and twenty girls. Other censuses from both Rosario and Refugio show more boys than girls, roughly equal numbers of men and women, but only a small number of unmarried men at Rosario in the 1790s.[22] Other mission populations on the northern frontier of colonial Mexico had unbalanced age and gender structures characterized by more men than women and more adults than children.[23] The Rosario and Refugio censuses show a trend of gender imbalance among children, and the absence of men from the mission, particularly unmarried men who apparently left the mission with greater frequency.

A surviving set of baptismal and burial records from Refugio Mission for the years 1808–1828 provide additional evidence. There was an under-registration of burials, which suggests that many Karankawas baptized at Refugio later died away from the mission. The majority of the baptisms were of young children, including some children born to adults previously baptized and brought to the missions months or even, in one case, several years after birth. Moreover, the majority of baptisms of converts were of children: few adults converted and received baptism.[24]

The evidence shows that the Karankawas did not adopt sedentary life in the missions. Rather, the Karankawas incorporated the missions into the seasonal migration between coast and coastal prairie as an additional potential food resource, and most likely came to the missions when traditional sources of food were scarce.[25] The proliferation of herds of cattle and other livestock probably displaced wild game such as deer and bison, and made the choice to come to or remain outside the missions permanently or periodically somewhat more diffi- cult. By the 1770s and 1780s, Espíritu Santo and Rosario missions had herds of fifteen thousand and thirty thousand cattle, respectively, and in 1808 Refugio Mission counted five thousand cattle and small livestock. On the other hand, Karankawas could kill and eat mission livestock, and as early as the 1750s Spanish military officials expressed concerns that Karankawas would steal mis- sion animals.[26]

Few details of the economy of the Karankawas missions remain, other than the references to the approximate size of the mission herds. Archaeological excavations at Rosario Mission have allowed a reconstruction of the configura- tion of the mission complex. Earlier descriptions of the mission from the late 1760s and 1770s report that the buildings, including the church, were built of wood.[27] The Franciscans directed the construction of more permanent stone structures prior to the abandonment of the mission in 1779, the ruins of which can still be seen at the site today. Walls built for defense that were characteristic of most Texas missions surrounded Rosario, because of the threat of raids by Apaches or Comanches and their allies.[28]

MISSIONS FOR THE LIPANS APACHES:
SAN LORENZO AND CANDELARIA

After several decades of war, Spanish officials in Texas made peace with the Lipan Apaches, already being attacked by Comanches moving into the South- ern Plains. In 1758, Comanches and allied tribes destroyed San Sabá Mission, established for the Lipans in the previous year, but Spanish officials maintained a large garrison at San Sabá after the destruction of the mission. Lipan band chiefs continued to request missions, and one chief named Gran Cabezón promised to settle three hundred members of his band at a new mission. The commander of San Sabá Presidio assigned troops to protect new missions for the Lipans to be established on the Nueces River, and Franciscans from the Apostolic College of Santa Cruz de Queretaro established San Lorenzo and Candelaria missions on January 23, 1762, and February 6, 1762, respectively.[29] The presidio commander and college officials established the two new missions without the formal authorization of the viceregal government, and without government funds.

Initially, about four hundred Lipans settled at the two missions, but they also came and went as they pleased, to hunt bison or because of food shortages at the missions. Raids on Lipan rancherías (villages) in the Nueces River area by Comanches and allied tribes in 1762 forced the Lipans to leave the missions, but some Indians did return. In 1764, a smallpox epidemic killed Lipans at the missions. In October of 1766, a force of three hundred Comanches directly raided the missions for the first time, and periodically returned to attack the missions. By the summer of 1767, the Lipans abandoned the two missions and never returned.[30]

The mission program for the Lipan Apaches failed for several reasons. Most significantly, raids by Comanches and allied tribes forced the Lipans to flee from central Texas and, in the process, to abandon the missions. As many as twelve Lipan band chiefs contacted Spanish officials expressing an interest in missions.[31] The Lipans most likely were more interested in military aid for the war against the Comanches. Lack of support for the missions was also an important factor. As shown in Table 5.5, the college provided funds in 1762 for supplies for San Lorenzo Mission, but not enough to feed the Lipans throughout the entire year, which prompted the Indians to leave. Beginning in 1764, supplies sent by the college only satisfied the needs of the Franciscans at the mission.

In 1766, the Marqués de Rubí, conducting an inspection of frontier presidios, visited the two Apache missions. Rubí reported the presence of thirty soldiers from the San Sabá Presidio at San Lorenzo, a site he deemed poorly defended. The soldiers defended four missionaries, but there were no Indians and thus they constituted, in Rubí's judgment, a waste of resources.[32] Archaeological excavations of the San Lorenzo Mission site, located on the top of a small ridge close to the Nueces River, have shown that the mission structures, built of adobe, surrounded a rough square enclosed by walls that included two bulwarks.[33] However, from the perspective of a military expert the defensibility of the San Lorenzo Mission complex must have been limited.

CONCLUSION

In contrast to the California missions that accomplished the goals of the Spanish government, the Texas missions were expensive failures, as highlighted by the Rubí inspection in 1766. Military garrisons in Texas totaled 297 soldiers protecting missions staffed by 25 Franciscans. Many of the missions did not even have resident Indian populations: the two Apache missions on the Nueces River; three missions in east Texas; and the Orcoquisac Mission on the lower Trinity River. Five missions in the San Antonio area had Indian populations that totaled 809, and Rosario and Espíritu Santo had some 100 Indians.[34] Christianity and Spanish colonialism had little attraction for most Texas Indians. Groups such as the Lipan Apaches sought military alliances with the Spanish, but refused to adopt a sedentary lifestyle. Sedentary Hasinais Caddos in east Texas also rejected Spanish evangelization, and could easily trade with the French. A Franciscan inspection of the Texas missions in 1768 recorded few baptisms of Indians in east Texas over some fifty years: 12 at Guadalupe; 11 at Dolores de los Ais; and 103 at Los Adaes.[35] Raiding by the Comanches and other Indian tribes stalled Spanish settlement and the mission program. In the 1770s, the Spanish government reduced the number of settlements in Texas, and focused missionary activity in the San Antonio area and Espíritu Santo (modern Goliad). Refugio was the only new mission established after 1770.

The effort by the Spaniards to create sedentary indigenous communities on the frontier met with mixed short- and long-term results. The Franciscans in California settled thousands of Indians in the missions, and organized an economy that produced large quantities of grain, livestock, and craft goods such as textiles and leather products. However, demographic collapse undermined the stability of the mission communities. In Texas, on the other hand, the effort to reduce Indians to sedentary life proved less successful, as shown by the Karankawan and Lipan Apache missions. The Karankawas accepted the missions on their own terms, and the Lipan Apaches, pressed by the Comanches, rejected the missions altogether. In a real sense, the mission program did not work well at all. Only the San Antonio missions inhabited by Coahuiltecans, who most closely resembled the Indian populations of coastal California and were caught between Apache and Comanche raids, attracted and kept numbers of converts. However, as in California, the demographic collapse of the Coahuiltecan populations undermined the stability of the mission communities.[36]

TABLE 5.1

Grain Production at La Purísima Mission, in *Fanegas*

Year	Wheat Sown	Wheat Harvested	Corn Sown	Corn Harvested	Barley Sown	Barley Harvested
1789	15	331	2	357	0	0
1790	25	530	3	521	½	16
1791	76	800	4	653	0	0
1792	61	602	4	891	0	0
1793	55	1,102	6	200	0	0
1794	68	1,254	2	549	0	0
1795	96	308	3	502	0	0
1796	75	1,250	2	15	0	0
1797	65	1,700	2	0	0	0
1798	92	1,900	½	38	0	0
1799	92	2,500	1	15	1	70
1800	69	1,200	1	160	0	0
1801	165	1,600	10	130	⅙	8
1802	96	1,000	1	160	⅙	5
1803	161	500	1	125	0	0
1804	230	3,000	3	130	0	0
1805	140	3,000	2	100	0	0
1806	300	1,200	3	200	10	50
1807	400	1,000	3	400	10	50
1808	177	2,000	5	450	3	10
1809	175	1,800	6	600	6	60
1810	200	3,000	4	506	13	360
1811	180	3,000	4	450	25	800
1812	150	3,000	1	50	0	0
1813	150	3,600	7	2,000	100	2,000
1814	100	200	6	2,000	0	0
1815	180	2,000	6	400	3	50
1816	123	2,500	8	10	18	600
1817	157	2,800	8	1,000	39	500
1818	250	3,000	2	200	12	200
1819	180	2,900	6	900	6	200
1820	208	2,435	4	0	0	0
1821	240	4,000	6	400	13	334
1822	150	1,587	7	900	0	0
1823	150	1,500	4	200	0	0
1824	112	1,100	4	120	0	0
1825	90	2,000	5	200	3	30
1826	150	2,000	4	80	0	0
1827	120	2,000	4	800	12	60
1828	102	1,000	7	200	15	58
1829	90	300	4	400	10	80
1830	50	500	4	300	12	50
1831	70	700	4	100	14	56
1832	60	500	4	100	11	45

SOURCE: Robert H. Jackson and Edward Castillo, *Indians, Franciscans, and Spanish Colonization: The Impact of the Mission System on California Indians* (Albuquerque, 1995).

TABLE 5.2
Livestock Reported at La Purísima Mission, 1789–1812

Year	Cattle	Sheep	Horses
1789	124	371	16
1790	169	464	74
1791	232	603	87
1792	311	626	94
1793	380	1,142	143
1794	451	1,587	148
1795	607	1,503	121
1796	700	2,200	176
1797	900	3,300	192
1798	1,016	3,700	208
1799	1,400	4,000	224
1800	1,600	4,000	262
1801	2,000	4,300	288
1802	2,640	5,400	326
1803	3,230	5,400	320
1804	3,736	4,967	352
1805	4,372	6,800	400
1806	5,000	6,000	590
1807	5,000	7,000	700
1808	7,000	10,000	800
1809	10,000	11,000	1,350
1810	8,000	10,000	1,100
1811	7,000	9,000	1,080
1812	4,000	12,000	1,150
1813	5,000	12,000	1,160
1814	8,000	12,000	1,160
1815	8,000	12,000	1,110
1816	8,500	11,000	1,217
1817	8,500	11,500	1,300
1818	9,000	12,000	1,300
1819	9,000	12,000	1,110
1820	9,500	12,600	1,305
1821	11,000	11,000	1,344
1822	10,000	11,000	1,463
1824	10,500	10,000	1,445
1825	6,000	8,365	330
1826	10,100	6,150	1,200
1827	10,202	9,000	?
1828	10,200	9,000	1,000
1829	8,000	6,000	1,000
1830	13,000	6,000	?
1831	10,500	7,000	1,000
1832	9,200	3,500	1,000

SOURCE: Robert H. Jackson and Edward Castillo, *Indians, Franciscans, and Spanish Coloni-zation: The Impact of the Mission System on California Indians* (Albuquerque, 1995).

TABLE 5.3
Population of La Purísima Mission

Year	Population	Year	Population
1788	95	1813	1,010
1789	151	1814	982
1790	278	1815	1,019
1791	434	1816	1,018
1792	510	1817	958
1793	546	1818	937
1794	656	1819	888
1795	743	1820	840
1796	760	1821	808
1797	842	1822	764
1798	920	1823	722
1799	937	1824	662
1800	961	1825	564
1801	956	1826	521
1802	1,028	1827	471
1803	1,436	1828	445
1804	1,520	1829	406
1805	1,383	1830	413
1806	1,166	1831	404
1807	1,124	1832	372
1808	1,084	1833	343
1809	1,031	1834	407
1810	1,020	1838	242
1811	978	1839	142
1812	999	1842	60

SOURCE: Robert H. Jackson, *Indian Population Decline: The Missions of Northwestern New Spain, 1687–1840* (Albuquerque, 1994).

TABLE 5.4
The Population of Rosario and Refugio Missions in
Selected Years and Months

Year	Month	Rosario	Month	Refugio
1754		500		
1758		400		
1768		101		
1790	May	51		
	Dec.	67		
1791	July	57		
	Nov.	114		
1792	June	83		
1793	Feb.	138		
	Aug.	139	Aug.	125
1794	Sept.	92		
1795	Feb.	43		
	Oct.	107	Oct.	82
1796	Oct.	148		
	Dec.	97		
1797	June	254	June	175
1798	Dec.	70		
1802		63		
1804		61	Dec.	224
1809		122		
1815		115		
1822		21		

SOURCE: Robert H. Jackson, "Congregation and Population Change in the Mission Communities of Northern New Spain: Cases from the Californias and Texas," *New Mexico Historical Review* 69:2 (1994), 163–83; Robert Ricklis, *The Karankawa Indians of Texas: An Ecological Study of Cultural Tradition and Change* (Austin, 1996), 129.

TABLE 5.5

Value of Goods Supplied to San Lorenzo Mission by the Apostolic College of
Santa Cruz de Queretaro, 1762–1768

Year	Value of Supplies in Pesos/Reales
1762	907 p, 5 r
1763	411 p, 1 r
1764	98 p, 4 r
1765	156 p, 3 r
1766	131 p, 1 r
1767	258 p, 1 r
1768	54 p, 5 r

SOURCE: San Lorenzo Mission Account Book, Archivo del Colegio Apostolico de Santa
Cruz de Queretaro, Celaya, Mexico.

NOTES

1. Zephyrin Engelhardt, O.F.M., *Mission La Concepción Purísima de María Santisima* (Santa Barbara, 1932), 6–7.

2. Roberta Greenwood, "Obispieño and Purísimeño Chumash," in Robert Heizer, ed., *Handbook of North American Indians: California* (Washington, D.C., 1978), 529–23.

3. The interpretation of the mission program in this section is largely derived from Robert H. Jackson, *Indian Population Decline: The Missions of Northwestern New Spain, 1687–1840* (Albuquerque, 1994); Robert H. Jackson and Edward Castillo, *Indians, Franciscans, and Spanish Colonization: The Impact of the Mission System on California Indians* (Albuquerque, 1995); Felix Almaraz, *The San Antonio Missions and Their System of Land Tenure* (Austin, 1989).

4. This section is based on Norman Neuerberg, *The Architecture of La Purísima Mission* (Santa Barbara, 1987); Robert H. Jackson, "La colonización de la Alta California: Un analisis del desarrollo de dos comunidades misionales," *Historia Mexicana* 41:1 (1991), 83–110.

5. Quoted in Engelhardt, *Mission La Concepción Purísima*, 30–31.

6. Quoted in ibid., 32.

7. Jackson, "La colonización," 87.

8. Engelhardt, Mission La Concepción Purísima, 57.

9. La Purísima Mission Account Book, Santa Bárbara Mission Archive-Library, Santa Barbara, Calif.

10. Ibid.

11. Daniel Larson, John Johnson, and Joel Michaelson, "Missionization among the Coastal Chumash of Central California: A Study of Risk Minimization Strategies," *American Anthropologist* 96:2 (1994), 263–99; Philip Walker and John Johnson, "The Decline of the Chumash Indian Population," in *In the Wake of Contact: Biological Responses to Conquest* (New York, 1994), 109–20.

12. Jackson, "La colonización," 94–96, 109; Robert H. Jackson, "Causes of High Rates of Indian Mortality in the Alta California Missions: A Contemporary Analysis," *Prelado de los Tesoros: Noticias* 3:3 (1988), 6–9.

13. Jackson, "La colonización."

14. This section relies primarily on Engelhardt, *Mission La Concepción Purísima*, chap. 6; Sherburne F. Cook, *The Conflict between California Indians and White Civilization* (Berkeley and Los Angeles, 1976), pt. 1; Jackson and Castillo, *Indians*, chap. 4.

15. Cook, *Conflict*, 61, 119.

16. This section draws on Charles Hale, *Mexican Liberalism in the Age of Mora, 1821–1853* (New Haven, 1968); Michael Costeloe, *La primera república federal de México (1824–1835): Un estdio de los partidos políticos en el México independiente* (México, D.F., 1975); Robert H. Jackson, "The Impact of Liberal Policy on Mexico's Northern Frontier: Mission Secularization and the Development of Alta California, 1812–1846," *Colonial Latin American Historical Review* 2:2 (1993), 195–225.

17. Engelhardt, *Mission La Concepción Purísima*, 64–65, chap. 8.

18. Robert Ricklis, *The Karankawa Indians of Texas: An Ecological Study of Cultural Tradition and Change* (Austin, 1996), 70–71, 101.

19. Ibid., 163–67.

20. Ibid., 153.

21. Ibid., 118.

22. Ibid., 129; Kathleen Gilmore, "The Indians of Rosario Mission," in David Orr and Daniel Crozier, eds., *The Scope of Historical Archaeology: Essays in Honor of John L. Cotter* (Philadelphia, 1984), 163–91.

23. Robert H. Jackson, *Indian Population Decline: The Missions of Northwestern New Spain, 1687–1840* (Albuquerque, 1994).

24. Robert H. Jackson, "Congregation and Population Change in the Mission Communities of Northern New Spain: Cases from the Californias and Texas," *New Mexico Historical Review* 69:2 (1994), 163–83.

25. Ibid., 178; Ricklis, *Karankawa Indians*, 163–67.

26. Ricklis, *Karankawa Indians*, 148, 150.

27. Seymor Connor, *Texas in 1776: A Historical Description* (Austin, 1975), 93.

28. Gilmore, "Indians of Rosario Mission."

29. Curtis Tunnell and W. W. Newcomb, "A Lipan Apache Mission: San Lorenzo de la Santa Cruz, 1762–1771," *Bulletin of the Texas Memorial Museum* 14 (1969), 165–67.

30. Ibid., 170–75.

31. Ibid., 167, 169.

32. Connor, *Texas,* 27.

33. Tunnell and Newcomb, "Lipan Apache Mission," 3.

34. Connor, *Texas,* 27.

35. Ibid., 41–42.

36. Jackson, "Congregation," examines the congregation of Coahuiltecans and demographic patterns in the San Antonio missions.

CHAPTER SIX

MARGINALS AND ACCULTURATION IN FRONTIER SOCIETY

PETER STERN

"Every frontier," one ethnohistorian wrote, "is actually two: the frontier of those who are advancing and the frontier of those who are being advanced upon."[1] This essay will examine the phenomenon of marginality in New Spain, both in the colony as a whole and in the Borderlands frontier of New Spain. It will also ask what social, political, and economic conditions encouraged marginality, and examine the impact marginals may have had on European-indigenous acculturation on Mexico's northern frontier.

The Spanish Borderlands frontier was far from conforming to the old Turnerian idea of the frontier as "the meeting point between savagery and civilization."[2] The frontier was neither a line nor a barrier; nor was it a Manichaean division between Europeans and Indians, or between the forces of light and darkness. The Spanish Borderlands frontier was a complex zone of cultural, social, economic, genetic, military, political, religious, and linguistic interaction between many different groups of peoples. Within this zone a complicated process of cultural and social diffusion, acculturation, was an ongoing and continuing process. Acculturation, the transfer of cultural traits from one ethnic group to another, is both voluntary and involuntary, and it is rarely a one-way street, even in relationships between conquerors and conquered. In that interchange, cuisines, languages, weapons, artifacts, ideas, concepts, and, not least, genes are passed between peoples.

If we think of the border as a diffuse zone of acculturation, then the role of marginals who inhabit the Borderlands, those who could not fit neatly in either European or Native American culture, is easier to grasp. Marginals were people who could not or did not wish to live in a fixed societal role. In the Spanish

Borderlands they were escaped black slaves, mestizos, and mulattos chaffing at discrimination, runaway mission Indians, Spanish presidial deserters, itinerant miners and peddlers, and assorted malcontents—horse and cattle thieves, murderers, and renegades. It was this "underclass" that fed upon and contributed to the insecurity of the Spanish Borderlands frontier.

In the past decade the term *underclass* has come to be used widely in American sociological discourse; it is defined as "a social stratum consisting of impoverished persons with very low social status."[3] The underclass is certainly not a modern phenomena; it has existed in countless societies, both urban and rural, and those in it have been called by many names: vagabonds, *ociosos* (lazy), *léparos* (lepers) mendicants, beggars. Those in the underclass might be termed marginals, persons who for a variety of social, political, or economic reasons live on the margins of society, not integrated into nor defiant of the social and economic norms of society.

Marginality is an extremely old phenomenon, one often created in the past by natural catastrophes such as earthquakes, famines, droughts, or epidemic diseases. It can also be created by changes that alter or destroy the existing social or economic order, such as rebellion, war, or depression. The Enclosure Act of Henry VIII forced thousands of peasants off their lands and onto the roads of sixteenth-century England to beg or steal. The Great Depression of 1929, combined with a disastrous drought, created an enormous migration of impoverished farmers heading west in search of work.

It does not, however, take a catastrophe to create an underclass. The very social and economic structure of society can force people to the bottom of a hierarchical structure. Medieval Europe was plagued with a vast army of mendicant beggars, and governments throughout the continent were increasingly fierce in their efforts to control the movement of populations.[4] In 1547 an act of Edward VI of England decreed that all persons loitering or wandering, not seeking work or leaving it when engaged, were to be taken up as vagabonds. The penalties included branding and virtual bondage in chains.[5] Thirteen thousand people were actually detained in England for begging in 1596.[6] Early modern Spain was equally plagued: the Cortes of 1618 declared the number of beggars in Spain to be one million (probably an exaggeration).[7] Contemporary observers put the number of *vagos* as high as 200,000.[8] Charles I, in response to a plea from the Cortes, decreed the expulsion of vagabonds from the streets and plazas of Madrid. His decree was apparently of little use, for it was repeated in 1552 and later by Philip II in 1560.[9] Between 1730 and 1789 sixty-three thousand people were apprehended and punished in Spain as vagabonds.[10] Penalties included one hundred lashes and eight years in the galleys.[11] Official reports called the underclass by many names: *vicioso* (vicious), *ratero, holgazán, bor-*

racho (drunkard). Many were punished simply for being out of work: *inutil* (useless), *sobrante en el pueblo* (surplus or excess in the town), "without vice but without work" were common phrases.[12]

Marginality, then, was a familiar social phenomenon in Spanish society. All the conditions necessary for it to flourish were present in Mexico upon the conclusion of the conquest. War had destroyed the political and religious structure of the Mexica. Epidemic disease swept through Indian society, finishing the work of social dislocation. Miscegenation produced a growing class of mestizos (offspring of Spaniards and Indians), for whom no specified place existed within society; the importation of African slaves would soon add *mulatos* (persons of mixed Spanish, Indian, and African ancestry) to the ethnic mix of the colony. Conquistadors were transformed by peace from conquering soldiers into idlers. It was necessary to send them to pacify other areas of central Mexico as much to prevent civil war as to extend Spanish authority.

In 1528, just seven years after the conquest, the crown issued a proclamation on the treatment of the Indians, which noted that the intention of most Spaniards who had passed and were passing to the colony was not to settle and remain, but to rob and dispossess the Indians of what they had, so that they wandered like vagabonds from one village to another, taking what they wanted from the Indians to sustain themselves, and causing many injuries.[13] Many sailors and soldiers jumped ship as soon as they reached the Indies and lived like vagabonds in defiance of the law. Complaints like these reached the crown from Cuba, Veracruz, and Panama.[14]

The problem was that very few colonists came to Mexico to work with their hands. Most made the journey *para hacer América*—to make their fortunes in the New World, preferably through the labor and sweat of someone else. This attitude was compounded at various times by periodic economic depressions, which swelled the ranks of the vagabond class in New Spain. These vagabonds, commonly known as *saramullos léparos*, or *ociosos*, were regarded with distaste by the *gente decente*, the upper classes, of Mexico. They were said to mix with mestizos and mulattos, and to be the leaders of tavern and low life.[15] An Italian visitor to New Spain noted in 1698, after a visit to the courts, that "there were 400 prisoners Spaniards, and all for theft; for living idle, and like vagabonds, they must steal and cheat to live . . ." (He himself had his sword stolen while wearing it in the streets.)[16] A major drive against these vagabonds, launched by the viceroy in 1621, arrested so many that even after a number had been dispatched to Manila, the jails of Mexico City were filled to overflowing.[17] The government appointed both *capitanes de campaña* and an *alguacil de vagamundos* to deal with both rural and urban marginals.[18]

The problem of marginalization was further compounded by the very racial situation that lay at the heart of colonial society. The neat and tidy *república de españoles e indios* that the Spanish set out to erect on the ruins of the Aztec empire was undone from the start by *mestizaje*—racial mixing of Europeans and Native Americans. The first generation of mestizos may have been cherished by their conquistador fathers, but their descendants were not. Mestizos proved useful in the pacification of the Mesoamerican heartland, the fighting of the Chichimec wars, and the conquest of Chile. Nevertheless, they were stigmatized by their mixed ancestry. One colonial historian declared the word *mestizo* to be practically synonymous with "illegitimate."[19] Another declared:

> The mestizo, without a place in the economic scheme, found himself also without a place in the social order, because, not being Indian or black, he aspired to be white without the power to be so. Colonial society assigned him to a dangerous intermediary place, creating a psychology of resentment . . .[20]

Obviously many mestizos in the colony were absorbed into Spanish society as overseers, artisans, servants, stockmen, miners, and manual laborers. In addition, the stigma of mestizo origin lessened as time passed and their numbers grew. Nevertheless, both mestizos and mulattos were clearly second-class citizens. The restrictions on their activities were numerous. A *cédula*, or royal decree, of 1549 prohibited mestizos, mulattos, and illegitimate sons from holding *encomiendas*, or royal or public offices, without special license.[21] Mestizos were forbidden to be notaries, *corregidores*, or caciques (native chieftains).[22] Until quite late in the colonial period they were forbidden ordination.[23] Under restrictions of 1566, 1573, and 1575, mestizos, mulattos, and Indians were forbidden to carry arms. The penalty for carrying an arquebus illegally was death, an absurd restriction given the conditions in the Indies. In northern New Spain the unceasing war against Apaches and in southern Chile the struggle against the Araucanians were carried out largely by mestizo *presidiales*.[24]

That many of these restrictions promulgated in Spain were a dead letter in the New World is beside the point; they existed as part of Spanish legal and social doctrine. More revealing of a worried upper class than the restrictions on occupation were those on freedom of movement and association. Over and over again, mestizos were forbidden to reside in Indian villages or to wander about in the company of natives.[25] They were said to mistreat the natives, to teach them bad habits, laziness, and many vices. In 1558 a cédula suggested that towns be established in New Spain in which vagabonding Spaniards and mestizos be congregated to isolate them from the Indians.[26] In 1568 a decree of

Philip II stated that Spanish vagabonds were residing in Indian villages, where they caused much offense, damage, and intolerable nuisances. All royal officials were to ensure that vagos did not reside among Indians, and that they found masters to serve and learn a trade with which to occupy themselves. If they did not do this, they should be exiled from the province.[27] This regulation was issued in 1563, but the Recopilación de Leyes de las Indias states that it was confirmed and reiterated in 1578, 1581, 1589, 1600, and 1646 by successive monarchs. Under its terms, no Spaniard, mestizo, black, or mulatto was to live in Indian villages, because of reports that some of these men who lived, treated with, and traveled among the Indians were wicked men (*hombres inquietos, de mal vivir*), thieves, gamblers, vicious and lost men who caused Indians to flee from their oppression. It also stated that blacks, mestizos, and mulattos, besides treating Indians poorly, made use of their services and taught them bad habits, laziness, and also errors and vices, which spoiled and perverted the aim of the Spaniards: namely, the salvation and good order of the Indian republics.[28]

The frequency and repetitiveness of such royal proclamations against both the social mingling of Indians and *castas,* and the unregulated life of the *gente baja* point to a serious problem of social control and marginalization in New Spain. Much of the reporting describing a kingdom overrun by *léparos* was no doubt exaggerated. Lucas Alamán, a not-unbiased historian, when writing his history of the colonial period after independence described a "plague of bandits on the roads" and a population continually molested by thieves, who attacked their houses and despoiled them by night, even in the most public streets of the principal cities. The sierras and badlands of the country, he wrote, gave secure refuge to the malefactors, who abounded in the cities because of the large numbers of lazy, fallen, and vagabonding peoples who lived in them.[29]

Still, admitting that the streets of Mexico City were no safer than those of London, Paris, and New York in the seventeenth or eighteenth century, the existence of a large marginalized sector is indisputable:

Within the debased lower classes roamed the léparos, whom the authorities considered a class apart from the urban poor. According to both contemporaries and modern historians, léparos, or as they were often called, ociosos, were responsible for crime and the breakdown of public order in Mexico City. The term léparo depicted a special type of person in whom accumulated all vices known to cultured society. Léparos, the most "dissolute" and "abandoned" of all the poor, composed the dangerous class of "vicious people" who were "without honor, feeling . . . and religion." A léparo was typically a rootless, young Indian male or casta, unskilled in any trade who spent his day lounging in legal and illegal taverns, drinking, fighting, gambling, and stealing.[30]

Not only were popular attitudes prejudiced against mestizos and other gente baja, but the economic structure of the colony worked against the advancement of the marginalized. Economic corporatism, mercantilism, and industrial monopoly were features of Spanish economic policy. Regional industries in the colonies were highly restricted in order to prevent competition with the metropolis. Severe restrictions blocked most castas from belonging to the more skilled and prestigious craft guilds. Blacks and mulattos were prohibited, for example, from being silk workers, gold and silver leaf manufacturers, cloth shearers, or glove makers. They could be leather workers, but that was a relatively dirty and low-status trade. Blacks, mulattos, and *castes de color quebrado* (another term for Afro-mestizos) could not have licenses to become shopkeepers.[31] Economic monopoly placed control of mines and cattle ranches, two of the most prominent industries in New Spain, in the hands of the *peninsulares* and the wealthy creoles; agriculture was an occupation that demanded capital, to which the lower classes had no access (nor frankly, much inclination to pursue). One historian estimated that a good part of what he called the *plebe* of New Spain had little or no participation in the constructive economic life of the kingdom.[32]

The marginalized were not merely persons of mixed blood and unemployed Spaniards. Many Indians became "de-tribalized": separated voluntarily or involuntarily from their villages, their clans, and their cultures. The process of European-native acculturation was not a gentle or subtle one; native political and economic institutions were discarded or refashioned to suit Spanish objectives. In concrete matters of labor and tribute, compliance was mandatory; in matters of faith and culture, acculturation was a slower and more subtle process. Indians showed themselves far more willing to adopt Europe's material culture than its concepts. In dress, language, the adoption of plants and animals, firearms, and manufactured implements of labor, the Indians selectively chose to accept what benefited them and eased their lives. But further still, the breakdown of native structures enabled many to fashion new roles for themselves in the emerging colonial order. The constant refrain that Spaniards and other castes perverted and ruined the aim of the crown, the establishment of the neat and tidy república de españoles e indios, points to two worries that preoccupied royal government. The first was that these people were hurting Indian interests; colonial records abound in complaints of maltreatment, abuse, and exploitation at the hands of outsiders.[33] The other was the vague but constant fear that the marginals and Indians would combine to threaten the peace and stability of the kingdom.

The latter worry was not a fanciful one. One colonial historian stated that the threat to the tranquillity of Spanish society came from the union of disgruntled Europeans, mestizos, and *pardos*:

> Indians of the cities, Indians and blacks who fled from the mines and plantations, some whites who were not interested in, or had few opportunities to acquire salaried work, swelled the number of the *desocupados*—the unemployed or out of work—each year greater in the three centuries of the colony and the dividing line between permanent unemployment, crime, and prostitution came to be very difficult to draw.[34]

In the central area of New Spain, the threat from *cimarrones,* or escaped blacks and mulattos, was considered an especially dangerous one. The fear of an anti-Spanish alliance between cimarrones, Indians, and "Protestant corsairs" was prevalent.[35] Just two years after the conquest, at a time when Hernán Cortés was occupied in putting down rebellions among the Zapotec and Mixteca, a chronicler noted that there had fled to the Zapotec many black slaves, who wandered in rebellion throughout the land.[36] Historian Phillip Wayne Powell, in his study of the Chichimec wars of the later sixteenth century, found official complaints from Nueva Vizcaya, as early as 1543, that blacks who had escaped from bondage were allying themselves with Chichimec raiders between Zacatecas and Guanajuato, helping the nomads attack *estancias* and traffic on the roads.[37] Further reports detailed the participation of mestizo, mulatto, and other vagabonds (*gente perdida*) joining with Chichimecs.[38]

If there is no doubt that marginality was a serious threat to the stability of the colony's heartland, the question can then be posed, Did marginals also exist in the borderlands, and did they have a significant effect on European-Indian relations? Outside of an urban environment, no exact analogue of a léparo class could be said to exist, but Borderlands society, almost by its very nature, had to accommodate a significant marginal population, largely made up of mestizos, mulattos, blacks, de-tribalized Indians, as well as Spaniards. There is very little parallel, in Turnerian terms, between Spanish frontier society and a more familiar environment, the Anglo-American West; that is, the frontier as an escape valve from a restrictive society. The Spanish Borderlands did not see the rise of a more democratic society founded on free enterprise. One tenet of the Turner-Webb-Billington thesis might be argued to have partial validity for the

Spanish frontier: "free" lands provide a safety valve that undercuts authoritarianism, centralization, and subordination to traditional laws and customs.[39] Since a significant proportion of the frontier population was made up of non-Spaniards, distance from the metropolis, combined with the constant menace of Indian warfare, made for a less restrictive society with a greater latitude for individual action (often of a criminal nature). Still, while royal control was unarguably weaker in the Borderlands, frontier society differed little in social and economic terms from that of the metropolis.

The same prejudices that existed in the colonies' heartland were widespread on the frontier. Certainly, Spanish elites complained of a society peopled, as they saw it, by gente baja. In 1723, when the non-Indian population of Sonora could hardly have numbered more than a few thousand, a Jesuit *visitador* (inspector) complained that the largest segment of the European population of Sonora was made up of "*coyotes,* mulattos, and other scum of the earth *(hezes de la tierra),* who wandered like vagabonds in the province, without any other occupation than stealing, gambling, seducing women, sowing discord, and . . . other evils.[40] Padre Daniel Januske's complaints illustrate the basic outline of a frontier society. He bitterly condemned the Spanish justices, who did little or nothing to prevent people from wandering the countryside, allegedly in search of precious metals. There were numerous parties, he wrote, miners in name only, who had neither mines nor means to sustain themselves. Civil government, in his view, should take strong measures to restore good government and separate Indians from the *gente mala.* Coyotes, mulattos, and other vagabonds should be compelled to discharge their servants (presumably Indians), and be forced to serve *vecinos* (Spaniards). This would contribute a great deal to the peace of the province, the growth of mining, the increase of royal revenues, and the relief and quiet of towns disquieted by that class of men.[41]

Thirty years later, a civil inspector reported that the same gente mala were living the same bad life. Among the Indians there lived, he wrote, "vicious men of bad habits, thieves, gamblers, dissolute and lost men, who with their bad customs, laziness, mistakes and vices, could spoil and pervert . . . the salvation, growth, and peace of the Indians."[42] By the mid-eighteenth century many Indian towns in Sonora had sister communities nearby, towns of mestizos and mulattos; many land and water disputes arose from the presence of these settlements. One *regular* (missionary friar) complained that Spaniards and mulattos were not only living in Indian villages, but serving as lieutenants of the pueblos, and that they refused to abide by decisions of Indian officials.[43] Padre Reyes, in 1772, echoed Januske some fifty years before. The two main reasons for Sonora's deplorable state, he wrote, were the invasions of the enemy Indians (Apaches), and the vagabonding nature of the non-Indian population:

The Spanish traders, mulattos, blacks, and all castes have entered, and enter Sonora with the sole aim of using for themselves the first mines and placers that they find, until they find in another part a better one. With this they form their *reales* and pueblos, with such little cost and sustenance in furnishings and supplies that, on the first occasion which is suitable for them, they have no difficulty or loss in abandoning them. This is the reason that there is not in all the province of Sonora a proper and formal population of Spaniards.[44]

He cited a case where a rich silver strike at Saracache had caused a town to spring up "with well-built houses"; the discovery of placers at Alamillo twelve leagues away caused the abandonment of the town, which was shortly thereafter raided and burned by Indians.[45]

The two principal economic enterprises of the frontier were mining and ranching. Mining was an especially transient activity; the mining centers were the focus of such diverse social and ethnic groups that they formed the focus of northern mestizaje.[46] They were also the focus of the innumerable clerical complaints against the civil population. Padre Juan Nentvig, in his *Rudo Ensayo* of 1764, complained that the mission Indians of Sonora left their villages and sought work with Spaniards in their *rancherías* (small farms) and *reales de minas* (mining towns). There they found such instructors (*catedráticos*) that in two hours they learned everything necessary to the irremediable ruin of body and soul.[47] Padre Januske was of the opinion that the Opata, for example, were naturally a very docile people, of good inclinations, but they were upset by the bad examples and counsel furnished them by the coyotes, mulattos, and other vecinos, which necessitated unceasing vigilance and zeal on the part of the padres.[48] An illustrative example of what the missionaries feared is furnished by Padre Reyes; he told how a wandering peddler arrived at a *pueblo de visita* (outlying mission settlement) of Cucurpe Mission, swapping glass beads, ribbons, horns, and bells to the Indians in exchange for earthenware jugs of mescal. Their padre told his charges that the viceroy, governor, and justicias had forbidden them to manufacture mescal. When the peddler learned of the regular's interference, he "ordered [the Indians] to come together in the *casa de comunidad* (community house), and preached to them a sermon." He told them that they were fools to believe all that the padre had told them; they were free to do whatever they wished, and could not be prohibited from making mescal. The Spaniards, he declared, wanted to make them all slaves and deprive them of their liberty.[49]

The missionaries, many of them European born and contemptuous of Americans, especially of mixed-race Americans, had their own agenda: they desired the strict segregation of their charges from all outside influences. Ironically, the haciendas, ranches, and missions of Sonora found a ready market for their agricultural goods, mostly in support of the mining sector of the province.[50] Thus, the missionaries' bitter and constant complaints about the ephemeral nature of the mining sector and its itinerant casta population has something of a hypocritical note about it.

Still, the complaints of the missionaries were echoed by those of the civil and military authorities. Examples are numerous, from each end of the frontier: the *alcalde* (mayor) of San Antonio de Béxar ordered every ruffian and vagabond to find a master within three days of his decree, or leave the town, complaining that robberies were the consequence of so many persons who had no means of making a living. No person was to carry knives, pistols, or daggers, or walk through the city streets after curfew.[51] The captain general of Sinaloa complained of the "great number of vagabonding people, of bad life and habits" in the districts of Maloya, Copala, and Culiacán. The whole land, he reported, was infested with a growing number of thieves, who were causing great consternation and grief to settlers, threatening their haciendas and estancias. They robbed and destroyed with freedom, and a total absence of fear of God or the law. The captain general intended to make it his principal consideration to put a halt to these excesses committed in these deserted and depopulated places. He railed against thieves, highwaymen, arsonists, and men living in sin.[52] The *comandante general* of the Provincias Internas called the state of affairs in Chihuahua in 1784 a cancer, which he would attempt to cut out with the least possible shedding of blood. Although the greater part of the rebels were Indians (almost certainly Apaches), he noted among them many mulattos, coyotes, and people of other castes. Their numbers, he stated, were continually growing.[53] The castas of Sonora, declared one missionary, lived "*sin Dios, ley, ni Rey*" (without God, law, or the King).[54]

The protests of Spanish religious, civil, and military authorities, even taking into account exaggeration and racial prejudice, leave little doubt that the Borderlands were in a dangerous state of lawlessness. There was, of course, the continuing state of war between the Spaniards and the Indians: Tepehuanes, Tarahumaras, Yaquis, Seris, Pimas, Papagos, Lipanes, Chiricahuas, Mescaleros, Gileños, Jicarillas, Kiowas, Comanches, Utes, and many others all fought the Spanish, the French, and each other. There was never a time of peace; while some tribes or bands lived in the shadow of missions and traded peacefully at Taos or San Antonio, others were raiding towns, burning haciendas, stealing horses and cattle, and abducting women and children. Indian nations supposedly pacified and Christianized rose in rebellion; Indians ran from the custody of the Jesuit or Franciscan fathers to join Apache bands, or live among mestizos and mulattos in mining communities, or in renegade communities in the sierras. The continual shadow of war and the fear it engendered hung over the frontier from the Sea of Cortés in the west to the forests of Louisiana in the east. The governor of Nueva Vizcaya reported to the viceroy that in the years 1771–1776 Indian raiders had killed 1,674 people in his jurisdiction, taken 154 persons captive, and stolen over 66,000 head of livestock.[55]

The war was undoubtedly a principal element in the instability of the frontier. Another was the lack of viable economic enterprises; the semiarid nature of the land confined agriculture to limited areas with sources of water: the valley of the Río Grande in New Mexico and the ranchería communities of the Ríos Sinaloa, Yaqui, Fuerte, and Sonora. Mining was the only alternative to cattle ranching; both were hazardous due to Apache raids. The north was thinly populated and precariously held. The repopulation of the colony after the great demographic catastrophe of the sixteenth century was a slow process; there were never any teeming masses spilling over the mountains into sparsely populated Indian land, as in the British colonies far to the north. To complete the picture, pernicious attitudes toward the multiple castes of New Spain alienated the very settlers needed to give the frontier stability.

Who, then, were the marginals of frontier society? Many were castes, Euro-, Indo-, and Afro-mestizos (to use Aguirre Beltrán's terminology)[56] who rebelled against a society deeply prejudiced against them. Presidio deserters went over to the enemy Indians. Cattle rustlers ran stock across provincial boundaries. Captives served as translators, negotiators, and even warriors for their adopted cultures. Mission Indians rejected their forced acculturation and ran away to join castes and rebel Indians in the mountains. French, English, and American traders lived and treated with Indian bands in Spanish territory, in defiance of the strictest of royal regulations against intercourse with foreigners. These marginals acted as agents of acculturation, serving as intermediaries between the European and the indigenous, in a process which predated even the Spanish conquest. Hernán Cortés, landing in Mexico in 1519, found two castaways living among the Calachion Indians. One thankfully rejoined his countrymen. The other, the notorious Gonzalo Guerrero, had turned Indian; tattooed, married, and the father of mestizo children, he warned his adopted people to attack the European intruders immediately.[57]

The proximity of the frontier, with its complex skein of Indian-Spanish relations, was especially conducive to transculturation or marginalization. Many individuals, who conform less to Hobsbawm's model of revolutionary social banditry[58] and more to our modern ideas about asocial criminal psychosis, chose to escape Hispanic society and either live in native society or as marginals between the two. Their behavior was a constant headache for the Spanish civil and military authorities.

One individual illustrates this phenomenon particularly well; indeed, his record constitutes virtually a one-man crime wave on the eastern Texas frontier. Juan José Peña, alias El Bocón (Big Mouth), made the transition from European to Indian society and back again with apparent ease, to the despair of the commander at Nacogdoches. Peña began his career by robbing Frenchman Juan Bosque of six horses and some merchandise meant for the Indians on the Río Brazos in 1786. Caught in April 1788 without a passport by some *carneadores* (beef jerkers) on the banks of the Río Colorado, he was thrown into jail in Nacogdoches, secured by shackles. He nevertheless managed to escape, stealing a musket and some ammunition, two horses and a cow (which he ate). He fled to the settlement of some Hasanais Indians, but when he tried to sexually assault an Indian woman, she resisted and he beat her. Her screams alerted her tribesmen, who sent El Bocón to Nacogdoches, where his feet were put into the stocks. He broke jail again, robbed three citizens of their clothing and horses, and was chased and caught, having put up "tenacious resistance." He was hauled in front of Captain Antonio Gil Ybarbo, the commander of militia at Nacogdoches, and imprisoned for three months. Falling ill, he was taken out of jail and led to a house, from which he promptly fled again. He was heading for Nachitoches, the neighboring French settlement, when he was apprehended and imprisoned once more.

Once again he broke out of jail, and headed for Louisiana. There he robbed a man, enticed two slaves to run away from their owner, and stole some horses that belonged to the commander of Nachitoches. Caught and jailed by Gil Ybarbo, he escaped again, and this time rode boldly up to the commander's home, "with the intention to kill him . . ." He called out to Gil Ybarbo to come outside, as he had something to tell him. But the Spaniard's wife recognized his voice, and the captain yelled for his men to catch Peña, who ran, this time to the Tonkawas Indians, stopping to steal some horses along the way. He spent a winter with the Tonkawas, living with an Indian woman. Then he apparently fell out with his hosts, and went back to Spanish Texas. Caught stealing horses by some Tejanos (Texas Indians), he was jailed once again by the long-suffering Gil Ybarbo. This time he had shackles on his feet, handcuffs on his wrists, and his feet in stocks. In spite of these precautions, he was found missing in August 1790. Gil Ybarbo dryly wrote that he was making inquiries into how Peña had managed to free himself from all his fetters.

Some traders who spent the winter among the Tawakonis reported on their return that Peña had been seen there. He had joined with some other ruffians, including a Frenchman. The three left on the pretext of going hunting, and disappeared for several months. When Peña reappeared, it was with some horses. He headed for La Bahía del Espíritu Santo, where he stole arms, ammunition, clothing, and other items from the houses of citizens living there. He also stole some horses, and then apparently moved up to kidnapping: "On the sixth day he took from the *rancho* of Antonio Ariola the woman whom he found alone in the house." (Later court testimony indicates that it was more of a lovers' triangle than a kidnapping.) Peña was caught, and sent this time to San Antonio de Béxar, with an escort of a corporal, four soldiers, and six militiamen.[59]

Although El Bocón seems to have been an especially energetic career criminal, he was by no means unique. The reports from places like Texas are full of reported criminals. In 1781 Juan José El Sordo (Deaf) and Francisco Pacheco were accused of stealing horses and clothing and as punishment were given twenty-five lashes; not surprisingly, they confessed. After breaking jail, they were caught and whipped again, one of them proclaiming his innocence and accusing his companion of the murder of a Spaniard. Both were jailed, but escaped a few days later.[60] Another man, Damasio Gutiérrez, was a horse thief and cattle rustler, whom the report noted had been jailed twice before for theft, and was imprisoned once again for stealing mules. In 1793 the governor of Texas had José Vasques and José María Rico prisoners in the presido at La Bahía del Espíritu Santo. The pair was charged with stealing mares and trying to sell them to Indians who were out hunting on the Río de la Trinidad.[61]

Sometimes the actions of criminals had wider repercussions: two vaqueros (cowboys) in Texas, Pedro Javier Salinas and José Reymundo Días, whom the authorities said could not be ignorant of the fact that the Lipan Apaches were at present allies of the Spanish, nearly wrecked the peace in Texas for their own gain. The Lipanes "were admitted to the province of Texas in peace, entering and leaving without any hostile act." The pair helped a group of Tonkawa Indians to steal forty horses from the herd of the Lipanes near the Paraje de Durazno. The Lipanes caught the men, took them to the governor, and demanded justice (an interesting comment upon Indian-Spanish relations; the pair was lucky not to be summarily killed). The governor decided to make an example of the men, and they were given one hundred lashes apiece in the plaza of San Antonio de Béxar, in the presence of the greatest number of Lipanes who could be assembled in the town. They were then sentenced to four years' hard labor at the presidio public works, shackled, with rations but without pay.[62]

One factor that must have encouraged high rates of both military desertion and civilian crime was the way in which criminals were tidily disposed of by being sent to the frontier. The Acordada, a court in Mexico City, used the presidios as dumping grounds for criminals. A sentence to hard labor on public works was a common one, giving the crown a cheap source of labor and a convenient way to rid itself of troublemakers at the same time.[63] In 1780, Teodoro de Croix wrote to Governor Cabello of Texas asking what duties or labor he could propose for criminals he had to sentence; Croix wished to end their incarcerations, for they were costing the crown money.[64] Such men were predisposed to commit antisocial acts and to add to the climate of insecurity on the frontier, already wracked by the near-continual state of war with various Indian nations.

Others rebelled for more fundamental reasons: they were already perpetual outsiders in Hispanic society. Afro-mestizos remained behind in New Mexico with Franciscan fathers after Coronado's expedition returned to New Spain in 1542; others ran away from De Soto's *entrada* into the southeastern United States in 1538. The latter lived among the Indians some twelve years after the Spaniards left La Florida.[65] The permanent African presence in the Borderlands is linked to mining and ranching: Africans and Afro-mestizos were vaqueros, itinerant placer miners, and overseers in Zacatecas and Parral. They also made up a sizable component of the frontier presidio and militia force.[66] Their interaction with Indians took place on many levels. Despite royal prohibitions, they were employed as *alguaciles* (constables), *ministros de justicia,* and *fiscales* in mission villages, where they often abused both their office and their charges.[67] Others were taken captive by *indios enemigos.* Two mulatto shepherds were caught spying for Apaches in Durango in 1773. They had been captured by the Indians, but admitted that under the influence of a steady diet of "the root they call peyote" they had "persevered voluntarily in their apostasy."[68] A striking case is that of Gaspar Francisco, a mulatto slave, who in 1627 "fled from the service of his master in the company of others who committed various excesses." Captured and sent to the mines in Nuevo León, he fled again, stealing a horse. Recaptured again, he ran away once more, having "little fear of God and less esteem for royal justice." He fled with a companion to Coahuila, "the land of the Chichimecs, and in offense of God our Lord and in hurt to his conscience being *ladino* and Christian," he danced with the Indians of the province, was tattooed, and drank "bones of death" (ground-up bones of war victims, a common practice among some nomadic tribes). He was also allegedly named a war captain, and lived in concubinage with an Indian woman. He was tried and sentenced to hang. Besides his alleged crimes against society, the Spanish were afraid of what he might teach the Indians ("*daría extender algunas cosas a los dichos yndios*").[69]

Merely being an African or Afro-mestizo often evoked suspicions of collusion from a nervous populace ever wary of Indian depredations. José Augustin Alvarado, a forty-year-old mulatto who lived on an estancia in Nuevo León, was arrested for allegedly having had communication with an Indian suspected of leading raiders, in July 1794, through the Valle de San Pablo de los Labradores. The mulatto did not deny that he had a close Indian friend who sometimes slept on the floor of his *jacal* (hut), but he swore that neither he nor his friend had ever committed any crimes against the community. Alvarado was lucky; several people came forward in court to swear to his good reputation.[70] Not so lucky was another mulatto, Francisco Pacheco, also of Nuevo León. When an Apache bow and arrow were found in his house, he claimed that he possessed them only for his own defense, but he was still thrown into jail. He was sent to the governor of the province for judgement.[71] More serious, if equally insubstantial, was the case against Julián de Lugo y Cabrera, a free mulatto, accused by the Spanish in Saltillo of accompanying Apaches on their raids. A witness told of hearing a little girl who had been taken captive swearing that the mulatto danced and played a guitar while Apaches violated and killed captured women. The mulatto was later freed for lack of evidence.[72]

Despite many false accusations arising from anxiety and prejudice, there were many instances when Spanish fears were well realized. Various members of outcast groups could on occasion act in concert, as well as rebel individually. *Palenques* (communities of escaped slaves and other marginals) were established in the New World from a very early date;[73] the Spanish mounted an expedition against an especially troublesome palenque in the vicinity of Veracruz in 1690. This community of escaped slaves gained additional members by mounting raids against neighboring haciendas and liberating fellow captives, under the leadership of a charismatic African named Yanga. The viceroy sent a force of some 450 soldiers, Indians, mestizos, and mulattos against Yanga's community. After an inconclusive battle, the slaves fled. Eventually a peace accord gave their settlement legal status—provided they ceased their raids of liberation.[74]

Palenques are also known to have existed in the Borderlands. Less racial than social in nature, they were magnets for attracting all manner of rebellious and dissatisfied people. One of the most vivid descriptions of such a community comes from Nueva Vizcaya. It begins: "Yesterday about two in the afternoon there entered into this real José Tomás de la Trinidad, fifteen years old, son of Juan Trinidad, my sheepherder, who among others was taken prisoner by the Indians and mulatos when they raided my hacienda of San Salvador de Orta [Horta]." All their raiders and their captives had escaped on foot and, after circling to throw off pursuit, returned to their palenque in a canyon in the Sierra Madre Occidental.

José Tomás told the Spaniards that the palenque was comprised of four rancherías. The largest had about three hundred men (probably men, women, and children). Its captain was an Indian, very old and lame, so crippled that he went about on horseback. Nevertheless, he exercised authority over the other settlements, which consisted of about two hundred persons each. Their leaders were also Indians, one of them a Tarahumara. All four settlements were comprised of rebels, mulattos, *lobos*, coyotes, Tarahumaras, and other "wild Indians." Each one lived in whatever manner he wished; they had as many women as they liked, and a great many children. There were also several old invalids, as well as two dark young Africans *(negros atezados mozos)*.

The cimarrones raised maize, squash, and melons in irrigated fields, herded cattle and buffalos, and drank a great deal of pulque, "with which they make themselves drunk." The young captive described the horse and mule herd as "innumerable," and said that "they turn the plains black." The herd was comprised of stolen animals, with many different brands, and was little cared for, because it largely furnished food for the cimarrones.

The people in the settlement had an image of Our Lady of Sorrows "in her niche with a glass door," kept in a cave near the main ranchería, decorated with shawls, altar cloths, quilts, braids, and little jewels. The people kept the area around the image clean and swept, and lit tapers before it, dancing *mitotes* (ceremonial dances) accompanied by drum and whistle. The rebels also had much clothing of all types, many loose goods, and unopened bundles, all evidently stolen from Spanish settlements. They had many European arms—guns, powder, balls, and sheets of lead—but, declared the captive, it is the same as if they did not have them, because they did not know how to employ them, nor were they able to use more than the pike and the arrows, of which they had many. In the settlement of *el capitán cojo* (the lame captain) was a large buffalo-skin tent, in which clothing, goods, rebozos, boots, shoes, *calsones* (trousers), and clothing made of buckskins, which they themselves made, were stored, to be distributed among the people, and constituting their commerce. José Tomás did not see any reales (coins), nor did he see any Indians of other nations among the rebels.

The captive said that from the stubble and signs of old cultivation in the fields, the settlement appeared to have been in existence for many years. Its inhabitants did not live in houses, but in jacales (rude huts) of horsehide. "They live with much satisfaction, and do not fear that war will be waged against them there." By day spies were posted on the mountaintops, and the people slept carelessly, until after dawn. Among the women of the palenque were many captives from various parts, who were already accustomed to such a life that they did not remember their homes or their families. Most of the men and women of the camps wore buckskins (*gamuza*), putting on fancier dress only to parade and dance in.

The captive stated that the aim of the rebels was "to finish with all the *poblados* (settlements) of the frontier, and to make themselves masters of everything." The cimarrones had made a raid the previous month, in which mares, stallions, mules, and two children had been stolen. A raid against the haciendas of the Señor Conde de San Pedro del Alamo in Parras was being planned, and also against those of Señor Márquez and his brother. When José Tomás was kidnapped, the cimarrones had also captured his brother, two other boys, and a little girl. The journey had taken four days, with the party walking very slowly, sleeping all night long, and traveling with great carelessness and satisfaction. When they arrived at the ranchería, "people came out to receive them with skins of pulque, and that night all became drunk." Afterward, the rebels killed his brother and one other boy, leaving only himself and another boy, and the little girl alive. José Tomás was assigned by his master to rise early to guard the horse herd, and ran away. Lost in the darkness, he wandered about, eating mesquite, tunas, and other cactus fruits, dressed in ripped buckskins and a buffalo robe. It had not been difficult to escape, owing to the great carelessness with which the settlements were guarded.[75]

The captivity problem in the Borderlands furnished the greatest number of go-betweens. This interchange of cultural values and artifacts, termed *acculturation*, was in no sense an unequal or one-way exchange, from the European to the Indian. The process, defined as "culture change that is initiated by the conjunction of two or more autonomous cultural systems,"[76] was one that operated in both directions. All conquerors take on some aspects of the conquered, usually in language, dress, customs, habits, and cuisine. Nevertheless, they customarily expect what acculturation does take place to be primarily in one direction—theirs—that is, that their perceived cultural superiority will inexorably and eventually draw their "inferiors" to embrace the blessings and benefits of their way of life. It was therefore with a great degree of surprise that European colonizers began to realize that in many cases the exact opposite was occurring—that many of their fellow countrymen and women, when brought into close and sustained contact with aboriginal life, chose to abandon their mother society and culture and immerse themselves in Indian society—in short, to become, in the words of James Axtell, "white Indians," as did Gonzalo Guerrero.[77] Europeans, whether Spaniards or Englishmen, never ceased to be astonished that any person, without coercion, could abandon his or her society and choose to live in what was regarded as savagery. Unfortunately, there are no stirring literary narratives from Spanish captives (other than the remarkable *relación* of Alvar Núñez Cabeza de Vaca) to correspond with those from the

New England frontier. Nevertheless, a multitude of military, judicial, and religious documents attests to the "crossing over" of Spanish and Hispanicized transculturites.

Captives were deliberately seized by Indians, both for ransom and to reinforce band population. Women and children were favored, the latter especially if they were small children, most of whom adapted easily to a new way of life. In 1782, Comandante General Croix wrote to the commander at Janos presidio about a man named José María Gonzales, captured by Indians (probably Apaches) in December of 1771 in Sonora. About fifteen years old when taken captive, Gonzales was identified as having led an attack on the pueblo of Cucurpe, Sonora, in June of 1781. The raid was carried out by three hundred enemy Indians, who killed fifty-three persons (including Gonzales's father), captured forty-four others (including his two brothers), and stole the entire horse and cattle herd of the settlement. Croix described the young apostate in his communiqué, and added the information that Gonzales was known among the Indians as Cayetano, and apparently had a devoted following among them. He had married among the Indians and had fathered children; the whole family lived in a ranchería in the Sierra Madre Occidental. Croix urged that every effort be made to apprehend the said José María Gonzales, dead or alive (*el mayor esfuerzo para cogerlo muerte, o vivo*).[78]

In another instance, a young mulatto from Nuevo León named Marcelino, taken captive while tending sheep, was raised by Indians in Parral. Caught by the Spaniards when he offered to show them the whereabouts of a large horse herd allegedly stolen by the Apaches, he was accused of horse theft and the murders of many people. During the interrogation of this *apachito*, or little Apache as he was called, he could not make the sign of the cross, being "entirely ignorant of the mysteries of our holy faith." He testified that he had been taken captive at a very early age by a captain of the Mescalero nation. He denied that he had ever accompanied the Indians on any raids against the Spanish, but did testify that he knew of innumerable excursions of Apaches against Monclova and the presidios of Nueva Vizcaya, and many murders of Spaniards. The Spanish were disinclined to believe his protestations of innocence, and the comandante general ordered him sent in chains to Mexico City.[79] On the Argentine and Chilean frontiers, the captivity problem was as serious for frontier society as it was in the Borderlands of New Spain.[80]

There were, in addition, numerous cases of adults, both captive and free, "turning Indian." In 1693, the Franciscans abandoned their mission in eastern Texas when the Indians among whom they had been preaching, Caddos, warned them to leave lest they be killed. On the journey back to Monclova, four of the ten soldiers assigned to escort the priests deserted to remain with the

Indians. The missionaries, when reporting the apostasy of their escorts, attributed it to un-Christian lechery, "because as people with obligations, and abandoned to the vice of the Indians, they wanted more to live with them than among Catholics."[81] In fact, one of the deserters, José de Urrutia, spent seven years living among the east Texas Indians before rejoining Spanish society.[82] Another individual, Antonio Treviño, was escorting buffalo hunters from San Sabá in Texas when his party was attacked by Taovayas. He fought until severely wounded, but was finally taken prisoner by the Indians. His skill at arms and bravery prompted the Indians to spare his life. He lived among the Taovayas for six months, and showed up at Nacogdoches dressed only in a breechcloth, escorted by Indian warriors as an honored guest and friend.[83]

The problem of deserters was a particularly vexing one for the Spaniards. The muster rolls of the presidio at Janos, in western Nueva Vizcaya, indicate that in the last decades of the eighteenth century, 1 and sometimes 2 men deserted every month out of a total troop strength of less than 145 men.[84] The muster rolls are backed up by innumerable incidents that can be traced through the documentary record. Presidial commander Pedro de Nava wrote the commander at Janos informing him that Ignacio Mendoza had deserted from the *guarnición de caballada* (the guard on the horse herd), on October 18, 1796.[85] A party of eight Spanish dragoons was being escorted by a detachment of soldiers and Indian *flecheros* (bowmen) in Durango when they managed to free themselves from their shackles and flee. All had deserted from their regiment, some more than once, and had committed various crimes while on the run. The eight split up in the sierra, some taking refuge in churches; others were caught in Durango.[86] Athanase de Mézieres, the lieutenant governor of Nachitoches, wrote to Luis de Unzaga, the governor of Louisiana, in 1774, about the case of one Joseph Antonio Butieres, a deserter from Los Adaes, who was living a scandalous life with a black slave. This deserter was an idle man, whose sole occupation was to guide wanderers to the coast to carry on their illicit trade of smuggling. He also acted as interpreter to a troublemaker named Clermont, who was allegedly stirring up the Indians of eastern Texas. The comandante general, the Caballero Teodoro de Croix, in a proclamation issued in 1778, bemoaned the gravity of the desertion problem, which he blamed on the inefficient methods used to apprehend deserters, and on the cooperation and aid that inhabitants of the region gave the malefactors. He ordered stiff penalties, including whippings, imprisonment on a presidio or *obraje* (textile workshop), and banishment for anyone helping a deserter to escape justice.[87]

One particularly dramatic case of renegade activities occurred in Texas. Miguel Jorge Menchaca was the son of a former captain of San Antonio Presidio, but his family was often in trouble with the law (his father was once accused of rounding up strays after the legal deadline of the *mesta,* the cattle-man's guild, had passed). On the order of Governor Cabello, Miguel Menchaca was not allowed to enroll in the presidial cavalry company. A circular reported that Miguel Menchaca had fled from the presidio of San Antonio de Béxar on April 14, 1781 (the reason why was not related). Making his way toward Nacog-doches, Menchaca encountered a band of Comanches, who fired at him and knocked him off his horse, wounding him in the right leg. The Comanches took him captive, and no one heard of Menchaca for two years.[88] In Novem-ber, 1783, a Tacanes Indian, fluent in Spanish, appeared before the governor, sent by the missionaries at Nuestra Señora de la Purísima Concepción de Acuña with a strange story to tell. On the afternoon of October 31, he had been tending the mission flock near the junction of the Medina and San Antonio rivers, when an Indian walked out of a ravine on foot, carrying a bow and some arrows in his hand and a quiver of arrows on his back. The Indian whistled to him and indicated that he should approach. Pantaleón, the Tacanes, thought that it was perhaps one of his tribe who had run away a few days before. When he came close, to his astonishment he recognized Miguel Jorge Menchaca. Menchaca asked him if he knew him, but it seemed wiser to deny it. Menchaca told Pantaleón that he knew him, and identified himself. He asked where the royal horse herd was grazing. Pantaleón was frightened and lied, telling Men-chaca that it was grazing in an arroyo (canyon) west of the presidio. Menchaca replied that it was not, for he and fifteen other Indians had just scouted the area to no avail.

Just then two other Indians emerged from the ravine, one armed with a lance, the other with a musket. They spoke with Menchaca, who told Pan-taleón to go away and hide his sheep or the Comanches would kill them that night or the next morning. The Tacanes collected his flock, and then went to see his mission priest, who sent him to the governor. Pantaleón told Governor Cabello that the two men with Menchaca had their hair cut off in the manner of the *norteños,* but he did not believe their language was Comanche or Ton-kawa. Soon after, another man arrived to report an encounter with the rene-gade. Gaspar Flores, a resident of the Béxar, had been rounding up horses with his sons that morning two leagues north of the presidio. Menchaca, whom Flores had recognized, emerged from a bush, riding a horse, dressed like a Comanche, with breeches, boots, and chamois leggings, wearing hides from the waist up. He carried no arms. Flores was afraid as the renegade approached. Menchaca asked him what he was doing in that place, and then asked for news of his family. Flores told him that his father and mother were well, but that his *abuela* (grandmother) had died a short time before. Hearing this, Menchaca's eyes filled with tears. He warned Flores to get away, for other Indians were approaching.

Flores straightaway went to report to Governor Cabello, who was convinced that Menchaca had guided Comanches in an earlier foray against the town. He rounded up ten soldiers and fifty-five militiamen to chase after Menchaca. But they found no one.[89] The governor sent a circular to all presidios, and to the governor of New Mexico, as the Comanches often journeyed there to trade. Menchaca was to be apprehended if he showed up there, or perhaps the Comanches might be induced to turn him over to the Spanish. In any case, he was clearly too dangerous a man to be left at liberty.

In 1776, José de Gálvez wrote to the viceroy of Mexico of a series of robberies and murders of shepherds recently committed in Coahuila, probably by Apaches. A captive who had escaped from an enemy ranchería described the encampment as being under the command of a Spanish deserter named Andrés. Gálvez immediately ordered a surprise attack upon the camp.[90] The Spanish authorities displayed great concern over any real or imagined alliances between Spaniards and Indians, and both dismay and bafflement over the matter of persons who transferred their cultural allegiance from the Europeans to the Indians. In 1787, Comandante General Jacabo Ugarte wrote to the viceroy that no one could doubt that a great part of the robberies and murders in Sonora had been executed by gangs of raiders composed of Tarahumara Indians, fugitives from the missions, mulattos, mestizos, and other malefactors of diverse caste, sometimes in union with the enemy Apaches, and sometimes acting by themselves. He had irrefutable proof of this, and planned to destroy the culprits and extinguish the crime of *infidencia*—treason.[91]

Such occurrences were not unique to the frontier of New Spain. The same situation arose during the long struggle between Spaniards and Araucanians in colonial Chile. One early chronicler reported that there lived among the Indians more than fifty fugitives who were mestizos, mulattos, and Spaniards; these renegades took part in all depredations against the Spanish, and taught the Indians how to use European weapons, including muskets. Only a shortage of powder prevented the Indians from doing more harm than they had already committed.[92] In fact, historian Mario Góngora simply declared mestizos, mulattos, and *zambos* to be a perennial source of vagabondage in Chile. Horse stealing and *vagabundaje* were, in his opinion, inseparable elements of Chilean transculturation. Soldiers, tired of the discipline of the service and attracted by the liberty and power they would possess in Araucanía or in the *llanos* (grasslands) of Cuyo, deserted to live among the Indians. Europeans living among the Indians often assumed leadership roles, advising Apaches or Araucanians on Spanish tactics and weapons, and leading attacks on their countrymen.[93] Military commanders on the Argentine pampa frontiers frequently reported the flight of persons to the Indians.[94] Two black slaves, for instance, had fled in 1758 to the *tolderías* (Indian camps) of cacique Rafael Iai.[95] On an expedition led by Comandante Don Manuel de Pinazo, a herder fled to the Indians, to "introduce among them a thousand mischiefs."[96] Soldiers also deserted; one José Ferreira was picked up placidly sleeping in an Indian settlement.[97] The transculturite phenomenon involving military men was not unique to the Spanish empire: Portuguese sailors went native in the fifteenth century in West Africa, bringing their weapons and knowledge to the African tribes of the coast; Englishmen deserted from their armies in India and signed on as gunners in the armies of Indian princes, to fight for loot and against Portuguese India.[98]

Still another marginalized group within Spanish Borderlands society were Indians, many in a state of transition between native and European society. Since the object of Spanish civil and religious policy was to transform Indians into peaceful Hispanicized farmers, no matter their mode of life before the intrusion of the Europeans, any Indian who ran away after being baptized was legally an apostate and a renegade. When Spanish "sovereignty" had been extended over whole nations, like the Tarahumaras, Tepehuánes, Yaquis, and Seri, rebellions and individual acts of infidencia were almost the norm. Flight, joining rebels in mountain areas, and participation in secret and forbidden rituals were manifestations of a continuing struggle against the Spanish. *Hechiceros* (shamans and sorcerers) conducted old rites; Indians met in underground kivas and danced their ceremonial dances covertly or in public, sometimes with the encouragement of the civil authorities, who were often feuding with the missionary friars. Acts of open rebellion, such as stealing horses and joining with Indians who rejected Spanish rule, especially the many Apache nations, were frequent.

Not all Indian marginals were renegades; some had left their villages because the Europeans had disrupted or altered traditional economic or social patterns. Many went to work voluntarily in the mines in Sonora, Parral, or Zacatecas. Others worked for Spaniards as stockmen and herders and agricultural laborers, or were taken by the Jesuits to help them in the missions. Some were dispossessed of their lands and forced to wander, seeking food and work. Others simply took advantage of a changing world to cut their ties to their communities and seek what fortune offered them. There were many in the sierras to shelter such people, and many enemies of the Spanish to welcome them into their ranks.

Pedro de Nava suspected the Tarahumara and Tepehuán Indians of such infidelities. He had, he wrote, evidence that fugitives from their missions and other castas were committing murders, robberies, and other acts, which had been attributed to the Apaches. He proposed ordering one hundred men to sweep through the *alta* and *baja* Tarahumara country, and through haciendas, *poblaciones*, and rancherías.[99] Ugarte complained that the situation among the Tarahumaras could hardly be otherwise, when rancherías of pagan Indians were located near the towns of Christian Indians, giving shelter and welcome to fugitives from the missions, and asylum to malefactors from diverse parts. It would be best to deprive them of this refuge; the villages were of uncertain or insecure Christianity, and represented "stains" or "blots" of *gentilismo*—heathenism.[100] The Spanish military believed that among the population of Nueva Vizcaya there resided *enemigos domésticos encubiertos*—concealed domestic enemies—who were united and allied with the Apaches, and served as spies and auxiliaries, communicating to them information that helped them in their raids.

A concrete case of infidencia surfaced in November of 1772. Five men and three women were killed by raiders on a ranch near the Villa de Chihuahua. Two who managed to escape told of an attack by mounted Indians, among whom was a Tarahumara known to the Spanish. The man, Felipe Tanaderas el Bernardo, was arrested and confessed to the assault in the company of six Apaches, as well as to long-standing ties of friendship and cooperation between the Apaches and Indians in several towns in Nueva Vizcaya. The authorities, determined to root out sedition, detained more than two hundred suspects, many of whom conveniently confessed to cooperation with the Apaches. Sadly, as the principal leaders and captains of the rebels could not be taken, and since the authorities could not afford to keep so many people in jail, the prisoners were released to work at several local haciendas and on public works. Not surprisingly, some of them fled; if they had not been enemies of the Spanish before, their experiences with Spanish justice had made them so.

Indian experiences with Spanish missionaries, Jesuits and Franciscans, were particularly apt to breed resentment and treason. Padre Antonio Reyes, surveying Sonora for the viceroy in 1772, sadly admitted that after a century of effort he and his brother clerics had failed utterly in their tasks: "after a thousand years, though the missionaries might be apostles, these missions and Indians will be in the same, or worse, state."[101] Although the padres tended to blame their failure on the intractably wicked nature of native society, the proximity of heathen nations was also held to blame. Padre Nentvig, in his *Rudo Ensayo* of 1764, observed that friendly and enemy Indians continually visited one another. The Seris, he wrote, had always been unquiet and rebellious toward the laws of God. Even those reduced to Christianity and peace in a number of villages had daily communication with their heathen brethren; in that way, information was channeled to the cimarrones.[102]

The commander of the presidial company at Río Grande del Norte complained to the viceroy of the intolerable contact between the Indians of the mission of El Carrizo, in Coahuila, and the Mescaleros and other enemies who lived near the mission. Such contact, he wrote, required continual attention and wariness, and absorbed attention that could have been focused on other enemies. He desired the troublemakers to be transported to Havana, or any other place far away from Coahuila.[103] Another presidial captain reported encountering a group of enemies, composed of Apaches, norteños, and Colomes, with a mixture of others who were called *criados,* who had been raised by Spaniards from birth and now returned to their own people and to the Tarahumaras. These criados were trained in war, and attacked with their faces covered to remain incognito. Over fifty people had been killed in his district by this alliance of *indios bárbaros.*[104]

Indian spies were utilized by both sides in their complex dance of war and peace. The Spanish used Opatas and Tlaxcaltecos as auxiliaries, and even established communities of *genízaros* and *nijoras* or de-tribalized Indians and redeemed Christian Indian captives to act as guards and assistants around missions.[105] But the Spanish were particularly plagued by the problem of spying; every ranchería or village newly converted to Catholicism and allegiance to the Spanish crown was a pool of potential recruits for Apache raiders or rebel neophytes. In 1773, Joseph Fayni wrote the viceroy that there was no doubt that disloyal Tarahumaras were mixing in with the general population and acting as spies for the Apaches.[106] He went on to assert that the Tepehuanes, Altos, and Bajos, were entirely distrusted by their own friars because of their innate love of the deserts and badlands, and their boredom with civil life and Catholic institutions. When civil and religious authorities joined to force the Indians to live in their new mission settlements, the Indians ran off, stole women, wandered through the countryside, and sustained themselves by robbery.[107]

The two mulatto shepherds caught spying for the Apaches in Durango were acting on behalf of a group supposedly composed of as many as seventeen hundred men, led by a man named Calixtrin and his son, and a Spaniard named Antonio de la Campa. The party was comprised of a few Apaches, but mostly apostate Tarahumaras, Cholomes, and *gente de razón*: mulattos, blacks, lobos, and other castes. The party sheltered in a mountain range named Rosario, where they kept their horse and mule herd. They traded with deerskins and other goods with the Indios bárbaros (probably Apaches). They divided themselves into raiding parties of twenty or so men to commit their depredations. In every hacienda and town, the spies confessed, there were other spies who hid or disguised the raiders. Some Tarahumara women voluntarily accompanied the rebels; other women were captives, who, having been crudely used, "became sick with fear, and died." Among the rebels were Tepehuán Indians who could handle firearms.[108] (The large size of the group is almost certainly an exaggeration.)

But two could play the game of using Indians as spies, translators, scouts, and fighters. The comandante general of the eastern Provincias Internas questioned his counterpart in the west as to the advisability of employing *espías* (in this context, scouts), and how much to pay for their services. The officer replied that he had used more than twenty spies on his last campaign, and he placed total confidence in them. They knew the terrain and streams where his soldiers campaigned.[109] An ensign from San Sabá Presidio took thirty-eight men from three presidios and eight Indians as scouts on a campaign. He described in his diary how he dispatched the scouts every day to reconnoiter the terrain ahead of the main body. But he was betrayed: several of his scouts failed to return after a fight with enemy Indians, and some soldiers from the Río Grande presidio expressed doubts about their loyalty. They knew the Julimeños and believed they had gone over to the enemy, fighting with the loyal scouts during the night. Ensign Pérez could not doubt that those who had misled his troops were traitors.[110]

Three interesting incidents illustrate just how quickly the many Indian nations of the Borderlands adapted to the evolution of the frontier. In each, the Indians demonstrate an intelligent and deliberate utilization of European ways for their own ends. The first is from 1690: Governor Vargas of New Mexico, after raiding Taos to obtain corn, was crossing Ute territory in southern Colorado when he was attacked:

> just before dawn, the camp was raided by a group of Utes armed with bows and arrows and war clubs. The Spaniards were taken completely by surprise, and six were wounded before the alarm brought resistance. After eight Utes had been killed, the others fled across the river. From there they waved a buckskin as a flag of peace, and cried out "Anche pastiche," meaning in their language "My friend and brother." Then they recrossed the river and mingled peacefully as if nothing had occurred. They were given gifts of maize, dried meat, a horse, and numerous European trifles. There were about three hundred of them counting the women.

Their apologetic explanation of the reason for their surprise attack was quite plausible. They pointed out how before the revolt of 1680 they had been friends of the Spaniards, but had always been enemies of the Tewas, Tanos, Picuries, Jemez, and Keres. During the period of pueblo independence these rebels had often come to this region to hunt buffalo disguised as Spaniards, mounted, and with leather jackets, leather hats, firearms, and even a bugle, all of which they had taken from the Spaniards at the time of the revolt. Whenever they went on these excursions the Utes had attacked them, hence the recent misfortune, a result of mistaken identity.[111]

The second incident occurred in 1760, when Bishop Tamarón encountered a strange form of European-Indian contact in New Mexico:

a little farther on . . . we found a black cross about a vara and a half high and as thick as a man's thumb at the side of the road, and at its foot a deerskin sack containing two pieces of fresh venison and a deerskin. The Apaches, who must have been in the Doña Ana sierra, put it there. By this means they indicated that they were at peace and that we should give them food and buy the deerskin. The experienced guides gave this inter-pretation. And therefore they left a knife in exchange for the deerskin and kept putting pieces of bread and tobacco leaf in the sack. And a short distance away, for we were on the lookout, two Indians on horseback were sighted. They were coming to see what had been left in the sack.[112]

The third incident is also from 1760. As the Spanish were about to conclude a general peace with a number of norteño tribes in Texas, the Apaches did their best to wreck it:

The Apaches would go out to rob and kill Indians of the north, taking with them a number of hats and other things worn by our soldiers, all of which they left artfully along the way, as if by carelessness, in order to convince their enemies that the Spaniards were perpetrators of their crimes. At the same time they would provide themselves with arrows and shoes of the kind used by their enemies [los norteños] and would then commit depredations in the neighborhood of our presidios and missions, where, when the tracks were examined and the arrows found, it was thought the Indians of the north were the authors of the evil.[113]

Every society has an underclass, a marginalized group or groups. By their very nature, frontiers breed marginals, whether they are persons simply mar-ginalized economically or socially or are, in fact, renegades, people who have rejected one cultural norm for another. Many persons, especially those living in a fluid cultural or political zone like east Texas or the grass steppes south of La Plata, passed between the two worlds, European and aboriginal, at will. Others were marginalized or forced to be transculturites against their will. Whether voluntarily or involuntarily, these European or Hispanic marginals found common ground with apostates and rebels of Indian groups:

> Such groups eventually set up their own nexus of social contact and joint interest. Men of both border populations, working together in this way, become a "we" group to whom others of their own nationality, and especially the authorities, are "they." To this extent it is often possible to describe the border populations on both sides of a frontier taken together, as a joint community that is functionally recognizable though not institutionally defined. It is not surprising that the ambivalent loyalties of frontier people are often conspicuously and historically important.[114]

The European, mestizo, mulatto, and Indian marginals of the borderlands formed such joint communities, functionally recognizable to the authorities as threats to Spanish and Christian polity. The Europeans gave the Indians their arms, their goods, their intelligence, and their skills (when the Indians did not simply take these for themselves). The Indians, in return, often provided marginals with sanctuary from the laws and norms of their own society. Spanish civil, military, and religious officials preferred "official" paths of acculturation: the mission, the presidio, the trade fair, the corregidor, or fiscal. The marginals provided alternative pathways to cultural exchange. To the end of the frontier (that is to say, the end of independent Indian polities in the Borderlands), they posed a threat to the peace and stability of the Borderlands, but at the same time, a bridge between radically different cultures and ways of life.

NOTES

1. Robert L. Reynolds, "The Mediterranean Frontiers, 1001400," in Walker D. Wyman and Clifton B. Kroeber, eds., *The Frontier in Perspective* (Madison, 1957), 23.

2. Frederick Jackson Turner, "The Significance of the Frontier in American History," in George Rogers Taylor, ed., *The Turner Thesis: Concerning the Role of the Frontier in American History*, 3d ed. (Lexington, Mass., 1971), 3–4.

3. *The Random House Dictionary of the English Language*, 2d ed. (New York, 1983), 2060.

4. Andrew McCall, *The Medieval Underworld* (London, 1979), 90.

5. Charles Ribton-Turner, *A History of Vagrants and Vagrancy, and Beggars and Begging* (London, 1887), 89–90.

6. Norman Martin, *Los vagabundos en la Nueva España* (México, 1957), x.

7. Rosa María Pérez-Estévez, *El problema de los vagos en la España del siglo XVIII* (Madrid, 1976), 85.

8. Ibid., 86.

9. Martin, *Los vagabundos*, xv.

10. Pérez-Estévez, *El problema de los vagos*, 94.

11. Charles I, Monzón, Nov. 25, 1552; Philip II, Toledo, 1560 (n.d.), in *Novísima recopilación de las leyes de España*, 6 vols. (Madrid, 1805–1807), 12:31:4.

12. Pérez-Estévez, *El problema de los vagos*, 65–66.

13. Charles I to the Audiencia of Mexico, Toledo, Dec. 4, 1528, in *Colección de documentos ineditos relativos al descubrimiento: conquista y organización de las antiguas posesiones españoles de ultramar* (Madrid, 1885–1932) 1:19.

14. Real cédula, Philip II, Valladolid, Mar. 7, 1559; Vajadoz, Sept. 1, 1580; San Lorenzo, Mar. 31, 1584, in Alfonso García Gallo, ed., *Cedulario indiano recopilado por Diego de Encinas*, 4 vols. (Madrid, 1945), 5:iv, 24–25.

15. Jonathon Israel, *Race, Class, and Politics in Colonial Mexico, 1610–1670* (London, 1975), 77.

16. John Francis Gemelli Careri, *A Voyage Round the World*, vol. 4, A. Churchill, comp., *A Collection of Voyages and Travels* (London,), 543.

17. Israel, Race, Class, and Politics, 78.

18. Carta de Exmo. Sr. Conde de Priego, Virrey de la Nueva Espaila a S. M. el Rey dn. Felipe III, Mexico, Feb. 26, 1622, in Antonio Vásquez de Espinosa, *Descripción de la Nueva España en el siglo XVII . . .* , ed. Mariano Cuevas (México, 1944), 216. Statement of Martín Fernández de Esquibias, Mexico, Jan. 25, 1624, in "Documentos relativos al tumulto de 1624: Colectados por D. Mariano Fernández de Echeverría y Veita," in vols. 2 and 3 of *Documentos para la historia de México*, 2d ser., 4 vols. (México, 1854–1855), 2:414.

19. Martin, *Los vagabundos*, 97.

20. Sergio Bagu, *Estructura social de la colonia* (Buenos Aires, 1952), 123.

21. Real cédula, Charles I, Valladolid, Feb. 27, 1549, in Richard Konetzke, ed., *Colección de documentos para la historia de la formación social de hispanoamerica, 1493–1810*, 3 vols. in 5 pts (Madrid, 1953–1962), 1:256.

22. Real cédula, Philip II, San Lorenzo, Sept. 5, 1584, in ibid., 1:553–55; real cédula, Philip II, Madrid, Jan. 18, 1576, in ibid., 1:491–92.

23. Real cédula, Philip II, Pardo, Dec. 2, 1578, in García Gallo, *Cedulario indiano recopilado por Diego de Encinas*, 4:344.

24. Capitulo de carta que su Majestad escrivió al Licenciado Castro, Año de 1568, in ibid., 4:345.

25. Real cédula, Philip II, Madrid, Nov. 25, 1578, in ibid., 4:341.

26. Real cédula, Philip II, Valladolid, Oct. 3, 1578, in ibid., 4:342–43.

27. Real cédula, Philip II, Madrid, May 2, 1563, and Nov. 25, 1578; Tomar, May 2, 1581; Madrid, Jan. 10, 1589; Philip III, Tordesillas, July 12, 1600; Philip IV, Madrid, Oct. I and Dec. 17, 1646, in *Recopilación de leyes de los reinos de las Indias . . .* , 6:3:21. See also real cédula, Philip II, Aranjuez, Nov. 1, 1568, and Philip IV, in his Instrucción de Vireyes, 1628, in ibid., 7:4:1.

28. Real cédula, Philip II, Madrid, May 2, 1563, and Nov. 25, 1578; Tomar, May 2, 1581; Madrid, Jan. 10, 1589; Tordesillas, July 12, 1600; Philip IV, Madrid, Oct. 1 and Dec. 1, 1646, in ibid., 6:3:21.

29. Lucas Alamán, *Historia de Méjico,* 5 vols. (México, 1968), 1:41.

30. Michael Scardaville, "Crime and the Urban Poor: Mexico City in the Late Colonial Period" (Ph.D. diss., University of Florida, 1977), 15–17.

31. Manuel Carrera Stampa, *Los gremios, mexicanos: la organización gremial en Nueva España, 1521–161.* (México, 1954), 238–39.

32. Norman Martin, "La desnudez en la Nueva España del siglo XVIII," *Annuario de Estudios Americanos* 29 (1972), 263.

33. See Magnus Morner, *La corona española y los foraneos en los pueblos de América* (Stockholm, 1970), 105; see, also, Konetzke, *Colleción de documentos para la historia de la formación social.*

34. Bagu, *Estructura social,* 113.

35. Morner, *La corona española,* 99.

36. Antonio Herrera de Tordesillas, *Historia general de los hechos de los castellanos en las islas y tierra firme del mar oceano,* 17 vols. (Madrid, 1934–1957), decade 3, book 5, chap. 7:59.

37. Philip Wayne Powell, *Soldiers, Indians, and Silver: The Northward Advance of New Spain. 1550–1600* (Berkeley, 1952), 62.

38. Ibid., 172.

39. See Joseph L. Wieczynski, *The Russian Frontier: The Impact of Borderlands upon the Course of Early Russian History* (Charlottesville, 1976), 8.

40. Padre Daniel Januske, San Francisco de Borja (n.d., probably 1723), Archivo Historico de Hacienda Temporalidades (hereinafter cited as AHH-T), 2–782.

41. Ibid.

42. J. Rafael Rodríguez-Gallardo, *Informe sobre Sinaloa v Sonora,* ed. Germán Viveros (México, 1975), 27.

43. Padre Reyes to Bucareli, México, Apr. 20, 1772, AGN-M, t. 14, exp. 3, f. 16.

44. Ibid.

45. Ibid.

46. Cynthia Radding de Murieta, "La minería en la economía colonial de Sonora," *Revista universitaria de Sonora* 2 (1977), 4, 8.

47. Juan Nentvig, *Descripción geográfica: natural y curiosa de la provincia de Sonora por un amigo del servicio de Dios y de el Rey Nuestro Señor,* ed. Germán Viveros (México, 1971), 101.

48. Padre Daniel Januske, San Francisco de Borja (1723), AHH-T, 278–2.

49. Padre Reyes to Bucareli, México, Apr. 20, 1772, AGN-M, t. 14, exp. 3, f. 64.

50. See Peter Stern and Robert Jackson, "Vagabundaje and Settlement Patterns in Colonial Northern Sonora," *The Americas,* 44:4 (April 1988), 461–81.

51. Titulo de comisión para Don Joseph de Loaisa, Jurisdición de Copala, Apr. 28, 1755, Archivo Franciscano no. 2045, 33/694.1, f. l–4v.

52. Ibid.

53. Neve to Gálvez, Arispe, May 31, 1784, no. 116, AGI, Guadalajara, 285, cited in Luis Navarro-García, *José de Gálvez y la Comandancia General de las Provincias Internas del norte de Nueva España* (Seville, 1964), 442.

54. Hubert Howe Bancroft, *History of the North Mexican States* (San Francisco, 1886), 1:566.

55. Croix to Bucareli, Durango, Sept. 27, 1777; annex to letter from Dn. Felipe Barry,

Durango, June 30, 1777; in *La administración de D. Frey Antonio María de Bucareli y Ursula* (México, 1936), 1:376.

56. See Gonzalo Aguirre Beltrán, *La población negra de Mexico*, 2d rev. ed. México, 1946).

57. Bernal Díaz del Castillo, *The Discovery and Conquest of Mexico, 1517–1521* trans. A. P. Maudslay (New York, 1956), l2, 44–46.

58. See Eric J. Hobsbawm, *Bandits* (New York, 1969).

59. Gil Ybarbo to Muñoz, Nacogdoches, Mar. 22, 1791, Béxar Archives (hereafter cited as BA) 21/273277; Muñoz to Gil Ybarbo, San Antonio de Béxar, Jan. 4, 1792, BA v. 1–13.

60. Criminal contra el Yndio Franco Pacheco acusado de Ladrón, Hacienda de Nra Sra de Candelaria de la Sienaga de Flores, Mar. 23, 1781, Joseph Miguel Cantú, juez, Archivo Municipal de Monterey—Causas Criminales, no. 404.

61. Córdoba to Muñoz, Nacogdoches, Dec. 8, 1793, BA 13/890–897.

62. Galindo Navarro to Nava, Chihuahua, July 9, 1793, BA 23/631.

63. See Colin M. MacLachlan, *Criminal Justice in Eighteenth Century Mexico: A Study of the Tribunal of the Acordada* (Berkeley, 1974).

64. Croix to Cabello, Arispe, Feb. 10, 1780, BA 13/890–897.

65. Garcilaso de la Vega, *The Florida of the Inca: A History of the Adelantado, Hernando de Soto . . .* , ed. and trans. John Grier and Jeanette Johnson Varner (Austin, 1951), 333–34; Carl Sauer, *Sixteenth-Century North America* (Berkeley, 1971), 168; *United States De Soto Expedition Commission, Final Report . . .* (Washington, D.C., 1939), l89.

66. See Richard J. Morrisey, "The Northward Expansion of Cattle Ranching in New Spain, 1550–1600," *Agricultural History* 25 (July 1951), 129–20; Robert C. West, *The Mining Community in Northern New Spain: The Parral Mining District* (Berkeley, 1949), 53; Christon Archer, "Pardos, Indians, and the Army of New Spain: Inter-Relationships and Conflict, 1780–1810," *Journal of Latin American Studies* 6 (November 1974), 229–33; Max L. Moorhead, *The Presidio: Bastion of the Spanish Borderlands* (Norman, 1975), 182–83.

67. See Evelyn Hu-deHart, *Missionaries, Miners, and Indians: Spanish Contact with the Yaqui Nation of Northwestern New Spain, 1533–1820* (Tucson, 1972), 62–63.

68. Fayni to Bucareli, Durango, June 19, 1773, AGN-PI, t. 43, f. 11.

69. Cerralvo, May 1, 1627, Contra Gaspar Francisco, Mulato, por haverse huido del servicio de su Amo en campañía de otros que cometieron varios excesos, AMM-C, v. I , exp. 6; material furnished to the author by José Cuello.

70. Cuasa criminal contra José Augustin Alvarado, México, Dec. 1, 1794, to the fiscal del crimen, AMM-CC, v. 29, no. 517.

71. Contra Francisco Pacheco, por haberle encontrado en su case un arco y flecha de indio apache, Josef Agabo de Ayala, alcalde mayor interino, San Pedro, gobernación, del Nuevo Reino de León, Aug. 10, 1782, AMM-CC, no. 411 (1782).

72. Diligencias que se practicán de oficio de justicia sobre la averigación de si Julián Lugo y Cabrera tenia alguna mexcla o acompatiaba a los Yndios apaches, Juan Manuel del Campillo, alcalde mayor, Saltillo, June 8, 1790, AGH-C, carpeta 6, exp. 24.

73. See Richard Price, ed., *Maroon Societies: Rebel Slave Communities in the Americas* (New York, 1973), for essays on palenques in Cuba, Venezuela, Colombia, Brazil, Jamaica, and elsewhere.

74. For an account of this episode, see Colin A. Palmer, *Slaves of the White God: Blacks in Mexico, 1570–1650*, (Cambridge, Mass., 1976), 126–28; see also Francisco Javier Alegre, *Historia de la provincia de la Compañía de Jesús de Nueva España*, ed. Ernest J. Burris and Felex Zubillaga, 4 vols. (Rome, 1959–1960), 2:176.

75. Fayni to Bucareli, Durango, July 17, 1773; enclosing declaration of captive, Real de Mapimí, July 8, 1773, AGN-PI, t. 43, ff. 192–196.

76. Social Science Research Council Seminar in Acculturation, 1953, "Acculturation: An Exploratory Formulation," *American Anthropologist* 56 (1954), 974.

77. James Axtell, "The White Indians of Colonial North America," in James Axtell, ed., *The European and the Indian: Essays in the Ethnohistory of Colonial North America* (New York, 1981), 168–206.

78. Croix to Peró, Arispe, July 16, 1782, Janos Archives, 72/73, folder 4, section 3, 23.

79. Testigo de las Diligencias contra Marzelino cautivo entre los Yndios . . . Rodríguez to Ugarte, Ugarte to Croix, Presidio de San Juan Bautista, Monclova, May-June 1770, AGH-C, carpers no. 4, exp.56.

80. See Susan Socolow, "Los cautivos españoles en las comunidades indigenas: el contacto cultural," *Anuario IEHS*, Universidad Nacional del Centro de la Provincia de Buenos Aires, no. 2 (1987), 99–136.

81. Informe del Capitán Domingo Ramón sobre el inicio de la entrada a Texas, notifíca la deserción de soldados, Corral de las Piedras, Mar. 17, 1716, Archivo Franciscano, no. 17, 1/1.7, f. 30v.–31v.

82. Elizabeth A. H. John, *Storms Brewed in Other Men's Worlds: The Confrontation of Indians, Spanish, and French in the Southwest, 1540–1795* (College Station, Tex., 1975), 192.

83. Ibid., 370; Calahorra y Sanz to Navarrete, Nacogdoches, Mar. 20, 1765, BA, 10/375.

84. Reports from the presidio of Janos, Antonio Cordero, commander, Mar. 1, 1778, Janos Archive (hereafter cited as JA), 114/219, folder 5, section 2, 219; Cordero, Sept. 1, 1788, JA 114/243, folder 5, section 2, 242; Cordero, Nov. 1, 1788, JA, 115/251, folder 5, section 2, 251; Captain Manuel Rengel, Sept. 2, 1795, JA 229/87, folder 12, section 1, 87.

85. Nava to comandante de Janos, Chihuahua, Nov. 9, 1796, JA 238/177, folder 13, section 1, 5.

86. Camino y Montero to the auditor of Durango, Sombrerete, Mar. 13, 1789, AGN-PI, t. 27, exp. 3, ff. 308–399 (numbering is irregular).

87. Proclamation, El Caballerode Croix, Chihuahua, Nov. 2, 1771, BA, 12/646 647; BA transcripts, 75:179–83, Julia G. Cruz and Patricia Flores, trans.

88. Cazorla to Pacheco, La Bahía del Espíritu Santo, Aug. 2, 1787, BA, 18/202–203.

89. Pacheco to Ugalde, San Antonio de Béxar, Sept. 15, 1787, BA transcripts, 146:78–84, John Wheat, trans.; Pacheco to Ugalde, San Antonio de Béxar, Nov. 22, 1787, BA 18/472–474.

90. José de Gálvez to Bucareli, Coahuila, Dec. 27, 1776, AGN-CV, t. 86, no. 2639.

91. Ugarte y Loyola to the viceroy, Arispe, Dec. 10, 1787, AGN-PI, t. 354, f. 29.

92. Alonso González de Najera, Deseano y reparo de la guerra del reino de Chile, vol. 48 (1866) of *Colección de documentos ineditos para la historia de España*, 112 vols. (Madrid, 1842–1895), 48:213, 219.

93. Mario Góngora, *El vagabundaje en la frontera chilena* (Santiago, 1966), 6.

94. See Carlos Mayo, "Los renegades de la frontera bonaerense (1750–1810)," *Todo es historia* 18:220 (August 1985), 67–71.

95. AGN (Argentina), IX–I–5, Comandancia de Fronteras, cited in ibid., 67.

96. AGN (Argentina), IX–I–4–2, cited in ibid.

97. AGN (Argentina), IX–12–6–10, sumarios militares, cited in ibid.

98. Charles Boxer, *The Portuguese Seaborne Empire, 1415–1825* (New York, 1969), 31, 137.

99. Order to Pedro de Nava, Valle de Santa Rosa, Sept. 17, 1790, AGN-PI, t. 224, f. 29.

100. Jacabo Ugarte, Informe general del Comandante General de Provincias Internas, Arispe, Dec. 10, 1787, AGN-PI, t. 354, f. 36.

101. Reyes to Bucareli, México, Apr. 20, 1772, AGN-M, t. 14, exp. 3, f. 31.

102. Nentvig, *Descripción geográfica*, 123–24.

103. Rodríguez to Croix, Presidio de San Juan Bautista del Río Grande del Norte, Mar. 16, 1770, AGN-PI, t. 22, ff. 56–59.

104. Fayni to Bucareli, Durango, Feb. 28, 1772, AGI, Guadalajara, leg. 512 (106–614), Bancroft Library manuscript, Chapman no. 1916.

105. See Henry F. Dobyns, Paul H. Ezell, Alden W. Jones, and Greta S. Ezell, "What Were Nixoras?," *Southwestern Journal of Anthropology* 16 (Summer 1960), 230–58; see also Noel M. Loomis and Abraham P. Nasatir, *Pedro Vial and the Roads to Santa Fe* (Norman, 1967), 417.

106. Fayni to Bucareli, Durango, May 8, 1773, AGN-PI, t. 43, f. 116.

107. Fayni to Bucareli, Durango, May 8, 1773, AGN-PI, t. 43, ff. 122–123.

108. Fayni to Bucareli, Durango, June 19, 1773, AGN-PI, t. 43, ff. 6–14.

109. Preguntas hechas por el Comandante General de Oriente Don Ramón de Castro al del Poniente Don Pedro de Nava y sus respuestas, Saltillo, Mar. 30, 1791, AGN-PI, t. 224, exp. 5, f. 298.

110. Diary, José Antonio Pérez, Valle de Santa Rosa, Aug. 6, I- , AGN-PI, t. 22, f. 396.

111. J. Manuel Espinosa, "Governor Vargas in Colorado," *New Mexico Historical Review* 11 (April 1936), 186–87.

112. Eleanor B. Adams, "Bishop Tamarón's Visitation of New Mexico, 1760," *New Mexico Historical Review* (pt. 3) 28 (July 1953), 199.

113. Juan Agustín Morfí, *History of Texas, 1673–1770*, trans. Carlos Castañeda, 2 vols. (Albuquerque, 1935), 11:394–395.

114. Owen Lattimore, "The Frontier in History," in *Relaziono del X Congreso Internazionale di Scienze Storiche*, 1: Metodoligia Problemi Generali (Florence, 1955), 106–7.

PART II

FLORIDA AND THE SPANISH CARIBBEAN COMPLEX

INTRODUCTION

The first Spanish colonies in the Americas were in the Caribbean, on Hispaniola, Cuba, Puerto Rico, and surrounding islands. Colonization of the Caribbean followed different lines than in colonial Mexico. Until about the second decade of the sixteenth century, the Caribbean was the most important arena of Spanish colonization, but was rapidly eclipsed as a result of the demographic collapse of the indigenous population and the conquest of new territories on the American mainland in Mexico, Central America, and the Andean region, which offered greater rewards. The exhaustion of placer-gold deposits on the islands also contributed to the exodus of Spaniards to the mainland.[1]

During most of the colonial period the Caribbean remained a sparsely populated and contested frontier, with an economy based on ranching and farming and at a level of self-sufficiency supplemented by some commercial crops, such as tobacco. It was only in the middle and late eighteenth century that slave-based sugar production expanded in Cuba, Puerto Rico, and the section of Hispaniola that remained in Spanish hands.[2]

In the late sixteenth and seventeenth centuries the Caribbean became a contested frontier, as Spain's European rivals occupied islands such as Barbados, Grenada, and Guadeloupe, bypassed by the Spaniards, and won control of islands such as Jamaica and western Hispaniola, only lightly settled by the Spaniards. Moreover, a floating multinational population of pirates preyed upon shipping and raided Spanish settlements, and during periods of formal warfare proved to be useful auxiliaries. Spain's attention shifted to defending major ports and securing the shipping lanes used by the *flotas*, the flotillas of merchant ships escorted by warships that carried the bounty of Spanish America to Europe.

Spain adopted a new colonial policy in the Caribbean. The government shifted funds from the mainland colonies to subsidize defense costs in the Caribbean, and built large stone forts in major ports such as Veracruz, Havana, San Juan, and Cartagena, to name a few. Until 1762, Spanish defensive strategy rested on holding invaders at the ports. Florida fit into this defensive strategy, and for the period of Spanish occupation (1565–1763, 1783–1819) was a northern military outpost. Spain initially colonized Florida in response to the building of a French outpost called Fort Caroline. For several hundred years the military outpost and town San Agustín was the most important settlement in Florida. English colonization of the Carolinas and later Georgia only enhanced the strategic important of Florida.

The mission program was also different from the missions of the northern frontier of Mexico. The native peoples of northern Florida and the Georgia coast, the Timucuas, Apalaches, and Guales, were sedentary agriculturists, and the Franciscans built their mission complexes (church and convent) on the edge of existing villages. Indigenous social and political institutions, such as council houses, persisted. The mission evangelization program resembled more mission activity in the Caribbean among sedentary agriculturists, and not the *congregación* that characterized northern Mexico. The Florida missions also fell within the episcopal jurisdiction of Cuba. Finally, the Florida missions were victims of the contested frontiers, and were largely destroyed by English attacks.

The Seven Years War (1755–1763) had a greater impact on Florida than the Mexican frontier. The English occupied Havana during the war, and traded Havana back to the Spanish in exchange for Florida. In the aftermath of the war, Spain escalated the level of militarization in the Caribbean by instituting a large-scale military-reform program. Reliance on port fortifications proved to be illusionary, and Spain created professional armies supported by disciplined militias.[3] When reconquered from the English during the American Revolutionary War (1775–1783), Florida remained a strictly defensive frontier.

NOTES

1. James Lockhart and Stuart Schwartz, *Early Latin America: A History of Colonial Spanish America and Brazil* (Cambridge, 1983), 61–77.

2. On the development of sugar monoculture in Cuba, see Laird Bergad, *Cuban Rural Society in the Nineteenth Century: The Social and Economic History of Monoculture in Matanzas* (Princeton, 1990).

3. On the program of military reform in the Caribbean, see Allan Kuethe, *Cuba, 1753–1815: Crown, Military, and Society* (Knoxville, 1986). Other studies of Bourbon military reform include Allan Kuethe, *Military Reform and Society in New Granada, 1773–1808* (Gainesville, 1978); Christon Archer, *The Army in Bourbon Mexico, 1760–1810* (Albuquerque, 1977).

CHAPTER SEVEN

THE SPANISH COLONIAL FLORIDAS

PATRICIA R. WICKMAN

Any examination of the history of Florida and its relationship to the story of post-1492 Euro-dominion of the Americas must begin with a clear understanding of the very name itself, because misunderstanding has resulted from a tendency to judge its past by its present. Prior to its being claimed by the Spaniards, no variant of the name *Florida* existed as applied to any segment of what is now the southeastern United States. There is no reason to believe that any of the indigenous inhabitants of this region saw themselves as anything beyond a member of an elan (an extended-family group), or a village, a tribe, or regional polity called by anthropologists a chiefdom, with taxons based upon power animals, status individuals, and linguistic or geographic affinities. Thus, for example, an individual might be a member of Bear Clan, in the village of Abihka (the name of the headman of the village), in the Abihka tribe (which might have alliances with other similar villages nearby), all of whom were tributaries of the Coga kingdom.[1]

At the same time, it is also clear that discrete clans and tribes carried and transmitted information sets concerning other, and competitive, tribes and kingdoms whose territories ranged for hundreds of miles beyond the regional in scope. The Spanish historian Herrera reports such an example, during Juan Ponce de León's voyage of discovery in 1513 (or 1512, there is some difficulty in understanding the account). The natives of the Lucayan Islands (today's Bahamas) knew the Florida peninsula as Cautio.

They [the Spaniards] could not know, in the beginning, the name Florida had, in the opinion of the discoverers, because seeing that any point of land came out so that they had it for an island, and the Indians [whom they had with them as guides and interpreters] as it was a mainland, spoke the name of each province, and the Castilians thinking that they were deceiving them, but in the end, for their importunities, the Indians said, that it was called Cautio, a name that the Indians of the Lucayos put to that land, because the people of it carried their secret parts covered with leaves of palm woven in the manner of a plait.[2]

Juan Ponce de León, already a veteran explorer and governor of San Juan, Puerto Rico, had obtained a three-year charter from the crown to explore and settle Bimini, an island thought to be north of the Lucayos. Ponce de León left San Juan, sailed along the Atlantic side of the Bahamas, and sighted land somewhere on what is now the state's northwest coast.

And thinking this was an island, they called it la Florida, because it had a very beautiful view of many cool groves and it was level and uniform; and because, moreover, they discovered it in the time of the Feast of Flowers [the Christian ecclesiastical celebration known as "Easter" in English], Juan Ponce wished to conform to the name with these two reasons.[3]

But the name *Florida*, as it is applied in geopolitical terms by anyone who can open an atlas today, is also historically misleading. The Florida of the twentieth century comprises only a small portion of the area claimed by the Spaniards. The geographic trajectory of the territory, called during the First Spanish Period (1513–1763) La Florida, and during the British Period (1763–84) and Second Spanish Period (1784–1821) "the Floridas," and reunited by the United States (1821) as a single entity Florida, has been steadily downward. Consequently, when speaking of any aspect of the almost five hundred years since its initial expropriation by representatives of the Spanish crown, it is necessary to specify the synchronic borders, in order to establish the diachronic frontiers.

Europeans began their explorations of the North American continent at La Florida. But the frontiers of the territory claimed by Juan Ponce de León were directly influenced by a very limited knowledge of the physical characteristics of the land that he was claiming. As a consequence, the early sixteenth-century representations of the area are, in reality, a mixture of that limited knowledge and artists' conceptions of all the southern and eastern portion of what is now the United States, with the words *La Florida* superimposed.

There is, however, a critical and very real difference between what one may claim and what one may hold.

In the case of La Florida, the extent of the claim ultimately would be decided by the limits of Spain's royal purse, which was limited indeed in the sixteenth century. Within the century, after a sea-lane across the Atlantic was inaugurated by the Castilian representative, Cristóbal Colón, it was embarked upon by the Portuguese, the English, the French, and the Dutch in pursuit of their own economic aggrandizement. Subsequently, the monarchy at Castile became embroiled in what was, essentially, a two-faceted, three-continent struggle that began in 1492 and would not end, officially, until Spain's loss of its last "New World" colony, Cuba, in 1898. The sixteenth century demarcated the high point of the struggle.

As one facet, Spain's soldiers and colonizers in the Americas sought to dominate the indigenous inhabitants and the radically varying environments of the lands they claimed. At the same time, the Spaniards had to stave off the encroachments of competing European powers who adopted the legalistic position that "effective occupation" was the single criterion of sovereignty. Inextricably mixed with the Spaniards' struggles for secular success was a very real determination to turn the peoples whom they found away from what they saw as the harmful teachings of the "devil" and back toward their "natural" evolutionary path to "god"—in this case, the Roman Catholic god.[4]

Meanwhile, the overlords in Castile fought another facet of the war: politically, with words; militarily, with costly troops; and religiously, with all the real and imagined power of their particularistic god, to consolidate their hegemony and preclude the need for continuing physical confrontations that the Crown could ill afford.

Spain's coffers were being depleted constantly by the external demands of warfare in defense of Castilian prerogatives and the Roman Catholic faith in Europe and North Africa. Internally, its needs were to support a growing bureaucracy, which frequently was unsupported by recalcitrant quasi-autonomous states allied with the crown of Castile, and to consolidate monarchical power in the face of continuous and growing challenges from a nobility that constantly had to be bribed with greater prerogatives in order to maintain a tenuous alliance with that monarchy.

In the case of La Florida, as in other new realms of Spain across the Atlantic, this need to maintain a delicate balance between crown interests and the new possibilities available for enhancement of personal wealth and status would result in the granting of specific concessions to men (always men, literally) who would agree to increase the coffers of the crown by the fruits of their "discoveries." Standard facets of the *asientos*, or royal agreements, with the explorers included certain exclusive civil and military prerogatives and, sometimes, the legal right to pass them on; freedom from various taxes; and the claim to a significant portion of the profits. Responsibilities included financially under-writing most of the start-up costs (a sizable investment); founding a city and building a fort; and pacifying and converting the natives. in other words: discover, conquer, pacify, and populate. In the case of La Florida, as in many other areas of its new provinces, the crown would find parts of its profits smuggled away and its power usurped, and would feel itself forced to renege on its concessions in order to reestablish control.[5]

The creation of a European La Florida would be an outgrowth of all of these power struggles. Its ultimate loss, to the young United States in 1821, would be the result of Spains unwillingness to continue the struggle in the face of unacceptably diminishing politico-economic returns. In the meantime, how-ever, Spanish dominion of La Florida and the Floridas would last for 287 years. it will be the year 2108 before Florida will have been a part of the United States for as long as it was a part of the Spanish empire.

Many social scientists do not choose to view Florida, historically, as a part of the Latin America.[6] However, despite the fact that the primary language of the contemporary state is not Spanish, many Floridians nonetheless preserve a strong affinity for their Iberian heritage. Latin American economics, politics, and culture continue to have direct and significant impact upon Florida.

NATIVE AMERICANS IN THE SIXTEENTH CENTURY

Current archaeological evidence indicates that the ancestors of the indigenous groups who met the Spaniards in the Southeast in the sixteenth century mi-grated eastward across the great river now known as the Mississippi sometime around ten to twelve thousand years ago. However, the application of new facets of hard-science technology to the old question of exactly when Native Americans became "native" to the Americas is producing some exciting results. Biogenetic researchers, using the mitochondria of native DNA as a type of regressive genetic clock, have posited dates of twenty-one to forty-two thou-sand years since the first groups migrated from their Oriental gene pool.[7] Although their findings are not universally embraced by social scientists, the results are nonetheless provocative and worthy of pursuit.

Even as non-natives continue to discuss a past not their own, however, the descendants of the earliest Americans have held to their own views on their origins, which generally have been reported as "legends," and given little credence by non-Indian researchers. Among the Maskókî-speaking peoples of the Southeast (whom the British would later refer to generically as "Creeks"), there is a tradition that their ancestors did not migrate from anywhere else but, rather, were created in the Southeast.[8] If one views their occupation of the area in this light, it becomes even easier to understand why these Native Americans fought so ferociously in the nineteenth century against United States military forces and whites' unilateral determination to remove them from the land that gave them their very lives.

Among the Seminoles and Miccosukees of Florida, who are some of the cultural survivors and inheritors of these southeastern Maskókî-speaking groups, there is an alternative tradition held by some that their ancestors migrated to the Southeast, but by water rather than overland as non-Indian researchers posit.[9] Perhaps this is a cultural memory of trading contacts or limited migrations, from the seventeenth century and earlier, between peninsular La Florida groups and the indigenous peoples of the Caribbean.

The Seminoles, who live across south Florida today, are generally considered by Euro-American social scientists not to be descendants of the earlier inhabitants of that specific area, but, rather, to have migrated southward into that area in the nineteenth century and to have filled a void left by the extinction of the earlier groups.[10] The Seminoles, however, still maintain oral traditions linking themselves to peninsular ancestors and hunting grounds, irrespective of later Euro-American imposed geopolitical boundaries. The discrepancies between these Native Americans' views of their past and the views held by many non-native researchers have yet to be resolved. This is one point upon which the results of the DNA researches may shed important light.

At least one current researcher has recently posited that the language isolate that the Timuguanas (who lived in the area that is now northeast Florida) were speaking when the first Europeans reached them, in the sixteenth century, was a derivative of Arawak, a language originally spoken, and still spoken today, by indigenous groups in eastern South America and the Caribbean.[11] If this is correct (and the theory is controversial), then this cultural memory of the Seminoles becomes even more intriguing because the Timuguana speakers also are considered by Euro-American social scientists to have become culturally and genetically extinct by 1763. Their remnants are not generally considered to have been subsumed by their Maskókî neighbors, as were the survivors of other groups. Even if the Seminoles' oral tradition in this regard is only coincidental, it does not deserve to be disregarded.

In addition to controversies over their origins, there is also controversy over the number of natives who lived in the various areas when the Spaniards first encountered them. In the historical analyses of the last fifty years alone, estimates have ranged upward from about 10,000 occupants of the area now called Florida to a current high of from 200,000 to 400,000.[12] Two elements, at least, have facilitated these rising estimates. First is the growing database of archaeological and historical information that revises upward the estimate of the number of native settlements in various regions. Second is the increasing refinement of methods in floral and faunal analysis of archaeological materials. From this analysis researchers can posit the nutritional value of the food sources available within a given environmental niche, and the subsequent number of occupants that niche could have supported. Regardless of whether or not the current high figure is correct, two points are accepted: by 1492, Native Americans had become even more adept at exploiting the environmental niches available to them than has been thought; and earlier low demographic estimates are far too low.[13] This is another facet of southeastern history on which research continues.

In order to form some picture of the Native American world in the Southeast, both spatially and culturally, as it existed when the Europeans arrived, it is useful—but by no means definitive—to use language as a delineator. Such information is not definitive because archaeological and documentary evidence indicates that the territories of linguistic groups sometimes overlapped and that normally competing polities could also form political and military alliances for reasons of expedience not associated with cultural affinities. Current research indicates that the major linguistic families used in the Southeast at the time of contact were the following.

Miskokean, a widely used language, later would be called "Creek," arbitrarily, by the British, although this generic term did, and continues to, obscure much social and political diversity. Its speakers lived in today's western Georgia and eastern Alabama, in parts of lower Tennessee, Mississippi, and Lousiana, and southward throughout the peninsula of Florida. As the frontiers of La Florida diminished, over the colonial period, it was the Maskókî speakers whose history would remain most closely linked with the area and many of whose descendants would make their final, half-century-long stand against removal inside the foreshortened borders of the territory and the state. Mikosukî, the language of most of the members of today's Seminole tribe of Florida, is a Maskókî dialect, and other Seminole tribal members are known today simply as "Creek" (Maskókî) speakers.

Iroquoian was, and is, represented by the Cherokees, whose territory ranged across the mountainous regions of eastern Tennessee and western North Carolina. Catawban appears to have been spoken in the Carolina Piedmont, and bands of Algonquian-speaking Shawnees lived in the upper Southeast also, although little is known of them. At least two language isolates may have existed, although their uniqueness is controversial. One, Yuchi, may also have been Siouan, and was the language of a group generally considered to have lived west of the Appalachian Mountains in eastern Tennessee. The other,

Timuguana, was the language spoken by a large number of residents of the northeast Florida area, included the crown of the peninsula, eastward from Apalachie to the Atlantic, southward up the St. Johns River, northward to Jekyl Island (Georgia) on the coast, and inland to the lower reaches of the Altamaha River. As mentioned earlier, this may even have been an Arawakan dialect.

The remaining major groups of peninsular La Florida and its western coast were also speaking forms of Maskókî. The Tequestas ranged across the lower eastern peninsula, in what are today Broward, Dade, and Monroe counties (Fort Lauderdale and Miami to Key West), and inland, probably into the hammocks of the Everglades. We have only limited information about this group. The Calusas, about whom we know somewhat more, were aggressive and successful and dominated the lower southwest coast, from around Tampa Bay southward, and inland to the lake we know as Okeechobee (from the Maskókî words, u-kee [water] + ho-bee [big]). Their political and military influence extended across the peninsula: the Tequestas were their tributaries and may have been tied to them by blood kinship as well.

The Abalachi, whose domain extended from the Aucilla River westward just beyond the Ochlockonee River and from the Georgia border to the Gulf of Mexico, are much better known because they were one of the two groups with whom the Spaniards had the most interactions. The largest of the seventeenth-century missions was in Abalachi, and its agricultural production was an important element of La Florida Mississippian society. Warriors were high-status individuals, were accorded privileges and exemptions, received honorific titles, had their own discrete symbology, and controlled their followers with a greater degree of autonomy than their European counterparts of the period.

In warfare, prosecuted either as single, decisive confrontations or as hit-and-run attacks, each side sought to destroy their enemies' villages; to bring home slaves or human trophies; and to capture enemy women who were incorporated into the victorious tribe as sexual objects or wives. Far too little has been made by historians of the activities of these women as principal instruments of a dynamism that was a central feature of southeastern Native American culture, through their roles as cultural mediators and transmitters economy. The other group about which we have much information is the Timuguanas, whose territory was described, above. The Timucuanas comprised at least six major subgroups, with whom the Spaniards had extensive interactions over their colonial period.[14]

The polities sharing a primary language had, for the most part, commonalities of clan and tribal affinity systems, political structures, and cosmogonies, although there existed numerous regional variations on the central themes. Many of these themes had been incorporated into the lives of tribes across the

Southeast and into the northern and central peninsula over the preceding two to four hundred years, as facets of what archaeologists call Mississippianism or the Mississippian Religion. This complex belief system was manifested in an expanded elite class, including hereditary rulers, priests, and warriors; the construction of temple mounds and ceremonial centers; the production of specific ceramic types; an esoteric cosmogony supported by many unique symbols; complex funerary rites; and an annual liturgical cycle punctuated by ceremonial events, which included a ritual ball game that bridged the spiritual and temporal worlds. By the time the Spaniards arrived, however, the ideological force of the cult may have begun to wane and, culturally, much of the Southeast already may have been in a transitional phase.[15]

Within the geographic extensions of the cultural systems, there were usually a number of dialects of the primary language, any of which may or may not have been mutually intelligible to its speakers. In addition to sharing certain organizational and ideological systems, most of the members of these extended cultural families also had in common an internal hierarchical structure of political allegiances.

Social scientists use several taxonomies to describe these systems of political allegiance, all centering on the English word *chief*; they are called "simple," and "compound" or "paramount" chiefdoms. A simple chiefdom generally implies two levels of authority: one leader exercised control over several villages. Many such systems existed within a larger framework, as well: a paramount chief might control several simple chiefdoms, and receive tribute in goods and/or service.[16]

However, it is important to remember that, as employed by Native Americans, the concept of a chief differed in several important ways from the European concept generally implied by this word. First, the power structure that accrued to the title was horizontal as well as vertical. That is, decision making was not a unilateral process that traveled up a vertical chain of command and stopped at the top. Rather, it was in many ways a horizontal process that required that a consensus be reached by the leader and his headmen (secondary tier of leaders), in conclave. Second, the office of chief was neither purely elective nor appointive. The accession to the position of chief was a combination of heredity, personal ability, and the approbation of constituents. As such, there was a direct element of reciprocity of expectations in this type of leadership that is not present in quite the same manner in the European concept.

Furthermore, kinship systems in the Southeast were (and remain) matrilineal. That is, inheritance of clan affiliation, for example, passed through the mother, and inheritance of leadership passed through the chief's eldest sister to her son. In order to further strengthen clan control, therefore, elites sometimes took their own sisters as first wives. It appears that this option was not available to other social strata, although sororate polygyny (the practice of taking multiple wives who were close kin to each other) was, and continued to be an option, at least into the warrior ranks.[17]

By the sixteenth century, there existed throughout the Southeast a number of complex chiefdoms, separated from each other by what we might refer to as buffer zones. Across these zones, members of one chiefdom carried on recurring wars against others. These wars served, externally, to increase territorial control and the tribute base of a chief. Internally, they also perpetuated and expanded a warrior class that was a salient of social values, lifeways, and language. They deserve much more study.

Within these complex chiefdoms, life was not always static either, however. Dissension sometimes arose between or among villages and war ensued. At other times, a chief at one level or another might feel that he or she (chiefs were not always males, but female leaders seem to have been much fewer in numbers and to have existed only within certain tribes) was powerful enough to break away from his condition of vassalage and to rule independently. Inevitably, the matter would be settled by warfare. If the subordinate chief proved himself and his followers strong enough to defy the paramount chief, a new chiefdom would come into being. The coming of the Europeans, with their advanced weaponry and their separate politico-military agendas, would altar this system irrevocably.[18]

The economies of the tribes were based on agriculture, internal production, hunting and gathering, and trade. There were exceptions to this, especially the Calusas and Tequestas of the southern peninsula, for whom no significant evidence of sedentary agriculture has thus far been found. Even among those groups that had long since domesticated corn and pumpkins and beans, and begun to produce a surplus for extended use, the economies still relied substantially upon seasonal rounds of hunting/fishing and gathering to provide game, fish, nuts, berries, and edible and medicinal plants, and to permit sites of intensive occupation to recover from resource depletion.[19] Internal production included the fabrication of utilitarian, decorative, and ceremonial items, such as ceramic cookwares and funerary wares; shell and metal pectorals and pendants; and bone, wood, and lithic tools and ornamental items. Hides provided much clothing, but the peoples of the coastal areas and peninsula, where the aerophyte today known as "Spanish moss" was available, were also using it as a body covering.

The trade systems established by the southeastern natives were extensive and well used, and their networks of trails provide further evidence of the dynamic nature of Native American life.[20] Tribes hundreds of miles apart maintained trade relations and, in the case of war parties and diplomatic missions, contacts sometimes extended for fifteen hundred miles. Long-established trails intersected at natural geographic and social "hubs," such as those at (present-day) Nashville and Chattanooga, Tennessee, and Montgomery, Alabama. River valleys, such as those of the Savannah, Coosa, and Chattahoochee rivers, provided natural arteries of transport for goods and information.

On the peninsula of La Florida, a major east-west artery ran from Jacksonville along the Gulf Coast all the way to Mexico. Native representatives from the interior of the continent could send goods southward to Jacksonville and, from there, up the St. Johns River to the ports of the lower southeastern coast and thence to the Bahamas and Cuba. Along the west coast, water routes connected the interior and Apalachicola Bay, Tampa Bay, and Cuba.[21] By the time the Spaniards arrived, many of these routes had carried regional wares, such as shells and other decorative and ceremonial items, northward and copper, galena, and mica southward for hundreds of years. The geographic position of La Florida made it a special area of intersection with the Bahamas and the Caribbean. Bird feathers were regular exports and turtles were imported.[22]

With the coming of the Europeans, there would be a literal explosion of new trade goods available, along with numerous "gift" items that the Spaniards, and later the English and the French, used not only as elements of their own colonial economy, but also as overt tools of cultural manipulation and social control. The eighteenth century would mark a high point in traversing these land and water networks. In the competition for control of native populations, however, the Spaniards would not be the winners in the long run, for two principal reasons.

First, the cost of supplying such goods rose geometrically throughout the colonial period as the natives' dependence on them rose and as the Spanish crown's ability to afford them declined. Second, as French and English colonization physically and politically diminished La Florida, over the seventeenth and eighteenth centuries, the quantity and quality of their trade goods (especially the English wares) outstripped those of the Spaniards. By the Second Spanish Period (1784–1821), not only the British and French but the citizens of the new United States as well would be on Spain's doorstep in the Floridas and their competition would finally prove too costly for Spain.

Given the rich, complex, and interrelated world depicted here, it would be impossible to overstate the importance of dynamism as the central element of the pre-contact paradigm. Such an image, however, directly contradicts the static model of life among the southeastern Native American groups that has been envisioned by many researchers up until the last generation, and thus changes completely the way we must envision the impact of the Europeans on their evolutionary trajectory. In the static model of native-European contact, through the agencies of technologically enhanced warfare, social manipulation, and profound population decline brought about by the inadvertent introduction of European pathogens and by labor exploitation, the post-contact evolutionary path of Native American culture has been viewed as a rapid and continuous decline, to and including the climax of extinction in the cases of most southeastern tribes.

While it is incontrovertible that thousands of Native Americans died as a result of European contact, we must begin to refocus on the living. In a dynamic model, we must view the coming of the Europeans not as a permanent interruption of a closed (static) system, but, rather, as a new variable (albeit a major one) that was introduced into an already continuously evolving (dynamic) social equation.

The Mississippianism of the southeastern indigenous groups was already evolving when the Spaniards entered La Florida. If we view change as a constant, then, we can more clearly realize what Native Americans have known all along: that they are not historical orphans—the flotsam and jetsam of a horrendous battle for primacy on a cultural sea—but, more correctly, the proud and enduring inheritors of a heritage of cultures over twelve thousand years old and far more flexible and resilient than those by which they are surrounded, today.

ARRIVAL OF THE SPANIARDS

By 1513, Spanish explorers had traversed the Caribbean and the Gulf of Mexico, partially reconnoitered the coasts of what is now Mexico, the Yucatán peninsula, and parts of the coasts of Central and South America. In that year, Balboa crossed the isthmus at Darien (now Panama) to the Pacific Ocean. But the excitement of discovery was, in no guise, satiating. It only served to increase enthusiasm for discovery as the explorers, conquerors, and colonizers decided that none of those places offered sufficient natural resources, or population bases robust enough, to bear the extended burden of recompensing them for the Herculean efforts, including the all-or-nothing personal financial investments, which had been required to make the push across the Atlantic.

Juan Ponce de León, the Spaniard who established Castilian claims and gave the world the name La Florida, was neither the first Spaniard nor, probably, the first European to reach the peninsula. The records of the Casa de Contratación (Spain's House of Trade) show that Spanish ships, undoubtedly slavers, stopped on the southwest coast of the peninsula at least from 1510.[23] The Calusas, who dominated this area and were themselves in the business of forming tributary settlements of the Caribs who came to their coast, may have resented the competition.[24] They certainly formed a rapid and abiding dislike of the Spaniards and their bellicosity soon became a known factor among Spanish explorers who, in the early years of movement into La Florida, traveled frequently to the harbors of the western coast.

The exploration and settlement of La Florida proceeded in two separate phases. From 1513 to 1557, the crown repeatedly offered the standard rewards and concessions to the succession of men who attempted to establish a permanent Spanish presence. As the conquest of New Spain (Mexico) proceeded, from 1519, and as information concerning the Gulf Coast grew, the settlement of La Florida also included the objective of linking the two Spanish realms by an overland route protected by fortified missions and settlements. This plan never materialized, although Spain tried. The Spaniards explored much of the Southeast, learned a great deal about what they could expect from future investments, and effected numerous settlements, which ultimately failed.

The second phase began in 1557 when Philip II of Spain, reiterating the determination of the French to target any areas not effectively occupied by the Spaniards despite ongoing negotiations with his government, decided that the strategic importance of La Florida outweighed any other considerations and that a permanent Spanish presence must be effected there. Consequently, in 1565, Pedro Mendéndez de Avilés established a settlement called San Agustín (now St. Augustine) that has endured for 432 years.

PHASE I: EXPLORATION

Following the establishment of their claim in 1513, a steady stream of Spanish explorers focused their attention on the potential of La Florida. Diego Miruelo reached Abalachi Bay in 1516. Francisco Hernández de Cordova also sailed to the southwest coast, in 1517. Alonzo Alvarez de Pineda prepared the first map of the Gulf Coast in 1519. In a second, and final, attempt to settle his grant of peninsular La Florida, Ponce de León subsequently made another voyage to the lower west coast, in 1521. This attempt failed also, however, because the natives (probably the Calusas again) drove him off. This try cost Ponce de León not only his investment, but also his life.

In that same year, however, two Spanish slavers, Pedro de Quejo and Francisco Cordillo, encountered a native land on the Atlantic Coast, which they reported in such glowing terms that their sponsor, Lucas Vásquez de Ayllón, took its story to Spain in 1523 and told it to his friend, Pietro Martiere d'Anghiera (Peter Martyr).[25] Martyr's account of "Chicora," together with the stories that Ayllón told, gave rise to a legend of a "New Andalucía," filled with all the natural abundance of its Iberian counterpart. Throughout the sixteenth and seventeenth centuries, it would lure the French and English into direct competition with the Spaniards for that part of La Florida between 32° and 39° north latitude.[26]

A second legend, born of the explorations of a French-sponsored Italian, Giovanni da Verrazzano, in 1523–24, stepped up the race for dominion of the North American continent. Verrazzano, like so many others, sought a westward passage to the Orient. He claimed to have found a river, originating on the east coast, which connected very closely with the Pacific Ocean. Cartographers placed it variously at points between 34° and 45° north latitude, and it came to be known as Verrazzano's "false sea."[27] Needless to say, neither the sea nor the passage existed, but together the legends of a "New Andalucía and a Way to the Orient" would provide impetus for almost two centuries of North American exploration and settlement in which a dwindling La Florida played a continuing role.

Lucas Vásquez de Ayllón made two further attempts at settlement. In 1523 he sent Pedro de Quejo to reconnoiter, and in 1526 he established San Miguel de Gualdape (on the Georgia coast). He carried six hundred seamen, plus Spanish men, women, children, and black slaves as settlers. The colony lasted only three months. The grant obtained by Panfilo de Narváez, Ayllón's old enemy, in 1528, was more productive, in terms of information, but still failed to plant a settlement. Narváez landed an army of four hundred, with forty horses, near Tampa Bay, with the objective of exploring the land from the peninsula westward to New Spain. He marched northward, into Apalachie territory, where illness halted his trek. He ordered boats built to continue the trip by water, but lost almost all of his men to the sea. Only five, including Alvar Núñez Cabeza de Vaca, survived, and after eight years of captivity among Texas natives, they reached Mexico in 1536. Narváez himself disappeared.

Cabeza de Vaca wrote of his fascinating experiences and also told Spaniards that La Florida was the richest country in the world. However, he turned down an opportunity to return with Hernando de Soto, and it would be left to the Soto expedition (1539–43) to give Europe its first detailed account of the interior of the Southeast, including firsthand accounts of some of the most complex native societies on the northern continent.

Soto and his five hundred to seven hundred soldiers (accounts disagree), with horses, pigs, and myriad supplies, marched up the peninsula and, ultimately, across what are today nine southern states. They stopped at or near native villages; took hostages and bearers from one village as guides to the next; and left a trail of ill will, along with European beads, hawk bells, armor parts, and other items that archaeologists are still encountering.[28] Although Hernando de Soto died in 1542, somewhere near the Mississippi River at present-day Natchez, survivors reached Tampico, on the Panuco River in New Spain, on September 10, 1543. They had participated in the single largest *entrada* into the southeastern continent that Spain would ever make. Ultimately, four written accounts would document the expedition, offering vivid accounts of an indigenous world in the throes of kaleidoscopic change.[29]

Evidence for the most obvious facet of this change came not only from the accounts of the Soto expedition, but also from Tristán de Luna y Arellano, who attempted, in 1559–61, to locate some of the chiefdoms and villages that Solo had encountered, and thereby learned of this major consequence of European contact.[30] Luna named his landing place Bahía de Santa María Filipina (Mobile Bay), moved on to Pensacola Bay, and searched inland from there for Coca, a paramount chiefdom described by the survivors from the Soto expedition as large and wealthy (it covered much territory in present-day Tennessee, Georgia, and Alabama). Instead of wealth, he found that many of the formerly populous, thriving villages were empty and deserted. The natives told them that the people had died of disease.

Juan Pardo, the leader of the next major expedition across part of the southeastern interior (1566–68) would find the effects of disease as well.[31] Smallpox, measles, colds, and influenza more than decimated the indigenous populations in the century following initial contact. Their effects would decrease over time, but not as radically as the native population would decrease. This demographic collapse has been the focus of increased research in the last two generations, as social scientists attempt to calculate the rate of population decline and the impact of radical population loss on the cultural coherence of the groups involved.[32]

The impact of the pathogens introduced by the Europeans would be hard to overemphasize; it has been called "the worst demographic disaster, the worst holocaust, in the history of the world . . ."[33] The rate of demographic loss in La Florida is calculated at a factor of ten for the first 170 years following contact.[34] That is, even if the base population is assumed at a conservative estimate of several hundred thousand, that number dropped to less than twenty thousand by the end of the First Spanish Period, in 1763.

Even beyond the consequences of population loss among the indigenous groups, the consequences of cultural loss became permanent factors of native life, and major factors in their intercourse with European residents after 1565. Disease does not respect age, gender, or status. Death took not only those men and women at the lowest end of the socioeconomic spectrum, whose work propelled society as their children replenished it; it also removed those in high-status positions, whose guidance regulated the internal functioning of society (family, clan, and village leaders). It took as well those who managed the external relations of the towns and the chiefdoms (in diplomacy and war), and mediated between society and the cosmos (shamans, priests, and informal keepers of memory and traditions).

The lives of the Native Americans henceforth would be a delicate balance. Cultural continuity, the maintenance of warfare as balance-of-power politics, and tribal autonomy would have to be balanced constantly against cultural realignment in the face of demographic decline, pressures to assimilate (constant, but fluctuating in intensity) in the forms of Spanish colonization and evangelization, and the lure of European trade goods. The fact of their descendants' survival to this day is, however, proof of their success with the process. The flexibility and resilience of their cosmogonies continue to be strong survival mechanisms.

PHASE II: SETTLEMENT

The Spanish explorations of the first phase left the crown with a fairly clear image of La Florida. There were no major stores of gold or silver. The freshwater pearls and quartz crystals that were found were of insufficient quantity and quality to justify further expenditures of men and matériel. The land available offered some hope of creating an agricultural base, but the human resources—the Native Americans who would comprise the labor force—were, from the Spanish point of view, at worst too belligerent to pacify easily and, at best, mobile and relatively few in numbers and hard to control. By mid-century, the Spaniards had not found their New Andalucía or a shortcut to the Orient. Why bother to keep trying?

The answer to that question lay not in La Florida, but in the Caribbean and in France. Twice in 1555, French corsairs captured Havana ("Pearl of the Antilles") was the critical rendezvous point for the *flotas*, the treasure fleets that assembled in the "New World" to transport its riches to the Old World. The crown came close to losing control of the Caribbean. In 1556, Spain and France temporarily settled trade disputes in the Indies with the treaty of Vaucelles, which forbade the French to navigate, traffic, or trade there without license from Philip II.[35] The treaty had political, but very little real, value. By 1557, the Spanish crown decided that its claim to La Florida must be upheld, for strategic reasons. The route of the treasure flotas lay too close to the coast of La Florida to allow its ports to fall into enemy hands.

The unsuccessful Luna expedition was the first of four attempts in the period 1559–64 to develop a port and fortified settlements across the southeast. On the Atlantic Coast, Martín Díaz (1560) and Angel de Villafane (1561) failed to settle near Santa Elena (now Beaufort, South Carolina). Lucas Vásquez de Ayllón the Younger also failed, in 1563, to settle further northward (near present Chesapeake Bay).

The French, pursuing their own belief that land unoccupied was land unclaimed, raced to the Atlantic Coast also. Jean Ribault established a short-lived colony at Charlesfort (South Carolina) in 1562. In 1564 and 1565, two further expeditions finally brought the two countries into a military confrontation that impeded French incursions on the Atlantic Coast. Both were promulgated by Gaspard de Coliny, first admiral of France, and both were composed almost exclusively of Huguenots (French Calvinists), an additional affront to the Roman Catholic Spaniards. The first, under Rene Goulaine de Laudonnibre, in 1564 constructed Fort Caroline, at the mouth of the River of May (today's St. Johns River near Jacksonville, Florida). The following year, Ribault sailed back to reinforce the colony, but not before the Spanish crown had set upon a course of action to interdict French claims. Pedro Menéndez de Avilés was captain general of the fleet of New Spain and one of the best seamen in Spain. He sailed in 1565 with a royal asiento to destroy the French settlement and establish, once and for all, Spanish hegemony in La Florida. The story of his swift military action and the destruction of the French and their fort is an exciting one and contains all the classic elements of Spanish New World zeal.[36] Its climax was the surprise attack on the fort during a hurricane, and its denouement was the execution of French prisoners at an inlet about fifty-five miles south of the fort, which is still known today as Matanzas (a place of slaughter).

By his actions, Menéndez not only destroyed the French settlements, but also succeeded where all of his predecessors had failed. He established two presidios, or fortified colonies: San Agustín (1565) and Santa Elena (1566). The former, now St. Augustine, Florida, was intended as a secondary fort and mission site. It, however, endured as the first permanent European settlement in what is now the United States. The latter, which Menéndez intended as his capital of La Florida and the Atlantic doorway to New Spain, enjoyed a brief period of success but ultimately failed and was abandoned in 1587.

LA FLORIDA DURING THE FIRST SPANISH PERIOD

Over the period 1565 to 1572 (when he returned to Spain), Pedro Menéndez set in place all the basic elements of the transfer of Spanish culture to La Florida. His initial colonists included not only soldiers for defense of the colonies, but also men and women chosen for their possession of specific skills necessary to the order and functioning of a community. Santa Elena and San Agustín were stratified communities, with all the social classes present in other Spanish towns represented, except that of grandees. His economic base was a tightly woven blend of personal investments (his own and many family members') and crown support. Menéndez was to prove a master in manipulating these accounts to his own advantage in order to satisfy the objectives of the crown, even as he turned profits back into the settlement process, and tried to recoup personal costs. In this, he was really doing no more than many other New World opportunists, but he did it well.

To institute civil government, Menéndez exercised his authority as *adelantado* (a governor with military as well as civil authority and with special tax exemptions) to fill as many administrative positions as possible with members of his extended family, creating what a biographer called an "Asturian dynasty" within La Florida's government.[37] Local government included a standard town *consejo* or council, with its governing *cabildo*, treasury officials, military commanders, supply keepers, and notarial officials. Along with order came typical disorder—smuggling, bribery, embezzling, malfeasance, and even mutiny— with a classic Spanish penchant for litigiousness at their nexus. This family rule lasted beyond the lifetime of Menéndez, but over the late sixteenth and early seventeenth centuries the crown slowly regained control by filling local offices with individuals loyal to itself rather than the Menéndez family and bringing La Florida into its legal system of *audiencias* (supreme courts) and viceroyalties.

Menéndez planned to set up a defensive perimeter along the coast of the Spanish Southeast by setting up forts northward to Newfoundland, southward to Cayo Viscaino (Biscayne Bay, Florida), and around the peninsula. Ultimately, the few he could afford to set up failed because of uncooperative natives and lack of supplies. There was no viable system by which the Spaniards could defend all of La Florida. Over the remainder of this Spanish occupation, Spain was unable to stop the march of French and English settlements on the borders of "its" territory. At Roanoke, Charleston, and Savannah, the English gained footholds on Spanish-claimed lands. The Spaniards established Pensacola, on the Gulf, in 1698, as a counter to French incursions, but French control of the Mississippi River came to pass nonetheless. By 1763, Spain's southeastern presidio was virtually surrounded by opposing powers. La Florida never became self-supporting, although it did develop some aspects of an independent economy. Its principal income was from a *situado* or fiscal subsidy. First approved in 1570, the payment was to be collected annually and was based primarily on the number of *plazas*, or places, in the garrison. The first payment, in 1571, was calculated on rations and pay for 150 men, plus the cost of powder, ammunition, and "commodities."[38] The crown was paying only for its soldiers, of course, not for dependents. In the 1580s, the population included 240 women and children as well as black slaves (less than 100). The subsidies came first from the Tierra Firme treasury (Panama), then from Veracruz (1573), and finally from Mexico City (1594 on). Despite early researchers' contentions that the situado frequently was in arrears and San Agustín constantly teetered on the edge of starvation, it now appears that payments were more often regular than irregular, at least up to the mid-seventeenth century.[39]

To present an image of La Florida as a secure, well-subsidized presidio on the Carrera de Indias would be erroneous, however, at any point in its colonial history. But the time has come to put aside the earlier image of a constantly starving garrison outpost, marginalized by Spain and the world. All of the basic elements of Spanish society existed there, and they flourished—abbreviated only by geography and resources. Spanish civil, military, and religious institutions constituted the traditional bases of life in La Florida, just as in other Spanish enclaves, and although the reports of their officials contain myriad complaints about things they did not have, much recent archaeological and documentary research has begun to put these in perspective by shifting the focus to the quality and range, if not the quantity, of things they did have.

Members of the colony, whatever their primary professions, frequently engaged in auxiliary commercial enterprises. Craftsmen and merchants sold European and local wares in San Agustín, and a farmer's market offered agricultural goods. Corn was the staple crop in La Florida, rather than wheat. In their off-duty hours, soldiers provided fresh game for local tables. In the seventeenth century, a growing cattle industry centered on the plains of the north-central peninsula (around present-day Gainesville). Hides and tallow traveled down the Suwannee River to the Gulf and to Cuba for sale, along with agricultural surplus from the Abalachi missions. A typical range of colonial entrepreneurial activities supplied colonists and soldiers with a wide variety of standard goods, from shoes to charcoal to chickens, but also with suits of cotton-padded armor that the Spaniards found far more effective than their own metal armor for repelling native arrows. Fish and shellfish were abundant; shipbuilding and the production of naval stores were other "natural" segments of the economy.

An interesting example of the citizenry of La Florida and the typical values that they embodied and transferred to the new Spanish-colonial microcosm was one Alonso de Olmos, from Castile.[40] Señor Olmos and his wife and their large family left Spain in 1569 to begin a new life at Santa Elena. By profession, he was a tailor and, with one of his sons, he made not only clothing, but also the cotton-padded armor that the Spaniards found they needed in La Florida. Olmos was also an enterprising man, not content to starve his family on a tailor's income. He raised hogs, ran a tavern (always a good bet in a garrison town), and loaned money to his neighbors.

But Olmos was also a proud and contentious man and, in 1572, he ran afoul of Governor Don Diego de Velasco, also a proud—and powerful—man. Velasco was married to María, the illegitimate daughter of the adelantado, Pedro Menéndez de Avilés. When Velasco ordered all able-bodied residents to help rebuild their burned fort, Olmos refused to serve. He was no soldier, he said, to be ordered around. He was a free-born citizen of Castile and a *vecino* of Santa Elena, protected by ancient municipal privilege. The governor, enraged, knocked Olmos to the ground and ordered him hanged. Finally, a Jesuit priest intervened and, rather than being hanged, Olmos was sent to work on the fort in chains.

Despite this object lesson in the realistic applications of power, Olmos clung to his putative rights under Spanish law. Four years later, after a verbal confrontation, with witnesses who placed blame on each side, Olmos filed a lawsuit against his old nemesis, Velasco. He claimed that the governor had insulted his daughter, María de Lara, during the religious procession on the Day of the True Cross, shoving her out of line and calling her a "proven bitch," then taunting Olmos: "See the Lutheran going to the synagogue!"[41] At the trial, Velasco denied insulting the father, but said that Olmos was after all a tradesman (therefore inferior to himself, a nobleman), and his daughter's reputation was not any too good. Olmos, for his part, reminded the court that his family were "Old Christians" and "we hold ourselves, in our being, to be as honorable as he."[42] Unfortunately, no documents are available to tell us the outcome of the suit, but perhaps there is some symmetry in the fact that, in that same year, Velasco lost his governorship when he himself was arrested and charged with misappropriation of Santa Elena's payroll monies.[43] La Florida may have been small, but its settlers brought, within themselves, the same society that they had left in Spain, regardless of the size of the settlement.

By 1717, the colony also was engaged in exporting oranges (introduced to the Americas by the Spaniards), an enterprise that constitutes a major facet of Florida's economy today. In that year, the first shipload of the fruit went to the English settlement at Charleston. Residents of English colonies as far away as New York and Philadelphia also enjoyed La Florida oranges by the 1730s.[44] San Agustín and Charleston, not natural political allies, were natural geographical allies and they formed a critical, albeit illegal, trading relationship in the first quarter of the eighteenth century. Unfortunately, the Anglo-Spanish War of Jenkins Ear interrupted the trade later that decade, and Charlestonians began to grow and export their own oranges, doubtless with seeds from La Florida fruit. Illicit trade between the Spanish and English colonies continue, however, despite admonitions from Spain to use only the approved Indies supply system, and smuggled goods provided La Florida with (sometimes crucial) supplies right up to the moment of its cession to the British, in 1763.[45]

In addition to direct economic activities, La Florida also came to depend upon the agricultural by-products of the mission program, which developed a modicum of autonomy during its "golden years," in the mid-1600s, a century before the better-known California missions flourished. A major element of Spanish relations with the Native Americans, evangelization was initiated by the Jesuits (1566), but almost as quickly abandoned by them (1572) on the grounds that the natives were too nomadic and not inclined to stay at missions, and that the cruelty of the soldiers created an animosity among the natives that could not be overcome.

Franciscans took over the process, arriving first in 1572, a few years before the outbreak of the first revolt in Guale (southeastern Georgia), which took the Spaniards four years to suppress. A second uprising in 1597 sent natives migrating to nearby islands for refuge, and the coastal missions went into a long period of decline. After 1595 the Franciscans began to push eastward across Timucua and, after 1633, into Abalachi province, the western extent of the missions of La Florida. Including those missions established during the exploration period and others abandoned or moved, there were a total of 128 *doctrirías* (mission centers), *visitas* (villages, sometimes with churches, visited by friars), and villages where priests or lay brothers lived in the regions of Guale, Timugua, and Abalachi between 1566 and 1706. Seventy friars were authorized by the crown, but it is not known if the total ever reached the authorized number.[46]

The Spanish crown envisioned all the natives of La Florida as constituting a "Republic of Indians" with which it could deal diplomatically, on European terms. If the natives failed to cooperate fully in their own conversion and assimilation (as so often happened), the Spaniards believed that they were then justified in waging war against the natives, for the good of their souls as well as for the benefit of the Spanish crown.[47] in other words, the end justified the means. in the case of La Florida, many of the natives were used to following seasonal rounds and not always willing to be confined to sedentary lives at missions. Further, the number of natives, although diminishing, was still larger than the number of Europeans. Therefore, the ability of the Spaniards to subjugate and control them was predicated to a great degree on a process of negotiation. This process, which proceeded continuously throughout the occupations of La Florida, was viewed quite differently by each of the parties involved. Spanish law required that native elites be afforded deferential treatment, just as elite Spaniards were, and with all native peoples negotiation and gift-giving were principal elements of Spanish-Indian relations. But it is clear also from the documents that when gifts were withheld or not available, the natives saw themselves as equal participants, with the prerogative to withdraw their "loyalty."[48] Both crown and church wanted to bring the natives into obedience to the "law of God," but negotiation was just one side of the coin; fear and force were the other.

The *encomienda* system of native labor grants was used in La Florida, but not as extensively as in the core areas of Spanish colonization, where European population, land development, and labor exploitation ratios were much higher. At missions, native labor systems were co-opted, frequently with the cooperation of their leaders, for the production of basic and surplus goods. Natives also were required to pay tribute, whether they lived in a mission village or not, but this system was periodically modified in the face of native resistance. A form of *repartimiento*, or labor levy, required the natives to work on civic and private projects, such as the military fortifications of San Agustín and the fortified cattle ranches of the interior, but customary usage required reciprocity in dealing with the natives. When the governor called for laborers, they were to be provided with passage money and provisions, and given gifts when they arrived at their destination. Both natives and missionaries complained loudly when they considered the labor requirements excessive, but conditions were not always mitigated.[49]

The Abalachi missions proved particularly productive, both in terms of the human labor force they provided and in terms of indigenous agricultural products and Spanish-introduced varieties. Corn, hogs, beef, hides, and tallow, fruits, and fowl, among other things, augmented San Agustín's supplies or went to the markets of Cuba. A major export from Abalachi, however, was its people. More densely populated than other native regions, the Spaniards' labor requirements took a heavy toll on the Abalachi.[50] In 1676, Fray Alonso Moral, who had served for thirty-three years in La Florida's missions, described in graphic detail the lives of many whom we will never know as individuals:

All the natives of those provinces suffer great servitude, injuries, and vexations from the fact that the governors, lieutenants, and soldiers oblige them to carry loads on their shoulders to the Province of Apalachie and to other areas and also to bring loads from those regions to the fort of St. Augustine. And it usually happens that to enhance their own interests they pretend that this work is in Your Majesty's service, without paying them what is just for such intolerable work. And if now and again they give them something for that reason, it is a hoe or an ax or a cheap blanket or some other thing of such slight value to pay for their work, which involves carrying a cargo on their shoulders from the fort to the Province of Apalachie, which is eighty leagues distant, and the same to return. In addition to this, in order to employ them further, they detained them in St. Augustine for as long as they wished, with very short rations, such as giving them only two pounds of corn a day and giving them for pay, at the most, one real for each day of work, which sum is usually given them in the form of old rubbish of little or no value or utility to them. Add to this the further vexation or injury of being snatched by force from their homes and villages, not only for tasks at the fort but also for work for private citizens, and this in the rigor of winter (when they come naked) or in the middle of summer, which is when they are most occupied in the labor of their crops on which solely depends not only their sustenance and that of their wives and children but also the victuals necessary for the relief of the garrison. Each year from Apalachie alone more than three hundred are brought to the fort at the time of the planting of the corer carrying their food on their shoulders for more than eighty leagues with the result that some on arrival die and those who survive do not return to their homes because the governor and the other officials detain them in the fort so they may serve them and this without paying them a wage. This is the reason according to the commonly held opinion that they are being annihilated at such a rate.

The same missionaries who complained frequently about the harsh treatment given the natives by the soldiers felt justified at the same time in whipping natives who did not attend mass regularly.[51] Elites were treated deferentially as long as they conformed to Spanish expectations, and if they did not they were not exempt from retribution. Polygamy, for example, was a major and constant point of contention between missionaries and chiefs. Spanish authorities ultimately resorted to unilaterally deposing chiefs for noncompliance, and the chiefs, maintaining their prerogatives, frequently led their people in revolt. The Spaniards would then feel justified in using whatever force was at their disposal, including enlisting the aid of Christianized native groups (who might coincidentally be traditional enemies of the rebellious tribe), and the recalcitrants would be subdued, until the cycle began anew.

As centers of acculturation, La Florida missions certainly were successful in introducing European material culture to the tribes and creating a dependency. The intensive sedentary agriculture required at missions created a reliance on European implements and decreased seasonal hunting and gathering among converted natives. At the same time, however, deerskins were a major focus of Spanish-Indian trade and over-hunting of deer herds, predicated upon a growing desire for the European wares that the hides purchased, sent many tribes migrating beyond their seasonal grounds and into increasing competition for a diminishing resource.

As regards the introduction of ideological culture, if assimilation is used as the yardstick, the assessment of the impact of the missions is more difficult to make. Even if the demographics of conversion are used, there are still too many variables to make a definitive judgment because conversion was many times extrinsic rather than intrinsic, and much ethnographic information has yet to be assessed. Between the years 1597 and 1717, population estimates for Christianized eastern Timuguanas were placed at a high of fourteen hundred (1595–1602).[52] In Abalachi, the total population was estimated at around thirty thousand in 1608, and one researcher posits the "virtual completion" of their conversion by 1670.[53] Throughout the rest of the peninsula, however, the mission program had very limited success and population estimates are lacking.

But juxtaposed against the conversion figures, there are still the mortality rates to be considered, and the rate of migration, which can only be viewed as high in either case. Then there is the fact that intensive Spanish acculturation of the natives lasted for little more than half a century. Massive uprisings disrupted the process periodically. In the later 1600s, the British, from their new base in the Carolinas, encouraged competing tribes to step up their attacks on the Abalachi and Timuguana villages and missions. Finally, in 1704–8, La Florida's missions came to a cataclysmic end. British governor James Moore from the Carolinas, in a daring drive all the way to the heart of Spanish power in the Southeast, had besieged San Agustín in 1702, during Queen Anne's War. Although the siege was ultimately unsuccessful, during its fifty-two days he destroyed all but twenty buildings of little consequence in the city, forcing most of its fifteen hundred inhabitants to take refuge inside the new stone fortress, El Castillo de San Macros. Over the next four years, he focused his attacks on weaker areas: together with native mercenaries, he attacked and burned the missions and killed or enslaved the inhabitants. The survivors migrated to the settlements at Mobile and San Agustín or down the peninsula. The destruction left a void across the area between San Agustín and Abalachi that slowly was refilled by a new amalgam. This new amalgam of southeastern Miskókî survivors whom the Spaniards called *cimarrones* (renegades) and the natives internalized as "yat'siminoli" or free people.

The British would not be daunted by the failure to take the Spanish stronghold. In 1740, James Oglethorpe, founder and governor of the new British province of Georgia, also attacked San Agustín, but again the attack was repulsed. In the following decade, however, when the Spanish crown belatedly entered the Seven Years War, the stakes rose dramatically for La Florida. British naval forces laid siege to Havana in 1762 and shocked the Spaniards by capturing the invaluable port. When the warring parties reached the treaty table, at Paris in 1763, it was decided (among other stipulations) that Britain would return Havana to Spain and, in trade, Spain would cede La Florida (what was left of it) to the British. About 600 Spaniards evacuated from Pensacola. At San Agustín a 1763 census showed 3,046 inhabitants, including 2,547 Spaniards, 315 black slaves and ninety-five free blacks, and eighty-nine Christian Native Americans, all of whom departed for Cuba. And so the first chapter of Florida's Spanish colonial history closed.

THE BRITISH FLORIDAS

As a direct result of the Seven Years War in Europe (1756–63), which spawned the French and Indian War in North America, Spanish control of the Southeast ended. Spain ceded to Britain all of her possessions "East or to the South East of the River Mississippi."[54] The French ceded Mobile and all their territory east of the Mississippi except New Orleans. Several basic changes were made in La Florida during this period. First, the British did not treat the area as a single entity, either geographically or politically. They divided the territory along the south-north course of the Apalachicola and Chattahoochee rivers and established administrative centers for east Florida at St. Augustine and for west Florida at Pensacola. Thus, east Florida comprised the present state to that river, while west Florida extended through Pensacola and Mobile and northward to around 31°.

Next, the British offered land grants for individuals capable of turning the Floridas into successful participants in their colonial mercantile economy. Between 1764 and 1780, 241 grants were issued in east Florida and 41 in west Florida; together, more than all grants issued during the same period in New York, Nova Scotia, and Quebec combined.[55] Ultimately, however, few owners took up their claims. One notable exception was Andrew Turnbull, M.D., who, in 1768, brought approximately fourteen hundred Menorcan (Catalán), Greek, and Italian indentured servants to found the indigo-producing colony of New Smyrna.[56] The majority group, the Menorcans, subsumed the survivors, all of whom moved to St. Augustine when the colony ended in 1777. Their descendants still reside in St. Augustine today, as the oldest remaining Hispanic group in the state.

St. Augustine remained the larger of the two population centers throughout the period, and the base population of east Florida was around one thousand, including military and civilians and families, plus about three thousand blacks.

Population density rose dramatically, however, as loyalists fled the American Revolutionary War, stopping briefly in the British Floridas on their way to the Bahamas and other British-held areas. East Florida swelled by 5,090 white and 8,285 black refugees.

THE END OF THE COLONIAL ERA

Spain's problems were all too obvious as she reinstituted colonial government in the Floridas. One major preoccupation was an old story for, as the Spanish minister put it, "You can't lock up an open field." There was no way to defend even the reduced borders of the largely unpopulated territories. Most of the British had departed, although Spain had relaxed its old laws by 1784 and had permitted British landowners to remain if they so chose. The incoming governor of east Florida reported that 656 planned to remain, 155 were undecided, and 1,181 would leave.

In St. Augustine, 469 Menorcan survivors of New Smyrna (over 800 had died and a few chose to remain at the colony) constituted the core of the population. Although they did not speak Spanish, they were ethnic Cataláns, a part of the Iberian Spanish kingdoms. After a poor start as destitute refugees from the coastal colony, they quickly settled in to life in east Florida as fishermen, farmers, and crafts people, and made the town their own. Together with new Spanish residents, including the new garrison members, they also constituted the plurality of the population, which totaled about seventeen hundred, in the city and the province, by 1786.

About four hundred black slaves and less than one hundred persons of mixed blood lived in and around the town, but there was no significant mestizo (Spanish-Indian) population.[57] Although *mestizaje* was a feature of the first Spanish occupation, that stratum of the population never reached a significance comparable to that of other Spanish colonies, primarily because the population in general remained low. And since most Spaniards who evacuated in 1763 did not return in 1784, the population was almost starting from "scratch."

In west Florida, the number of inhabitants was considerably smaller. Less than 300 civilians, mainly Canary Islanders and French creoles, remained in Pensacola and the authorized strength of the garrison was one battalion, with 460 men. However, it was to west Florida that the scene of action would shift during this denouement of the colonial story. For it was west Florida that was geographically situated to receive two significant ethnic groups who would, by their coming, change the composition of the Floridas forever: the Americans and the so-called Creek Indians.

The crown knew that it could afford neither to defend nor populate the provinces adequately. Consequently, Spain decided upon the only course of action that seemed possible even though, in the long run, it brought the end of Spanish rule. First, it maintained administrative centers at St. Augustine and Pensacola, but transferred some civil and financial authority to New Orleans and other civil and religious authority to Havana.

Next, Spain offered religious toleration, land grants, and equal commercial privileges to non-Spaniards who would settle the land. To the young United States, whose population was already sufficiently large that it was moving beyond the Ohio Valley and the mountains of the Carolinas and inexorably down the eastern shore of the Mississippi, the opening of the Floridas was important. During the Second Spanish Period, the movement would be little more than a steady trickle, but it would mark a permanent demographic shift. Politically, it also would be a great boon, but not to the Spaniards. Thomas Jefferson was delighted. He said that permitting Americans free access to the Spanish Floridas would be like "settling the Goths at the gates of Rome." He continued, "I wish a hundred thousand of our inhabitants would accept the invitation. It will be the means of delivering to us peacefully what would otherwise cost us a war." He was right.

Then the Spaniards turned their attention once again to the "Indian problem." They had learned to their detriment that they could provide neither the quantity nor the quality of trade goods necessary to maintain an alliance with the natives, and a century of Spanish-French-British competition in the interior of the Southeast had made the survivors of that process very savvy. So the Spaniards determined to license traders, in hopes of directing the trade to their own advantage. It was not to be. West Florida and Pensacola, which became the headquarters of the powerful British firm, Panton, Leslie and Co., to whom the Spaniards gave a monopoly on the Indian trade, were the centers of this commerce. But the lucrative Indian trade attracted much more than just Indians.

British agents, secure in the inability of the Spanish government to stop them, entered west Florida at will. They conducted talks with the Native Americans, offered them bribes of alliance, and encouraged them to rebel against the Spaniards and not to allow themselves to be used, yet again, as pawns in an international struggle. Independent entrepreneurs, purporting to speak for the Native Americans, tried to set themselves up as power brokers between the British and the natives. When the Creek War of 1813–14 in Alabama ended, General Andrew Jackson forced a treaty on the tribes that deprived them of millions of acres of their homelands and set in motion an exodus that sent several thousand migrating into west Florida.

The Floridas were already home to the Seminoles, the survivors of the earlier tribes, and cultural relatives of the Creeks. By the 1810s, the groups numbered about five thousand in the Floridas. British intrigues, Indian depredations, and white retaliations, as all of the new Floridians elbowed for living space, made the United States government very nervous. As the United States watched the process warily, they considered what to do about their unruly neighbor.

The Treaty of San Ildefonso, in 1795, was the first step in Spain's final withdrawal from the Floridas. The thirty-first parallel became the official northern boundary of the territories, and the Floridas began their final decrease to the current borders. Then the Louisiana Purchase, in 1803, removed the French and the Spaniards altogether from the mouth of the Mississippi and the west Florida western border became disputed territory. But, in 1810, U.S. President James Monroe publicly claimed west Florida, from the Perdido River to the Mississippi, as a part of the Louisiana Purchase, and with that claim, which the Spaniards could not militarily deny them, the Floridas assumed the geopolitical shape that is known today as Florida. It had taken 297 years, however, to reach that point.

Then the impending war with Britain made it clear to the United States that coastal defense must be a high priority, and that as large a contiguous land mass as the Floridas could not be allowed to remain in the control of any foreign nation, although "control" was a moot point. Foreign adventurers were invading east Florida and summarily claiming portions as their independent kingdoms. In west Florida, American nationals rose up and proclaimed the area a republic in anticipation of U.S. possession. On July 10, 1816, United States sea forces near the mouth of the Apalachicola River fired upon a wooden fort, deserted by the British and left to the occupation of natives and escaped black slaves. Blacks from the "Negro Fort" had fired on a small boat party, and in retaliation Americans lobbed hot shot into the fort and exploded the magazine, killing 270 of the 344 defenders. In 1818, Andrew Jackson, by then the hero of the Battle of New Orleans, marched into west Florida on grounds of controlling the Native Americans. In April, he executed two British nationals whom he considered responsible for inciting the natives. Then he marched to Pensacola, where he arrived on May 22, and occupied the city and Fort Barrancas. He summarily informed the Spaniards that he would transport them wherever they might care to go; wrote a full account of his actions; and returned to Tennessee.

Spain and Britain protested loudly, and the United States was embarrassed, but U.S. citizens approved of Jackson's actions and, after twenty-seven days of debate, the U.S. Congress failed to censure him. Meanwhile, negotiations were under way in Washington, D.C., that would result in the Adams-Onis Treaty, signed on February 22, 1819, and ratified on February 22, 1821. Spain relinquished control of the troublesome Floridas to the United States. In return, the United States canceled five million dollars worth of Spanish debts to U.S. citizens, mainly spoilation claims dating back to the late eighteenth century and Spanish closure of the Mississippi River. Thus, the exciting colonial eras ended and Florida became a territory of the United States.

TABLE 7.1

Population Estimates for the Colonial Floridas

Period	Estimate	Population	Area
1510	200,000	Native Americans	Lower La Florida
1580s	150	soldiers	San Agustín
	240	women, children (include, <100 Blacks)	
1597–1602	15,000	Native Americans	Timucua
1608	30,000	Native Americans	Apalache
1633	16,000	Native Americans	Apalache
1689	3,380	Native Americans	Timucua
	9,600	Native Americans	Apalache
1702	1,500	total population (Spaniards + Blacks)	San Agustín
	8,000	Native Americans	Apalache missions
1715	3,700	Native Americans	Peninsular La Florida
1763	800	total population (Spaniards + Blacks)	Pensacola
	350	French	Mobile
	700	Native Americans (includes no reliable count for the southern peninsula)	Peninsular La Florida
	3,046	total population (2,547 Spaniards + 315 Black slaves + 95 free Blacks + 89 Christian Natives)	San Agustín & environs
1768	1,000	British	East Florida
	3,000	Blacks	
	1,400	Menorcans	
	800	total population	West Florida
1787	3,190	Spaniards, Menorcans, Blacks	East Florida
	760	Spaniards, Canary Islanders, French	West Florida
1825	5–7,000	Native Americans	The Floridas
	5,780	Anglo-americans, Spaniards, Blacks	W of Apalachicola River
	2,370	Anglo-Americans, Spaniards, Blacks	Between Suwannee & Apalachicola Rivers
	5,077	Anglo-Americans, Spaniards, Blacks	E of Suwannee R.
	317	Anglo-Americans, Spaniards, Blacks	Peninsular Florida

NOTES

1. See, for example, Hernando de Escalante Fontaneda, *Letter of Hernando de Soto and Memoir of Hernando de Escalante Fontaneda* (ca. l575), trans. Buckingham Smith (Washington, D.C., 1854), concerning the Calosas of the southwest coast and their tribute system, which ranged across the peninsula. See also the reports of the survivors of the Hernando de Soto entrada, especially in Lawrence A. Clayton, Vernon James Knight, Jr., and Edward C. Moore, eds. *The DeSoto Chronicles: The Expedition of Hernando de Soto to North America in 1539–1543*, 2 vols. (Tuscaloosa and London, 1993).

2. Antonio de Herrera y Tordesillas, *Historia general de los hechos de los castellanos en las islas y tierra firme del mar oceáno*, 4 vols. (Madrid, 1601–1615), decade 1, book 9, 53, cited in Edward W. Lawson, *The Discovery of Florida and Its Discoverer Juan Ponce de León* (St. Augustine, Fla., 1946), 18.

3. Ibid., 15.

4. For the most lucid exposition of the sixteenth-century Spaniards' philosophical/religious ideology and the rationale of its transfer to their New World, see Anthony Pagden, *The Fall of Natural Man: The American Indian and the Origins of Comparative Ethnology* (Cambridge, 1982).

5. For a table of comparative provisions of sixteenth-century asientos granted to explorers of La Florida and other comparable sites in the Americas, see Eugene Lyon, *The Enterprise of Florida: Pedro Menéndez de Avilés and the Spanish Conquest of 1565–1568* (Gainesville, 1976), 220–23.

6. Leslie Bethell, ed., *Cambridge History of Latin America* (Cambridge, l984), 1:4.

7. See: Theodore G. Schurr, Scott W. Ballinger, Yik-Yuen Can et al., "Amerindian Mitochondiral DNAs Have Rare Asian Mutations at High Frequencies, Suggesting They Derived from Four Primary Maternal Lineages," in *American Journal of Human Genetics* 40 (1990): 613–23; Douglas C. Wallace and Antonio Torroni, "American Indian Prehistory as Written in the Mitochondrial DNA: A Review," in *Human Biology* 64:3 (June 1992), 403–16; and Antonio Torroni, Theodore G. Schurr, Margaret F. Cabell et al., "Asian Affinities and Continental Radiation of the Four Founding Native American mtDNAs," in *American Journal of Human Genetics* 53 (1993), 563–90.

8. For creation stories of some of the Maskókî peoples, see Albert S. Gatschet, *A Migration Legend of the Creek Indians, with a Linguistic, Historic, and Ethnographic Introduction*, vol. 1 (1884; repr.: New York, 1969); also, personal interviews with Seminole tribal members, in the files of the author.

9. Personal interviews, 1993–94, in the files of the author.

10. See, for example, Andrés González de Barcia Carballido y Zúñiga, *Ensayo cronológico para la historia general de la Florida* (Madrid, 1723). In his *Chronological Essay on La Florida*, Barcia states that in 1698 the Calusas of the southwest coast were traveling to Havana, by dugout, in twenty-four hours.

11. Julian Cranberry, *A Grammar and Dictionary of the Timucuan Language*, 2d ed., Anthropological Notes, no. 1. (Horseshoe Beach, Fla., 1989).

12. Henry Dobyns, *Their Number Become Thinned: Native American Population Dynamics in Eastern North America* (Knoxville, 1983), 51, 291–95.

13. Elizabeth l. Reitz, "'Evidence for Animal Use at the Missions of Spanish Florida," in Bonnie G. McEwan, ed., *The Spanish Missions of La Florida* (Gainesville, 1993), 376–98.

14. John H. Hann, "Summary Guide to Spanish Florida Missions and Visitas with Churches in the Sixteenth and Seventeenth Centuries," in *The Americas* 46:4 (April 1990), 423–24. For further discussions of these groups, see, among other works, Jerald T. Milanich and Samuel Proctor, *Tacachale: Essays on the Indians of Florida and Southeastern Georgia during the Historic Period* (Gainesville, 1978); Jerald T. Milanich and Charles Hudson, *Hernando de Soto and the Indians of Florida* (Gainesville, 1993); and John H. Hann, *Apalachie: The Land Between the Rivers* (Gainesville, 1988).

15. For an up-to-date discussion of the southern manifestations of this belief system, see Mark Williams and Gary Shapiro, eds., *Lamar Archaeology: Mississippian Chiefdoms in the Deep South* (Tuscaloosa, 1990); and Jerald T. Milanich, *Archaeology of Precolumbian Florida* (Gainesville, 1994), esp. 371–87.

16. Karen M. Booker, Charles Hudson, and Robert L. Rankin, "Place Name Identification and Multilingualism in the Sixteenth-Century Southeast," in *Ethnohistory* 39:4 (Fall 1992), 401.

17. See, for example, Luis Gerónimo de Ore, *The Martyrs of Florida (1513–1616)*, ed. Maynard Geiger (New York, 1936), 101–2; Lewis H. Larson, Jr., "Historic Guale Indians of the Georgia Coast and the Impact of the Spanish Mission Effort," in Jerald T. Milanich and Samuel Proctor, *Tacachale*, 125–26.

18. Chester B. DePratter, "Later Historic and Early Historic Chiefdoms in the Southeastern United States" (Ph.D. diss., University of Georgia, 1983).

19. This is a feature of the "paired town" concept posited by archaeologists Mark Williams and Gary Shapiro. They have thus far identified ten paired towns, throughout modern-day Georgia, that appear to have been abandoned and reoccupied at intervals of 50–125 years. See Mark Williams and Gary Shapiro, "Paired Towns," in Williams and Shapiro, *Lamar Archaeology*, 163–64.

20. Helen Hornbeck Tanner, "The Land and Water Communication Systems of the Southeastern United States," in Peter H. Wood, Gregory A. Waselkov, and M. Thomas Halley, eds., *Powhatan's Mantle: Indians in the Colonial Southeast* (Lincoln, 1989), 6.

21. Ibid., fig. 1, 8.

22. Ibid., 13–16.

23. La Florida first appears on the Cantino Map, 1502. See Carl Ortwin Sauer, *Sixteenth Century North America: The Land and the People as Seen by the Europeans* (Berkeley, 1971), 25. In comparison, by 1521 Spanish slavers had already emptied the Bahama Islands of all of their inhabitants in their searches. See Archivo General de Indias [hereafter cited as AGI], Justicia 3, no. 3, fols. 40–41. For a short discussion of the primary sources supporting 1510 as the date of first Spanish discovery, see Buckingham Smith, "Notes by the Translator," in Fontaneda, *Letter of Hernando de Soto* Memoirs.

24. Fontaneda, Letter of Hernando de Soto, 17.

25. Pietro Martiere d'Anghiera, *Décadas del Nuevo Mundo, 1530*, ed. Edmundo O'Gorman 2 vols. (Mexico City, 1964–65), II:595.

26. Paul E. Hoffman, *A New Andalucía and a Way to the Orient: The American Southeast during the Sixteenth Century* (Baton Rouge, 1990), 4, passim.

27. Ibid. Hoffman, A New Andalucia, 106–14.

28. Jerald T. Milanich and Susan Milbrath, *First Encounters: Spanish Explorations in the Caribbean and the United States, 1492–1570* (Gainesville, 1989), 77–118.

29. The latest translations of these four accounts are available in Lawrence A. Clayton, Vernon James Knight, Jr., and Edward C. Moore, eds., *The De Soto Chronicles: The Expedition of Hernando de Soto to North America in 1539–1543* (Tuscaloosa, 1993).

30. Charles Hudson, Marvin T. Smith, Chester B. DePratter, and Emilia Kelley, "The Tristan de Luna Expedition, 1559–1561," in *Southeastern Archaeology* 8:1 (1989).

31. For a guide to the primary sources on this expedition, see Stanley J. Folmsbee and Madeline Kneberg Lewis, ""Journals of the Juan Pardo Expeditions, 1566–1567," in *East Tennessee Historical Society's Publications* 37 (1965), 106–21.

32. See, for example, Dobyns, *Their Number Become Thinned*; Milanich and Milbrath, *First Encounters*; Peter Wood, "The Changing Population of the Colonial South: An Overview by Race and Region, 1685–1790," in Wood, Waselkov, and Halley, *Powhatan's Mantle*, 35–04; and Marvin T. Smith, *Archaeology of Aboriginal Culture Change in the Interior Southeast: Depopulation during the Early Historic Period*, Ripley P. Bullen Monograph Series, no. 6 (Gainesville, 1987).

33. David E. Stannard, "The Consequences of Contact: Toward an Interdisciplinary Theory of Native Responses to Biological and Cultural Invasion," in David Hurst Thomas, ed., *Columbian Consequences*, 3 vols, (Washington D.C., 1989–91), vol. 3, *The Spanish Borderlands in Pan-American Perspective*, 535.

34. Wood, "Changing Population," 38, 51–56.

35. Hoffman, *New Andalucía*, 131.

36. The story is told in all its exciting detail in Eugene Lyon, *The Enterprise of Florida: Pedro Menéndez de Avilés and the Spanish Conquest of 1565–1568* (Gainesville, 1976).

37. Ibid., 71–77, 80–87, 95, 104, 106.

38. Amy Bushnell, *The King's Coffer* (Gainesville, 1981), 64.

39. Engel Sluiter, *The Florida Situado: Quantifying the First Eighty Years, 1571–1651*, Research Publications of the P. K. Yonge Library of Florida History, University of Florida, no. 1 (Gainesville, 1985), 2, 9.

40. AGI, Contaduria [CD] 941, St. Augustine Foundation Data Base ISAFDB 1398, cited in Eugene Lyon, "Richer Than We Thought: The Material Culture of Sixteenth-Century St. Augustine," *El Escribano* 29 (1992), 7–9.

41 . AGI Escribania de Camara [hereafter cited as EC] 1024–A, fols. 467–505, cited in ibid.

42. AGI EC 1024–A, fols. 467–505, cited in Eugene Lyon, *Santa Elena: A Brief History of the Colony, 1566–1587* (Columbia, S.C., 1984).

43. Hoffman, *New Andalucía*, 26.

44. Joyce Elizabeth Harman, *Trade and Privateering in Spanish Florida, 1732–1763* (St. Augustine, 1969), 22–23.

45. Ibid., 13, 75.

46. Hann, "Summary Guide," 417–514.

47. Amy Bushnell, "Ruling 'the Republic of Indians' in Seventeenth-Century Florida," in Wood, Waselkov, and Halley, *Powhatan's Mantle*, 136.

48. Bushnell, "Ruling 'the Republic of Indians,' " 137; Bushnell, *King's Coffer*, 66.

49. Bushnell, "Ruling 'the Republic of Indians,' " 143; Bushnell, *King's Coffer*, 11–13, 16–25, 37–46, 97–99, 106, 110–11; Hann, *Apalachie*, 139.

50. Hann, *Apalachie*, 140–41.

51. The mission fiscal, or beadle, administered the punishment. See Friars in chapter vs. Governor Juan Marques Cabrera, May 10–May 30, 1681, AGI, Audiencia of Santo Domingo 226, cited in Bushnell, "Ruling the 'Republic of Indians,' " 142, 147n. 29.

52. Kathleen A. Deagan, "Cultures in Transition: Fusion and Assimilation among the Eastern Timucua," in Milanich and Proctor, *Tacachale*, 95.

53. Hann, *Apalachie*, 3, 162.

54. Charles Locke Mowat, *East Florida as a British Province, 1763–1784* (Gainesville, 1964), 5.

55. Mowat, *East Florida as a British Province*, 59, 61.

56. E. P. Panagopoulous, *New Smyrna: An Eighteenth-Century Greek Odyssey* (Gainesville, 1966).

57. For a comparison of demographic data available for this period, see Sherry Johnson, "The Spanish St. Augustine Community, 1784–1795," *Florida Historical Quarterly* 68:1 (July 1989), 27–54.

CONCLUSIONS
Some Common Threads on the Northern Frontier of Mexico

ROBERT H. JACKSON

The major common thread found along the northern frontier of colonial Mexico was the effort to recreate on the frontier patterns developed in central Mexico. Chronologically, changes did occur in Spanish policy and institutions in central Mexico. In the first years following the conquest of central Mexico, private individuals organized most exploration and colonization expeditions and sought compensation in *encomiendas* and any sources of wealth encountered. A number of fortunate men discovered rich mineral deposits in the north, and Juan de Oñate, the colonizer of New Mexico, derived his wealth from northern mines. New Mexico fits into the pattern of sixteenth-century Spanish expansion. Oñate received extensive powers and rewarded the settlers he brought to New Mexico with encomienda grants. Later, colonization on the frontier in the seventeenth and eighteenth centuries was undertaken largely at government initiative and generally for strategic reasons, to create buffers against rival European colonial powers; in this respect, Texas and California are exemplary. The Spanish occupied both regions because of the perceived threat of possible French, English, and Russian settlement of areas located on the fringes of Mexico. Both areas failed to attract large numbers of settlers because of the lack of readily discovered mineral wealth, and the government attempted to bring settlers to the frontier. However, missions and presidios were the most important institutions, and asserted a stronger Spanish claim based on occupation.

Colonization of the frontier in the late seventeenth and eighteenth centuries also reflected greater government involvement on the frontier, particularly in the mid- and late-eighteenth century, during the period of the Bourbon reforms. The government was responsible for the occupation of Texas and California, but also assumed a greater role in older areas such as Nueva Vizcaya and Sonora. In the Pimeria Alta region of northern Sonora, for example, the government funded missions and established presidios. Settlement by colonists and the discovery of mines followed the government initiatives. Some government officials also advocated greater integration of the indigenous populations into Spanish colonial society and settlement by non-Indians in the mission communities.

Despite continued reliance on missions as a colonizing institution, missionaries did not enjoy the same influence as during the decades immediately following the conquest of central Mexico. Secular and anticlerical ideas became more influential at the end of the colonial period, and during the eighteenth century more civil officials criticized the missionaries. The expulsion of the Jesuits, an assertion of government authority, was symptomatic of the changing attitude of government officials toward clerics, as were the calls for greater integration of the indigenous population and reform of church wealth perceived to be held in a form of *mortmain* (dead hands).

On the northern frontier of Mexico, the late eighteenth-century reforms lead to a reorganization of the military and greater coordination in war with hostile groups such as Apaches and Comanches. It also resulted in the establishment of more controls over the missions. In Baja California, the government assumed direct authority over colonization and the management of the missions following the Jesuit expulsion, and made efforts to develop marginal silver mines and bring settlers to the peninsula. The government also demanded greater accountability from the missionaries, including the preparation of reports describing the spiritual and material progress of the mission communities. The onset of the French Revolutionary and Napoleonic wars (1792–1815), the political crisis in Spain following the French invasion of 1808, and the outbreak of the Mexican War of Independence in 1810 stalled the new pattern of frontier development ushered in with the Bourbon reforms. However, post–independence liberalism reflected, in some ways, the new orientation in Spanish policy.

INDEX

NOTES ON CONTRIBUTORS

SUSAN M. DEEDS is associate professor of history at Northern Arizona University. Her work on the indigenous peoples of northwest Mexico may be found in *Indian Women of Early Mexico*, ed. by Susan Schroeder, Robert Haskett, and Stephanie Wood (Norman: University of Oklahoma Press, 1997) and in the Cambridge *History of the Native Peoples of the Americas* (Cambridge: Cambridge University Press, to appear in 1998).

JESUS F. DE LA TEJA is associate professor of history at Southwest Texas State University, where he teaches courses on Texas, Spanish borderlands, colonial Mexican, and Mexican American history. He is the author of *San Antonio de Bexar: A Community on New Spain's Northern Frontier* (Albuquerque: University of New Mexico Press, 1995) and *A Revolution Remembered: The Memoirs and Selected Correspondence of Juan N. Seguin* (Austin: State House Press, 1991), as well as the managing editor of *Catholic Southwest* and book review editor of *The Southwestern Historical Quarterly*.

ROSS FRANK received his Ph.D. in history in 1992 from the University of California, Berkeley. Since that time he has taught courses on the history of Native Americans in the United States, cultural world views of Native Americans, social and economic history of the Southwest, and graduate seminars in ethnic studies. His research interests emphasize intercultural contact and culture change in Native America from 1750 to 1880 as well as more specifically the social and economic history of northern Mexico and the American Southwest. He has published several award-winning articles.

ROBERT JACKSON, a specialist in borderlands and Latin American history, received his Ph.D. in 1988 from the University of California, Berkeley. His books cover such topics as the demographic collapse among Indians in northwestern New Spain (1994), regional markets and agrarian practices in Bolivia (1994), the impact of the mission system on California Indians (with Edward Castillo, 1995), land reform in nineteenth-century Spanish America (1997), and race, caste, and status in Bolivia and northwestern Mexico (forthcoming). He teaches at State University College at Oneonta.

PETER STERN received his Ph.D. in history and a master's in library and information science from the University of California, Berkeley. He has written on borderlands history for *The Americas, Journal of the Southwest,* and the *Colonial Hispanic American Historical Review,* and on information technology in the humanities for *The Journal of Academic Librarianship* and the *Colonial Latin American Review.* He has also published an annotated bibliography on the Sendero Luminoso guerrilla movement. He is bibliographer for Spanish, Portuguese, and Latin American Studies and adjunct assistant professor of history at the University of Massachusetts, Amherst.

PATRICIA R. WICKMAN has worked in the fields of Florida and public history for twenty-seven years. She received her Ph.D. in Native American and Spanish Colonial Ethnohistory from the University of Miami; her latest book (forthcoming) deals with relations between Native Americans and Spaniards in Florida. In addition to organizing major permanent and traveling exhibits, writing catalogues, consulting to historical agencies and museums, and speaking extensively on southeastern and Florida history, she has taught at several Florida universities. She has spent the last five years living and working among the Seminoles of Florida and Oklahoma, at the invitation of the tribes.